Fingerprint Dictionary

An examiner's guide to the who, what and where of fingerprint identification

Michele Triplett

Fingerprint Dictionary

An examiner's guide to the who, what, and where of fingerprint identification

by Michele Triplett

Published by:
Steve Everist for
Two Rings Publishing, LLC
Bellevue, Washington
tworingspublishing@gmail.com

The purpose of this guide is to be a general reference for the fingerprint examiner. Every effort has been made for this reference guide to be as complete and accurate as possible. There may be mistakes in content and of a typographical nature. Due to the length of many website addresses, it was necessary to break them up over lines, and in some case pages, to list them in their entirety.

Much of the material is available online and through various other sources, including the most current version being available at www.fprints.nwlean.net. This book is not meant to be the complete source of information. Its purpose is to supplement all of the current literature available to fingerprint examiners. The author recommends that fingerprint examiners read all the available material, including those referenced in this book, in order to keep current in the field.

Second Edition, First Printing 2010

First Edition 2006

Printed in the United States of America

Foreword

In June of 1998 Michele Triplett and I became Latent Print Examiners with the King County Sheriff's Office. During our training, Michele began to keep notes regarding people, places, and terms that she thought important enough that she would want quick access to them. In some cases there were differing definitions, so she would list all of them and cite their sources. Over the next couple of years, there were so many entries that her notes had grown into several pages.

What was once a quick, personal reference page had grown to the point that it had become cumbersome to search for a specific entry. So she decided to put it into her word processing program and alphabetize it for easy searching. As this document grew over time, it became known as Michele's Fingerprint Dictionary. She has posted it online, at http://www.fprints.nwlean.net, so that others outside of our office could also access the information. Many other sites relating to fingerprint examination have linked her dictionary to their site.

With her dictionary now being available worldwide, she receives suggestions of other people, places, and terms that she should consider adding. Many of the currently active individuals in the field that have been included wrote their own entries at Michele's request. Currently the dictionary contains over 1000 entries.

As the document grew to over 100 pages, it became too bulky to print out and clip together. So the opportunity came up for Michele and I to work together to put her notes into book format for publishing. In 2006 we came together to have the First Edition published. Four years and hundreds of added and updated entries later, we've done it again and are happy to release the Second Edition of; **Fingerprint Dictionary – an examiner's guide to the who, what, and where of fingerprint identification.**

Steve Everist, CLPE
Bellevue, WA
July 2010

A-Naphaflavone
Chemical used in fixing Iodine processed friction ridge detail.
SWGFAST, Glossary - Consolidated 09-09-03 ver. 1.0

AAFS
American Academy of Forensic Science.

ACE-V
The acronym for the sequential process or modified version of the scientific method that is followed by friction ridge examiners: Analysis, Comparison, Evaluation, Verification. (See individual terms.)

ACE-V was first used for physical evidence about 1960 & ridge detail about 1980. Inspector Roy A. Huber, RCMP, formulated the ACE-V process and Staff Sergeant David Ashbaugh, RCMP, popularized this process within the friction ridge identification field.

A- Analysis: The unknown item must be reduced to a matter of properties or characteristics. These properties may be directly observable, measurable, or otherwise perceptible qualities.
C- Comparison: The properties or characteristics of the unknown are now compared with the familiar or recorded properties of known items.
E- Evaluation: It is not sufficient that the comparison disclose similarities or dissimilarities in properties or characteristics. Each characteristic will have a certain value for identification purposes, determined by its frequency of occurrence. The weight or significance of each must therefore be considered.
Verification: It (scientific method) insists upon verification as the most reliable form of proof.
Insp. Roy Huber, Identification News Nov. 1962

A- analyze - The first step, analysis, requires the expert to examine and analyze all variables influencing the friction ridge impression in question. This begins with an understanding of friction ridged skin and the transition of the three dimensional skin structure to a two dimensional image. When examining latent fingerprints, several factors must be accounted for and understood. Some of these factors are the material upon which the latent print has been deposited, the development process(es), pressure distortion, and external elements (blood, grease, etc.). The quantity and quality of the latent print ridges influences the examiners ability to perform the next phase. The conclusion of the analysis process is a determination as to whether

sufficient information exists to proceed to the next phase.
C- **compare** - The comparison process introduces the known exemplar with which the latent print is to be compared. At this point, there is also another analysis phase taking place. This analysis is of the known exemplar in an effort to determine the suitability for achieving the conclusion stated above. It is possible that the known exemplar may contain fingerprint images that are too heavily inked or smudged, and thereby unreliable, thus preventing a conclusive comparison. The comparison process begins with determining the general ridge flow and shape (Level 1 Detail) in an effort to properly orient the latent print with a corresponding area of the known exemplar fingerprints. This is generally followed by selecting key focal characteristics (Level 2 Detail), understanding their position, direction and relationship and then comparing this formation with the formations in the known exemplar. The quality and quantity of this information directly affects the ease or difficulty of this process.
E- **evaluate** - The result of the comparison is the evaluation process or making a conclusion. The general fingerprint community refers to the conclusions drawn as being one of three choices. First, the two impressions (latent fingerprint and the known fingerprint) were made by the same finger of the same person. Second, the latent impression was not made by any of the fingers of the exemplar fingerprints. And third, a conclusive comparison could not be achieved, generally due to the lack of adequate clarity or the absence of comparable area in the known exemplar. In order to establish an identification decision, this process must insure that all of the fingerprint details are the same and maintain the same relationship, with no existing unexplainable differences.
V- **verify** - The final process is verification. The general rule is that all identifications must be verified by a second qualified expert. This verification process by a second examiner is an independent examination of the two fingerprint impressions (latent fingerprint and known exemplar fingerprint) applying the scientific methodology of analysis, comparison and evaluation described above.
United States vs. Byron Mitchell Government's Combined report to the Court and Motions in Limine Concerning Fingerprint evidence.

The acronym for a scientific method: Analysis, Comparison, Evaluation, and Verification (see individual terms).
SWGFAST, Glossary 07-28-2009 ver. 2.0

ACPO
Association of Chief Police Officers. The ACPO leads and coordinates the direction and development of the police service in England, Wales and Northern Ireland.

ADA
The American Dermatoglyphics Association (ADA) is a non-profit scientific and educational organization with membership worldwide. The mission of the ADA is to encourage and advance the science and applications of dermatoglyphics, and to facilitate cooperation among the membership and others with similar aims. Applications of dermatoglyphics encompasses the fields of anthropology, medicine, primatology, law, identification, embryology, and genetics.
http://www.physanth.org/annmeet/prizes/dermato.html 08-13-2003

ADAMS
Authenticated Digital Asset Management System.

A computer program designed to authenticate and track digital evidence. Produced by Foray Technologies.

AFIS
Automated Fingerprint Identification System.

ALPS
Automated Latent Print System.

ALS
See Alternate Light Source.

APIS
Automated Palmprint Identification System.

ASCLD
American Society of Crime Laboratory Directors.

ASCLD/LAB
American Society of Crime Laboratory Directors/Laboratory Accreditation Board.

Accuracy
A measurement of how precise a conclusion or a set of conclusions is to the real value.

Acetone
Solvent used as a carrier in reagents; also used as a cleaning agent.
SWGFAST, Glossary - Consolidated 09-09-03 ver. 1.0

Acetonitrile
Solvent used as a carrier in reagents; also used as a cleaning agent.
SWGFAST, Glossary - Consolidated 09-09-03 ver. 1.0

Acid Fuchsin
Reddish protein stain used to enhance bloody friction ridge detail.
SWGFAST, Glossary - Consolidated 09-09-03 ver. 1.0
Also known as Hungarian Red.

Acid Yellow 7
A fluorescent dye stain used to visualize latent prints left in blood on nonporous surfaces. Optimum viewing is at 400-490nm, using a clear, yellow, or light orange filter (depending on the wavelength used).

Acidified Hydrogen Peroxide
A solution used to develop friction ridge detail on cartridge casings by etching the surface of the casing not covered with sebaceous material.

Adactylia
Congenital absence of fingers and/or toes.
Synonyms: adactyly, adactylism
Source: WordNet ® 1.7, © 2001 Princeton University

Administrative Review
A review to insure the organizational procedures of an agency are adhered to, such as arrangement and punctuation.

Aggregate
Combining parts to arrive at the whole. This usually refers to making an identification based on the combined information from characteristics in a simultaneous impression.

Alanine
Alanine is the second simplest amino acid and the most common amino acid found in proteins, occurring at a rate of approximately 9%. Since amino acids are one of the organic components of eccrine sweat, alanine is often used to test latent print chemicals for an amino acid reaction.

Albinus, Weiss Bernhardus Siegfried (February 24, 1697-September 9, 1770)
One of the most well known anatomists of the eighteenth century. Albinus studied in Leyden with Govard Bidloo, among other great medical scientists. He is most noted for his attempts at increasing the scientific accuracy of anatomical illustrations.

Alias (AKA)
1. A false name. 2. Another name an individual has used. (Also Known As)
SWGFAST, Glossary - Consolidated 09-09-03 ver. 1.0

Altered Fingerprints
See Mutilation.

Alternate Black Powder
Developed by the FBI in the 1990's as an inexpensive and effective means of developing friction ridge detail on adhesive surfaces and/or tapes. This method is basically mixing normal black powder together with a 50:50 solution of liquid detergent (or liqui-Nox) and water. Mix the ingredient until it looks like shaving cream and paint it on to the adhesive side of tape. Let it sit for 30-60 seconds and then rinse with tap water. Repeat for

better contrast as needed.
Source: FBI Academy, Quantico, VA

Alternate Light Source (ALS)
Any light source, other than a laser, used to excite luminescence of latent prints, body fluids, etc., now commonly referred to as a forensic light source.
SWGFAST, Glossary - Consolidated 09-09-03 ver. 1.0

Aluminum Chloride
A metal salt used to treat ninhydrin developed latent prints.
SWGFAST, Glossary - Consolidated 09-09-03 ver. 1.0

Ambient Lighting
A lighting technique where the light is surrounding an object from all sides.

Amido Black
Blue-black protein stain used to enhance bloody friction ridge detail. See Naphthalene Black.
SWGFAST, Glossary - Consolidated 09-09-03 ver. 1.0

A dye used to stain the protein present in blood. Synonyms: Naphthalene Black; Naphthol Blue Black.

The Water Based Amido Black was developed by John F. Fischer of the Forensic Research and Supply Company in Gatha, Florida in 1998.
Source: FBI Academy, Quantico, VA

Amino Acids
One of the organic components in eccrine sweat. Amino acids are the basic structure of protein, protein is a chain of amino acids. The human body uses 20 amino acids to build the various proteins for growth, repair, and maintenance of body tissues.

The 20 amino acids the human body uses are: Alanine, Arginine, Asparagine, Aspartic acid, Cysteine, Glutamine, Glutamic acid, Glycine, Histidine, Isoleucine, Leucine, Lysine, Methionine, Phenylalanine, Proline, Serine, Threonine, Tryptophan, Tyrosine, and Valine. Alanine and glycine seem to be the most common amino acids used to test latent print chemicals for an amino acid reaction.

Ammonium Chloride
A metal salt used to treat ninhydrin developed latent prints.
SWGFAST, Glossary - Consolidated 09-09-03 ver. 1.0

Analog
Chemistry. A structural derivative of a parent compound that often differs from it by a single element.
The American Heritage® Dictionary of the English Language, Fourth Edition Copyright © 2000 by Houghton Mifflin Company. Published by Houghton Mifflin Company. All rights reserved.

http://dictionary.reference.com/search?q=analog 12-26-2005

Analysis
The first step of the ACE-V method. The assessment of an impression to determine suitability for comparison.
SWGFAST, Glossary 07-28-2009 ver. 2.0

Separate anything into its parts; to find out what a thing is made of.
Quantitative-Qualitative Friction Ridge Analysis, David R. Ashbaugh 1999 CRC Press

More definitions listed under ACE-V.

Anastomosis (Anastomoses)
The connection of separate parts of a branching system to form a network, as of leaf veins, blood vessels, or a river and its branches.
The American Heritage® Dictionary of the English Language, Fourth Edition Copyright © 2000 by Houghton Mifflin Company. Published by Houghton Mifflin Company. All rights reserved
http://dictionary.reference.com/search?q=anastomoses

Refers to the epidermal connective tissue that grows from a primary ridge to a secondary ridge, known as a shunt. The growth of anastomoses creates dermal papillae in the secondary dermal ridges.

Anhidrosis
A medical condition that reduces or eliminates the ability of the body to sweat (sometimes called Hypohidrosis). Anhidrosis can be caused from a variety of reasons including a genetic disorder, damage to the skin, or the use of certain medications.

Anthropometry
Dealing with measurement of the human body.
Quantitative-Qualitative Friction Ridge Analysis, David R. Ashbaugh 1999 CRC Press

Apical
At the apex; situated at the tip of a conical figure; at the tip of a finger.
Quantitative-Qualitative Friction Ridge Analysis, David R. Ashbaugh 1999 CRC Press

Apocrine Gland
A large sweat gland that produces both a fluid and an apocrine secretion; in human beings located in hairy regions of the body
WordNet ® 1.6, © 1997 Princeton University
http://dictionary.reference.com/search?q=apocrine%20gland 02-27-03

Sweat gland opening into the hair follicle.
Quantitative-Qualitative Friction Ridge Analysis, David R. Ashbaugh 1999 CRC Press

A type of skin gland that is associated with the hair follicles.
SWGFAST, Glossary - Consolidated 09-09-03 ver. 1.0

A large sweat gland that produces an apocrine secretion.
Professor Julian Verbov 04-19-08

Appendage
An attachment or connection within friction ridges.
SWGFAST, Glossary 07-28-2009 ver. 2.0

Any one of various external attached parts, i.e., arms, legs, tails, fins.
Quantitative-Qualitative Friction Ridge Analysis, David R. Ashbaugh 1999 CRC Press

Applied Science
Using a pure science in practical application by scientific method or having a goal.
Examples:
physics (pure science), engineering (applied science)
mathematics (pure science), statistics (applied science)
dactylography (pure science), fingerprint identification (applied science)

Aqueous
Water based.
SWGFAST, Glossary - Consolidated 09-09-03 ver. 1.0

Arch - plain
A fingerprint pattern in which the friction ridges enter on one side of the impression and flow, or tend to flow, out the other side with a rise or wave in the center.
SWGFAST, Glossary 07-28-2009 ver. 2.0

Arch - tented
A type of fingerprint pattern that possesses either an angle, an upthrust, or two of the three basic characteristics of the loop.
SWGFAST, Glossary 07-28-2009 ver. 2.0

Ardrox
Fluorescent yellow dye used with UV light to visualize cyanoacrylate ester fumed friction ridge detail.
SWGFAST, Glossary - Consolidated 09-09-03 ver. 1.0

Art
1. A kind of knowledge that is typically considered nonscientific, the Liberal Arts. Traditionally this kind of knowledge has been considered nonscientific because it lacks one or more of the requirements of a science, such as having testable observations or being about a natural phenomenon. Examples: Accounting, Economics, and Religion. Educational institutions have begun offering liberal art degrees in areas of study that are typically considered scientific (Biology, Mathematics,

Psychology). The BA degree is usually general knowledge, and the BS degree is more specialized.
2. A skill, talent, or ability that one can possess innately or by study or practice. This definition of art can apply to an individual involved in the liberal arts, the sciences, or any craft, trade or activity. This is not an essential requirement for any occupation or activity but is certainly a benefit.

Artifact
1. Any distortion or alteration not in the original friction ridge impression, produced by an external agent or action.
2. Any information not present in the original object or image, inadvertently introduced by image capture, processing, compressions, transmission, display, and printing.
SWGFAST, Glossary 07-28-2009 ver. 2.0

A structure or feature not normally present but visible as a result of an external agent or action.
The American Heritage® Dictionary of the English Language, Fourth Edition Copyright © 2000 by Houghton Mifflin Company. Published by Houghton Mifflin Company. All rights reserved. 05-25-2004
http://dictionary.reference.com/search?q=artifact

Asbury, David
David Asbury was convicted of murder in a 1997 SCRO murder investigation based on fingerprint evidence. The conviction was later overturned but the SCRO refused to admit to an erroneous identification.

See Erroneous Identifications.

Ashbaugh, Staff Sergeant David R.
(Mar. 11, 1946-present)
Staff Sergeant David Ashbaugh worked for the Royal Canadian Mounted Police, retiring in May of 2004, in addition to being the Director of Ridgeology Consulting Services. He spent over 27 years doing extensive research on the scientific basis and identification process of friction ridge identifications. Among his long list of accomplishments he is credited with coining the term Ridgeology in 1982 and creating the terms level 1, level 2, and level 3 detail. He introduced the ACE-V methodology to the fingerprint field around 1980 and was a key witness for the Daubert Hearings. He sat on several committee boards and as well as serving on the Scientific Working Group on Friction Ridge Analysis, Study and Technology. In addition to publishing many papers on the identification process, in 1999 he authored the book "Quantitative-Qualitative Friction Ridge Analysis: An Introduction to Basic and Advanced Ridgeology", which

has become a fundamental and essential resource for all latent print examiners. Staff Sergeant Ashbaugh has received numerous awards and honors for his significant contributions to the science of friction ridge identification and is recognized as one of the leading experts in his field.

Authority

An accepted source of definitive information.

An expert in a specific field.

Webster's II New Riverside Dictionary, Office Edition. Houghton Mifflin Publishing Co. Copyright 1984, Berkley Addition.

Axiom

In logic: a proposition that is not susceptible of proof or disproof; its truth is assumed to be self-evident. WordNet ® 1.6, © 1997 Princeton University. 02-09-2004

A self-evident principle or one that is accepted as true without proof as the basis for argument; a postulate. The American Heritage® Dictionary of the English Language, Fourth Edition Copyright © 2000 by Houghton Mifflin Company. Published by Houghton Mifflin Company. All rights reserved.02-09-2004

B

Babler, Dr. William Joseph (May 24, 1949-present)
Dr. Babler is recognized as the foremost authority in the structure and formation of friction skin. He is an Associate Professor of Oral Biology teaching human anatomy and embryology at Indiana University School of Dentistry. In addition, he served as the President of the American Dermatoglyphics Association, where he received their Distinguished Service Award in 2003. Dr. Babler has spent over 20 years researching the prenatal development of friction skin, writing numerous articles explaining his findings. He has confirmed many scientific theories about friction ridge formation as well as developed new theories. He has established that the patterns on the fingers are a result of the shape of the volar pads when the friction skin begins to develop; high volar pads create whorls while low volar pads create arches. This was presumed by Mulvihill and Smith but Dr. Babler did the research that confirmed their hypotheses. Dr. Babler was also recognized as a leading expert in the Daubert Hearings.
Besides the significant contributions he has made in the scientific arena, Dr. Babler has also demonstrated himself to be a profound teacher. He has spent countless time educating forensic examiners and has continually made himself available as an educational resource.

Ball area
The large cushion area below the base of the big toe.
SWGFAST, Glossary - Consolidated 09-09-03 ver. 1.0

Balthazard, Dr. Victor (1872-1950)
A Professor of Forensic Medicine at Sorbonne. Balthazard is credited for his statistical model of fingerprint individuality, published in 1911. His model was very simplistic and ignored relevant information but was the foundation for others to develop improved statistical models. Balthazard's work was the basis for Locard's Tripartite Rule.

Basal Layer of Epidermis
See Stratum Basale.

Basement Membrane
A thin, delicate layer of connective tissue underlying the epithelium of many organs. Also called basement lamina.
The American Heritage® Dictionary of the English Language, Fourth Edition

http://dictionary.reference.com/search?q=basement%20membrane

A membrane separating the dermis from the epidermis. The basement membrane consists of three layers: the lamina lucida, the lamina densa, and the lamina fibroreticularis.
Professor Julian Verbov 04-19-08

Basic Fuschin
Fluorescent dye used with selected wavelengths of light to visualize cyanoacrylate ester fumed friction ridge detail. See Rosaniline chloride.
SWGFAST, Glossary - Consolidated 09-09-03 ver. 1.0

Basic Red 28
Fluorescent red dye used with selected wavelengths of light to visualize cyanoacrylate ester fumed friction ridge detail.
SWGFAST, Glossary - Consolidated 09-09-03 ver. 1.0

Basic Yellow 40
Fluorescent yellow dye used with selected wavelengths of light to visualize cyanoacrylate ester fumed friction ridge detail. See Panacryl Brilliant Flavone 10GFF. See Maxilon Flavone 10GFF.
SWGFAST, Glossary - Consolidated 09-09-03 ver. 1.0

Bayes, Rev. Thomas (1702-1761)
A British mathematician and Presbyterian minister, known for having formulated Bayes' theorem. Bayes Theorem was first introduced in "An Essay Towards Solving a Problem in the Doctrine of Chances" published in 1763.

Bayes Theorem
A mathematical approach to solving logic problem by looking at the probability of an event happening given that some other event has already occurred. This approach optimizes the probability by modeling the sample space after the realistic instead of after the entirety.

Bayle, Allan J. (Oct. 11, 1950-present)
Allan Bayle served with the Metropolitan Police Service for 25 years at New Scotland Yard as a Fingerprint Officer and later was regraded as an Identification Officer. This new grade encompassed expertise in fingerprints and forensic scene examination, completing five operational tours of duty, and examining all types of scenes of crime. In 1993, he received a commendation for outstanding scene examination. From August 1996 until May 2001, he lectured at the Scientific Support College for the Metropolitan Police Training Establishment in Hendon. Subjects included basic fingerprint foundation, advanced fingerprint, cadavers/chemical, and basic and advanced forensic awareness courses. He has been an advisor to the Association of Chief Police Officers (ACPO)

led Project Board for fingerprint training which included ridgeology and designing a ridgeology course for future experts in the U.K.
(This next line is not posted on the web version due to differing opinions) He provided crucial fingerprint evidence against al-Megrahi of the 1988 Lockerbie bombing where ridgeology was used for the first time in the United Kingdom. He also testified in Philadelphia before Judge Pollak in the US v Plaza case stating that he thought the F.B.I.'s proficiency tests was too easy.
His work on the McKie, Asbury and McNamara cases forced him to resign and start a consultancy, which includes lecturing, advising on all fingerprint, forensic scene examination matters, training and investigating miscarriages of justice world wide.

Beck, Adolf (or Adolph) (1895)
An early case of erroneous identification by eyewitness testimony and personal recognition. In 1896, Adolf Beck was sentenced to 7 years for defrauding women out of their jewelry in London. The main evidence against him was the testimony of 10 women who identified him as the man who had robbed them, William Thomas aka John Smith, yet Beck insisted he was innocent and he was not this man. He served 5 years of the sentence before being released on good behavior in July 1901. On April 15, 1904 Beck was again accused of stealing jewelry from a young lady. He was again found guilty but before being sentence, the real William Thomas was arrested for the same crimes and the fact that these two men seemed to be doubles of each other was discovered. On July 19, 1904, Beck was pardoned and given 5000 pounds for compensation. Although some claim there were remarkable similarities between these two men, there were obvious documented differences between them.

Benzidine
Once considered to be the best technique for developing bloody latent prints on nonporous items. Benzidine has been found to be a carcinogen and is no longer considered to be a viable process.

The Bepler Committee
In 1894, Britains Troup Committee enacted the procedure of adding fingerprints to Bertillon cards. At this time, these fingerprints weren't used for identification purposes. In the early 1900's, the British Home Secretary convened a committee to resolve the competing claims of anthropometry and fingerprinting. This committee was headed by Lord Henry Bepler and became known as The Bepler Committee. In Dec. 1900, this committee recommended taking fingerprints and classifying them by the Henry system. The implementa-

tion began in 1901.

Berry, John B.E.M.
Berry was born in 1926 in Birmingham, England. He served in the British Army from 1944 to 1948, stationed in Germany. Upon demobilization he entered the police service, joining the fingerprint bureau in 1955. He served in the bureau for 20 years, having the rank of sergeant from 1960 to 1975. He retired from the police service in 1975 and joined the Hertfordshire Constabulary Fingerprint Bureau as a civilian technician. This bureau was a hive of activity because The Fingerprint Society originated there. Berry edited The Society's journal FINGERPRINT WHORLD, the first issue was published in July 1975, and he subsequently edited 64 consecutive quarterly issues, until retiring from the bureau in 1991, after reaching retirement age. In 1989 he was awarded the British Empire Medal by H.M. The Queen for 'services to fingerprints'. In his retirement, Berry has continued with fingerprint research, publishing 25 annual editions of his brainchild 'Ridge Detail in Nature' (renamed 'Strabismus' in 1998), some issues having more than 100 pages. He is now in his 79th year (2005), and is in ill-health, but still settles in his den everyday, keeping up-to-date with fingerprint matters. He states that in his fifty years of working the discipline, he has found that when dealing with a really difficult crime scene imprint, a 'within a minute' decision is totally feckless. There should not be a time limit for the technician to make a comparison; the distortion factor may have a bearing on apparent dissimilarities.

Bertillon, Alphonse (April 22 or 23, 1853-Feb. 13, 1914)
Alphonse Bertillon devised a meticulous method of measuring body parts as a means of identification, known as 'The Bertillon Method of Identification' or 'Anthropometry'. It was first used in 1883 and was found to be slightly flawed in 1903 (known as the Will West Case). The West case didn't end the use of Anthropometry but it did establish that Anthropometry didn't individualize all people. Even though the Bertillon system didn't provide perfect results, it did provide sufficient results and was very useful in its day.
Bertillon is also credited with solving the first crime involving latent prints without having a suspect. Bertillon identified latent prints found on a piece of glass, from the murder scene of Joseph Reibel, as being left by Henri Leon Scheffer's. Bertillon found the identification by searching his files one person at a time. The date of the murder was October 17, 1902 and the identification was made on October 24, 1902. This is published in "Alphonse Bertillon: Father of Scientific Detection", Henry

Rhodes (1956).

Bertillon Method of Identification
See Bertillon, Alphonse.

Bertillonage
Bertillon's method of anthropometry. Quantitative-Qualitative Friction Ridge Analysis, David R. Ashbaugh 1999 CRC Press

Betts case- Ohio 1917
The Betts case may have been the first conviction based solely on palm print evidence. In 1917, Samual W. Betts was arrested and charged with burglary based on the fact that his palm print was found on a windowpane. George Koestle (one of Ferrier's students) was the person who took and compared the palm prints. 'Fingerprint and Identification Magazine', Dec 1942.

Another palm print case that happened around the same time, and also said to be the first palm print case to have a conviction, was a murder trial in Nevada. The defendant was Ben Kuhl.

Bewick, Thomas (1753-1828)
An English engraver noted for carving fingerprint stamps. Galton credits him as the first well-known person to study ridges as a means of identification ("Finger Prints", 1892 pg. 26).

Bias
An influence based on impertinent information rather than objective data, such as irrelevant contextual details surrounding an event.

See Cognitive Bias, Confirmation Bias, Contextual Bias.

Bichromatic ™ Latent Print Powder
A multi-colored powder used to process an object with the purpose of visualizing friction ridge detail. To avoid damaging a latent print, powders are best applied with a camel hair or fiberglass brush.

Bichromatic ™ Latent Print Powder is a combination of black and silver/gray powder which can be dusted on a light or dark surface. On a light-colored surface, the latent print will appear dark so it can be seen and photographed easily. On a dark-colored surface, it will appear light. When lifted with tape and placed on a white backing card, the latent print will appear dark.
http://www.redwop.com/technotes.asp?ID=85 07-11-2004

See Fingerprint Powders.

Bidloo, Govard (1649-1713)
An anatomist, credited with writing the first book, titled "Human Anatomy", with detailed drawings of fingerprints and pores in 1685.

Bifurcation
The point at which one friction ridge divides into two friction ridges.
SWGFAST, Glossary 07-28-2009 ver. 2.0

Divide into two branches.
Quantitative-Qualitative Friction Ridge Analysis, David R. Ashbaugh 1999 CRC Press

Biohazard
Biological agent or condition (as an infectious organism or insecure laboratory conditions) that constitutes a hazard.
SWGFAST, Glossary - Consolidated 09-09-03 ver. 1.0

Biological
Of plant and animal life.
Quantitative-Qualitative Friction Ridge Analysis, David R. Ashbaugh 1999 CRC Press

Biological Uniqueness (also see Law of Biological Uniqueness)
The Scientific Law that states that all items in nature are unique.

Black Box
Any complex system where the internal components cannot be directly assessed. Ideas about how the system works and it's performance are made from viewing the correlation between inputs and outputs.

In psychology, the mind is usually referred to as a black box.

Black Light
Black Light is the series of electromagnetic wavelengths in the Ultraviolet light spectrum with frequencies ranging from approximately 345-400nm. This frequency is referred to as black light because of the absence of color that occurs. Some objects can be seen using black lights that are invisible with normal lights.

Black Powder
A powder used to process an object with the purpose of visualizing friction ridge detail. Typically latent print powder is black but is available in a wide range of colors. To avoid damaging a latent print, powders are best applied with a camel hair or fiberglass brush.

See Fingerprint Powders.

Blaschko, Alfred (March 4, 1858-March 26, 1922)
Alfred Blaschko was a German dermatologist who did extensive studies on embryology and dermatology and how they related to each other. He is sometimes referred to in fingerprint books for his early studies of the dermal and epidermal layers (1884, 1887). Dr. Wilder credits Blaschko as the first person to emphasize differences in the integument and attempts a classification for these differences. He is most noted for describing a

system of lines on the human skin which the linear naevi and dermatoses follow, known as Blaschko lines.

Blind Testing
A valid scientific method of testing a hypothesis. This method is implemented by limiting the information given to practitioners analyzing the data with the intent of decreasing the amount of bias being introduced into an examination. For example, if practitioners aren't privy to previous conclusions, confirmational bias and conformational bias will be decreased. If practitioners don't know case information, contextual bias will be decreased. This method of testing is especially useful in areas of an examination that are inherently subjective (when the potential for bias is elevated). Deciding what information to restrict is dependent on what area of the examination is subjective. Blind Testing tests the reliability of a conclusion (the reproducibility) but it doesn't test the validity of the conclusion (how the conclusion was arrived at), therefore blind testing isn't considered a valid form of peer review. Restricting information may be beneficial in testing for bias but it may severely impact a conclusion if relevant information is being limited.

See Double Blind Testing.

Blind Verification
A valid scientific method of testing the reliability (reproducibility) of a conclusion by giving the same information to others to independently analyze without being influenced by knowing the conclusion of others.

The independent examination of one or more friction ridge impressions by another qualified examiner who has no expectation or knowledge of the conclusion of the original examiner. SWGFAST, Glossary 07-28-2009 ver. 2.0

See Double Blind Verification.

Boiling Technique
A method to re-hydrate the friction skin of a deceased person. In this method water is boiled and them removed from the heat. The hand is submerged in the water for approximately 5 seconds. If re-hydration isn't fully achieved the hand can be re-submerged for another 5 seconds. The hand is then dried before attempting to record the friction skin detail.

Bonnevie, Kristine Elisabeth Heuch (1872-1950)
A Norwegian zoologist and geneticist who wrote "Studies on Papillary Patterns of Human Fingers" in 1924, Journal of Genetics, Cambridge 1924: 15: 1-111. Her main areas of study were genetic inheritance of patterns,

cell division and chromosomes, the embryology of dermatoglyphics and how the height of the volar pad affects the pattern type. Bonnevie was the first to suggest that the basal layer of the epidermis grows faster than either the rest of the epidermis. The layers growing at different rates, creates buckling which produces ridges on the surface of the skin.

Bose, Hemchandra (1897)
Aka Rai Bahadur Hem Chandra Bose or Rai Bahadur Hemchandra Bose. One of the Indian Police Officers in Bengal who worked for Sir Edward Richard Henry and helped him develop the Henry System of Classification.
http://www.jpgmonline.com/article.asp?issn=0022-3859;year=2000;volume=46;issue=4;spage=303;epage=8;aulast=Tewari 02-15-2004

Bottom-Up Influences
One of the two cognitive influences with respect to observational knowledge. Bottom-up influences are objective in nature, guided purely by data.

See Top-Down.

Bracelet Creases
The creases located at the base of the palm. Usually where the friction skin ends.

Brachydactyly
Abnormal shortness of fingers and toes.
SWGFAST, Glossary - Consolidated 09-09-03 ver. 1.0

Brady v. Maryland (1963)
The court decision which states that the prosecutor is obligated to disclose exculpatory information that may be favorable to the defense.

See United States v Henthorn and Giglio v United States.

Branchings
Friction ridge bifurcation; divergence of a friction ridge path.
Quantitative-Qualitative Friction Ridge Analysis, David R. Ashbaugh 1999 CRC Press

Bridge
A connecting friction ridge between and at generally right angles to, parallel running ridges.
SWGFAST, Glossary 07-28-2009 ver. 2.0

Bulb of the Fingers (Thumbs, Toes)
The portion of the friction skin on the tips of fingers, thumbs, or toes in the distal phalanx, from one side of the nail to the opposite side of the nail.
SWGFAST, Glossary - Consolidated 09-09-03 ver. 1.0

Bureau of Criminal Identification (Dept. of Justice) / National Bureau of Identification

The Department of Justice created a Bureau of Criminal Identification in 1905 in order to provide a centralized reference collection of fingerprint cards. In 1907, the collection was moved, as a money-saving measure, to Leavenworth Federal Penitentiary, where it was staffed by convicts. Understandably suspicious of this arrangement, police departments formed their own centralized identification bureau maintained by the International Association of Chiefs of Police (sometimes referred to as the National Police Bureau). It refused to share its data with the Bureau of Criminal Investigation. In 1924, Congress was persuaded to merge the two collections in Washington, D.C., under Bureau of Investigation administration. As a result, law enforcement agencies across the country began contributing fingerprint cards to the Bureau of Investigation by 1926.

http://www.fbi.gov/libref/historic/history/lawless.htm 12-03-2003

C

CA or CAE
Cyanoacrylate Ester (superglue). An adhesive used in a fuming method to develop friction ridge detail.
SWGFAST, Glossary - Consolidated 09-09-03 ver. 1.0

See Cyanoacrylate Ester.

CARDPACT
An acronym that stands for "Combined Advanced Ridgeology, Demystifying Palm Prints, and Comparison Techniques". This was an advanced class taught by the most prominent experts in the latent print community; Pat Wertheim, David Ashbaugh, David Grieve, and Ron Smith.

CAS
Competency Assessment Services Ltd.

CFRE
Complete Friction Ridge Exemplars.

CFSO
The Consortium of Forensic Science Organizations. The consortium is composed of the IAI, the AAFS, ASCLD, NAME (the National Association of Medical Examiners), ASCLD-LAB, and FQS.

CIS
Canadian Identification Society.

CJIS
Criminal Justice Information Services Division. The CJIS Division was established in Feb. 1992 to serve as the focal point and central repository for criminal justice information services in the FBI. It is the largest Division within the FBI. Programs that were initially consolidated under the CJIS Division include the National Crime Information Center (NCIC), Uniform Crime Reporting (UCR), and Fingerprint Identification. In addition, responsibilities for several ongoing technological initiatives were also transferred to the CJIS Division, including the Integrated Automated Fingerprint Identification System (IAFIS), NCIC 2000, and the National Incident-Based Reporting System (NIBRS).
http://www.fbi.gov/hq/cjisd/about.htm

C.R.
Crown to Rump. This abbreviation is used to illustrate the length of a fetus during friction ridge development.

CRFP
Council for the Registration of Forensic Practitioners. A United Kingdom organization that started in 2001 and closed March 31, 2009 due to financial issues.

CSI Effect
The effect on jurors of watching the forensic science shows offered on television. After watching these television shows, the 'CSI effect' claims that jurors expectations of what evidence should be produced at trial are now higher. Jurors may now feel that if forensic evidence isn't produced in a trial, the police and prosecutors didn't do their jobs adequately. Due to these shows, jurors also have unrealistic ideas of what scientific techniques are available and how likely it is to find forensic evidence.

CSS
Crime Scene Search. A filter for an alternate light source. This wavelength works well for an overall crime scene search to visualize different types of trace evidence.

CTS
Collaborative Testing Services.

CV
See Curriculum Vitae.

Cadmium Chloride
A metal salt used to treat ninhydrin developed latent prints.
SWGFAST, Glossary - Consolidated 09-09-03 ver. 1.0

Calcar Area
Area located at the heel of the foot.
SWGFAST, Glossary - Consolidated 09-09-03 ver. 1.0

Wentworth and Wilder refer to the Calcar pattern as extremely rare. It occurs on the heel of the foot usually in the form of a single loop opening inwards.

Caldwell, Harry H. (1872-1957)
An inspector for the Oakland Police Department who founded the IAI in 1915 and was elected president of the organization for the first six years.

Canadian Identification Society
An organization founded in 1978 with the goal as having a place where experts could discuss mutual problems and exchange scientific & technical information that would enhance identification work in Canada.
http://www.cis-sci.ca/HistoryCIS.asp

The charter members of the CIS were Lloyd Dunham, Christopher Tiller, Howard Hall, Clayton Bigras, Roger Remillard, Richard Jordon, Allen Wrenshall, Donald Braithwaite, Harold Tuthill, Donald Guttman, and Ronald Duck. Honorary Members were Judge Rene J. Marin, Deputy Commissioner A.C. Potter and David C. Day Q.C. The Canadian Identification Society publishes a quarterly journal called "Identification Canada".

Carlsson, Kjell
Pronounced Shell Carlsson.
Kjell Carlsson was employed with

the Swedish National Forensic Lab for 10 years before working as a Forensic Scientist for the Stockholm Police Crime Laboratory, where he's been since 1975. Additionally he founded a research and development company, Kjell Carlsson Innovation, aimed at improving forensic tools. Among his most valuable inventions are Mikrosil, Wetwop, the Electrostatic Dust Lifter, the Electrostatic Vacuum Box, the Versa Light Box, and Snow Print Wax.

Carpal Delta Area
Area of the palm containing a delta formation nearest the wrist.
SWGFAST, Glossary - Consolidated 09-09-03 ver. 1.0

Catalyst
A substance, usually used in small amounts relative to the reactants, that modifies and increases the rate of a reaction without being consumed in the process.
The American Heritage® Dictionary of the English Language, Fourth Edition.
Copyright © 2000 by Houghton Mifflin Company.
Published by Houghton Mifflin Company.
http://dictionary.reference.com/search?r=2&q=catalyst 03-08-2004

Cella, Cesare J.
See People v. Crispi.

Certainty
A measurement of ones state of mind with reference to truth. An amount of confidence.
See Accuracy.

Certified
An endorsement by an influential organization stating you've met certain requirements and are officially recognized as being qualified in a particular field.

Chacko, L.W.
Wrote "The Dermal Papillae and Ridge Patterns in Human Volar Skin" in 1968 with M.C.Vaidya.

Chamberlain, Paul
Paul Chamberlain is a forensic scientist and scientific advisor for fingerprints with the Forensic Science Service (FSS), a major UK provider of forensic services. Paul has over 22 years experience in fingerprint detection and comparison. He started his career with the London Metropolitan Police before taking senior roles in two provincial police forces. He joined the FSS in 2000 initially working on the expansion of fingerprint services. He continues to undertake case work but is also involved in a number of projects. In addition to being involved with the probabilistic approach to fingerprint comparisons these include proficiency trials and case interpretation strategies. Paul is the Chair of the ENFSI (Euro-

pean Network of Forensic Science Institutes) European Fingerprint Working Group and leads on the production of their Fingerprint Best Practices Manual.

Champod, Dr. Christophe

Christophe Champod is Professor of forensic science at the school of criminal sciences / Institut de Police Scientifique, University of Lausanne, Switzerland. He has strong interest in statistical and inferential issues in identification evidence and has written articles on the frequency distribution of friction skin characteristics. In 2004, Christophe Champod co-wrote "Fingerprints and Other Ridge Skin Impressions" with Chris Lennard, Pierre Margot and Milutin Stoilovic. He is also an invited member of the Scientific Working Group on Friction Ridge Analysis, Study and Technology.

Characteristics

Features of the friction ridges. Commonly referred to as minutiae, points, or ridge formation morphologies. SWGFAST, Glossary 07-28-2009 ver. 2.0

Characteristics, types of (not a complete list)

Ending ridge
Fork or bifurcation
Island
Dot
Bridge
Spur
Double bifurcation
Trifurcation
Short ridge

Charlton, David Ashley James
(April 18, 1963-present)

Dave Charlton is an internationally recognized latent print expert from the United Kingdom. He began his career in 1987 and has since been involved in many aspects of latent print work including promoting worldwide communication within our industry, developing and implementing updated practices and procedures, as well as research.

Dave Charlton is an active member in several professional organizations. Since 2001, he has been the editor of Fingerprint Whorld, the educational and peer review journal of The Fingerprint Society and has been one of the principle organizers of several Fingerprint Society sponsored national conferences. He's a member of "the Third Level Detail Sub-Group", formed by the Association of Chief Police Officers to investigate the potential use of third level detail within the identification process. He is also an active member of the IAI, and sits on the editorial review board and the latent print subcommittee. He has authored several papers and given many presentations at educational conferences. From 1995 to 1999, Dave Charlton was instrumental in the development and implementation of the United Kingdoms National Automated Fingerprint Identification System, known as NAFIS.

Currently, Mr. Charlton is working for the Sussex Fingerprint Bureau. He spends much of his time collaborating with others in researching the cognitive aspects and psychological influences on the latent print decision making process. His most recent findings have been presented in the following publication, Dror, I.E., Peron, A. E., Hind, S.L., & Charlton, D. When emotions get the better of us: The effect of contextual top-down processing on matching fingerprints. Applied Cognitive Psychology, 2005.

In April 2006, Dave Charlton resigned as Chair of the Fingerprint Society as well as from the committee.

Chatterjee, Sri Salil Kumar (1903 or 1904-Sept. 12, 1988)
Salil K. Chatterjee, of India, is recognized for developing edgeoscopy in 1962. He is also recognized as developing the only practical soleprint classification system.

Cheiloscopy
The study of lip prints.

Chemical Hazard
Chemical agent or condition that constitutes a hazard.
SWGFAST, Glossary - Consolidated 09-09-03 ver. 1.0

Chiridia
Hands and feet.
Quantitative-Qualitative Friction Ridge Analysis, David R. Ashbaugh 1999 CRC Press

Chiridium
Hand or foot.
Quantitative-Qualitative Friction Ridge Analysis, David R. Ashbaugh 1999 CRC Press

Chiroscopy
Examination of the hand (i.e. palms).

Circular Reasoning
Circular reasoning is the term for the error in logic of using the conclusion that you're trying to prove as part of the proof itself. Basically this is using the hypothesis as a proven principle to support itself.

Citric Acid
Chemical used in the preparation of Physical Developer and other friction ridge development reagents.
SWGFAST, Glossary - Consolidated 09-09-03 ver. 1.0

Clandestine
Kept or done in secret, often in order to conceal an illicit or improper purpose.
The American Heritage® Dictionary of the English Language, Fourth Edition

Copyright © 2000 by Houghton Mifflin Company. Published by Houghton Mifflin Company.
http://dictionary.reference.com/search?q=clandestine 09-17-2004

Clarity
Visual quality of a friction ridge impression.
SWGFAST, Glossary - Consolidated 09-09-03 ver. 1.0

Clearness, i.e., how well friction skin ridge detail is recorded in a print.
Quantitative-Qualitative Friction Ridge Analysis, David R. Ashbaugh 1999 CRC Press

Class Characteristics
Characteristics used to put things into groups or classes, e.g., arches, loops, whorls.
SWGFAST, Glossary - Consolidated 09-09-03 ver. 1.0

Class characteristics are features that will be the same for every member of a group, i.e. all whorls have at least 2 delta formations, as opposed to individual characteristics.

Classical Probability
A finite number of outcomes.

See Empirical Probability and Subjective Probability.

Classification
The act of categorizing items into groups. This could include labeling fingerprints as an arch, a loop, or a whorl; could include labeling parts of a palm print as interdigital, thenar, or hypothenar; or could be the process of using an alpha-numeric system to categorize prints.

Alpha numeric formula of finger and palmprint patterns used as a guide for filing and searching.
SWGFAST, Glossary 07-28-2009 ver. 2.0

Classification Systems
The Henry Classification System - developed by Henry in the late 1800's.
Icnofalangometric System – the original name of the system developed by Vucetich in 1891.
Dactiloscopy – the new name of the system developed by Vucetich.
The Oloriz System of Classification - developed by Oloriz.
Identakey – developed in the 1930's by G. Tyler Mairs.
The American System of Fingerprint Classification - developed by Parke in 1903.
The Conley System.
The Flak-Conley System – developed in 1906 in New Jersey, an improved Conley System.
NCIC Fingerprint Classification System.
Collins System – a classification system for single fingerprints used in Scotland Yard in the early 1900's.

Jorgensen System – a classification system for single fingerprints used in the early 1900's.
Battley System - a classification system for single fingerprints used in the 1930's.

Clean Delta
A term popularized by Ron Smith to describe the delta in the interdigital area that is below the index finger. The angles of this delta are usually evenly spaced. This is referred to as the 'clean delta' because it is usually the clearest and most legible.

Clear Layer of Epidermis
See Stratum Lucidum.

Cluster Prints
More than one print grouped together. These may or may not have been deposited simultaneously.

See Simultaneous Impressions.

Cognition
The mental process of knowing, including aspects such as awareness, perception, reasoning, and judgment.
The American Heritage® Dictionary of the English Language, Fourth Edition
Copyright © 2000 by Houghton Mifflin Company. Published by Houghton Mifflin Company. All rights reserved.
http://dictionary.reference.com/search?q=cognition 06-08-2005

Cognitive Bias
Influences that may affect the reliability and validity of one's observations and conclusions.
SWGFAST, Glossary 07-28-2009 ver. 2.0

Cognitive Influences
Influences that direct decision-making. The two cognitive influences are bottom-up and top-down influences.

Cognitive Researchers
Dr. Itiel Dror
David Charlton

Ralph Haber
Lyn Haber

Dr. Thomas A. Busey
John R. Vanderkolk

Dean Bertram
Jon S. Byrd

Cole, Dr. Simon A. (1967-present)
Dr. Simon A. Cole is an Assistant Professor in the School of Ecology at the University of California, Irvine, Department of Criminology, Law and Society. Some people refer to Dr. Simon Cole as a fingerprint critic. In 2001, Dr. Cole wrote the article, 'The Myth of Fingerprints' and the book, 'Suspect Identities'. Dr. Cole questions the accuracy of fingerprint identifications.

Colloidal Gold
A reagent that reacts with amino acids to develop friction ridge detail. Colloidal Gold produces a weak colored print and usually needs additional enhancement. Colloidal Gold is the initial suspension in the multimetal deposition process.

Color Reversal
See Tonal Reversal.

Colored Superglue
In 2006, Avery L. Smith, a 7th grader at Raney Intermediate Middle School in Corona, California did a science fair project to test different ways of coloring superglue for easier visualization. She found that coloring the superglue with a pink highlighter prior to heating the superglue made the latent images glow under a black light. In addition to the science fair project, she presented this information at the 2007 IAI Conference in San Diego, published it in "The Print" and in "Forensic Magazine".

In 2006, Mountain State University received an NIJ grant that, under the guidance of David Weaver, will research dyed superglue for better visualization.

Commonwealth v. Terry L. Patterson
See State of Massachusetts v. Patterson. 'Commonwealth v. Terry L. Patterson' is the official name of this court case.

Comparator
A split image projection screen used to view fingerprint images. Invented by William Russell-Turner.

Comparison
The second step of the ACE-V method. The observation of two or more impressions to determine the existence of discrepancies, dissimilarities, or similarities.
SWGFAST, Glossary 07-28-2009 ver. 2.0

The act of comparing or finding likenesses or differences.
Quantitative-Qualitative Friction Ridge Analysis, David R. Ashbaugh 1999 CRC Press

More definitions listed under ACE-V.

Competency
Possessing and demonstrating the requisite knowledge, skills, and abilities to successfully perform a specific task.
SWGFAST, Glossary 07-28-2009 ver. 2.0

Complete Friction Ridge Exemplars
The new name for major case prints (proposed in 2006). This name change is designed to describe what's actually being recorded and eliminate misunderstandings associated with the term major case prints.

A systematic recording of all friction ridge detail appearing on the palmar sides of the hands. This includes the extreme sides of the palms; and joints, tips, and sides of the fingers.
SWGFAST, Glossary 07-28-2009 ver. 2.0

Complex Examinations
The encountering of uncommon circumstances during an examination; for example, the existence of high distortion, low quality or quantity, the possibility of simultaneity, or conflicts among examiners.
SWGFAST, Glossary 07-28-2009 ver. 2.0

Conclusion
A result stemming from an objective basis, not merely an emotional basis.

See Opinion and Determination.

Conclusions for Comparisons
The formal observations seen or recorded during a comparison may indicate one of the following conclusions:

Individualization (has consistency and sufficiency to establish individualization)
Match (could be consistent but not sufficient for establishing individualization)
Inconclusive-No identification or exclusion has been established.

-Incomplete. Exemplars don't include the area the latent print was left from (tips, palms, etc), different exemplars may change conclusion.

-Incomplete. Exemplars don't include the detail in the latent print (level 3 detail), different exemplars may change conclusion.

-No identification effected. This may be due to time constraints, abilities, etc.

-Consistent but not sufficient. Features are consistent but not sufficient for individualization. The latent print can not be individualized to the exemplars and the exemplars cannot be excluded as the donor. Exclusionary value only.

-Generally consistent but not sufficient. The majority of the characteristics are consistent or similar but an unexplained dissimilarity exists and the characteristics that are consistent aren't sufficient to establish an individualization.
No identification effected (may not indicate an exclusion)
Exclusion (not left by a subject)
No value for identification (may have exclusionary value)
No value for comparison (no value for identification or exclusion)
No value for determining simultaneity

Some reasons for 'no value' may be that a print lacks quality, quantity, clarity, or reliability.

Conclusive
Serving to end doubt or uncertainty. Webster's II New Riverside Dictionary, Office Edition. Houghton Mifflin Publishing Co. Copyright 1984, Berkley Addition.

Expressing finality with no implication of possible change; "an absolute (or unequivocal) guarantee to respect the nation's authority"; "inability to make a conclusive (or unequivocal) refusal".
WordNet ® 1.6, © 1997 Princeton University
http://dictionary.reference.com/search?q=conclusive 03-09-2003

Confirmation Bias
A form of selective thinking that involves focusing on data that confirms preconceived expectations while ignoring data that doesn't confirm ones beliefs.

To compensate for this natural human tendency the scientific method is constructed so that we must try to disprove our hypotheses.
http://www.fact-index.com/c/co/confirmation_bias.html 07-14-2004

The tendency to search for data or interpret information in a manner that supports one's preconceptions.
SWGFAST, Glossary 07-28-2009 ver. 2.0

Conflict
A difference of conclusion that becomes apparent during the application of an examination methodology.
SWGFAST, Glossary 07-28-2009 ver. 2.0

Conflicting Conclusions
Failure of the verification process to result in confirmation of a prior conclusion constitutes a conflicting conclusion. Three types of conflict can occur: 1) individualization versus exclusion, 2) individualization versus inconclusive or 3) exclusion versus inconclusive.
SWGFAST - Quality Assurance Guidelines for Latent Print Examiners, (9/28/06 ver 3.0)

Congenital
Of or relating to a condition that is present at birth, as a result of either heredity or environmental influences.
The American Heritage® Dictionary of the English Language, Fourth Edition Copyright © 2000 by Houghton Mifflin Company. Published by Houghton Mifflin Company. All rights reserved.
http://dictionary.reference.com/search?q=congenital 06-11-03

Constellation Method
See Pincushion Method.

Consultation
A significant interaction between

examiners regarding one or more impressions in question.
SWGFAST, Glossary 07-28-2009 ver. 2.0

Contemporaneous Documentation
To document the steps done as you are doing them. The value in doing this is to know what was done in situations that can't be redone (such as physical tasks).

Contextual Bias
The tendency to allow information or outside influences to interfere with the evaluation and interpretation of data.
SWGFAST, Glossary 07-28-2009 ver. 2.0

Convergence
Two or more ridges running parallel and then moving towards each other.

Cooke, Donald
Donald Cooke was the son of T.G. Cooke. He worked along side his father at the Institute of Applied Science and helped operate the IAS after his fathers death in 1952 until his own retirement in 1975.

Cooke, T. Dickerson (1911-1980)
T. Dickerson Cooke was the son of T.G. Cooke. After graduating from college Cooke worked with his father at the Institute of Applied Science. In 1952, he took over as director of the IAS and retired in 1975.

Cooke, Thomas Grant (1885-1952)
T. G. Cooke was a civil engineer who founded a correspondence school for railway signal engineers. In 1916, along with Captain William K. Evans, he established "Evan's University", later known as the Institute of Applied Science. He served as director of the IAS until his death in 1952. The IAS became instrumental in training experts in the identification field.

Coomassie Blue
Blue protein stain used to enhance bloody friction ridge detail.
SWGFAST, Glossary - Consolidated 09-09-03 ver. 1.0

Core
The approximate center of a pattern.
SWGFAST, Glossary 07-28-2009 ver. 2.0

Corium
Dermis; often referred to as the true skin.
Quantitative-Qualitative Friction Ridge Analysis, David R. Ashbaugh 1999 CRC Press

Correspond
To be in agreement, harmony, or conformity. To be similar or equivalent in character, quantity, origin, structure, or function
The American Heritage® Dictionary of the English Language, Fourth Edition Copyright © 2000 by Hough-

ton Mifflin Company. Published by Houghton Mifflin Company. All rights reserved. http://dictionary.reference.com/search?q=correspond 02-27-03

Crease
A line or linear depression; grooves at the joints of the phalanges, at the junction of the digits and across the palmar and plantar surfaces that accommodate flexion.
SWGFAST, Glossary - Consolidated 09-09-03 ver. 1.0

Two types of creases: Flexion creases disrupt the basal layer of the epidermis and have no ridge detail within the crease. White lines (or tension creases) disrupt the stratum corneum or horny layer of the epidermis and do have ridge detail within the crease.

See Bracelet Creases, Distal Transverse Crease, Metacarpo-Phalangeal Crease, Proximal Transverse Crease, Radial Longitudinal Crease, Occasional Features.

See Flexion Creases, Tension Creases and White Lines.

Crispi, Charles
See People v. Crispi.

Cross-Hatching
Cross-hatching is a term popularized by Ron Smith that describes the crease pattern in the thenar area of the palm. These creases intersect other creases running in a perpendicular direction.

Crowle's Double Stain
Blue protein stain used to enhance bloody friction ridge detail.
SWGFAST, Glossary - Consolidated 09-09-03 ver. 1.0

Crows Feet
A term popularized by Ron Smith to describe the ulnar side of the distal transverse crease. On the ulnar side of the palm, the distal transverse crease is a series of bifurcating creases resembling crow's feet.

Crystal Violet
See Gentian Violet.
SWGFAST, Glossary - Consolidated 09-09-03 ver. 1.0

Cummins, Dr. Harold (1893-1976)
Doctor Cummins is universally acknowledged as the Father of Dermatoglyphics. Harold studied all aspects of fingerprint analysis, from anthropology to genetics, from embryology to the study of malformed hands with from two to seven fingers. (13) He pulled together the diverse work of his predecessors, added original research and set the standards of the field still in force to the present. His famous Down Syndrome(14) studies predicted a genetic link to the disease based upon the presence of

the Simian Crease.
http://www.handanalysis.net/library/derm_cummins.htm 2-27-03

Cummins is also known for inventing the term dermatoglyphics in 1926 and writing the book "Fingerprints, Palms and Soles" with Charles Midlo in 1943.

Curriculum Vitae
A summary of one's education, professional history, and job qualifications,
as for a prospective employer.
The American Heritage® Dictionary of the English Language, Fourth Edition
Copyright © 2000 by Houghton Mifflin Company.
Published by Houghton Mifflin Company.
http://dictionary.reference.com/search?q=curriculum%20vitae 07-08-2003

Cuspal
When the ridges on a finger run vertically from the crease to the tip of the finger. Moenssens states that these patterns cannot be grouped into any of the Henry pattern types. Cummins states that they should be grouped into the accidental whorl category. Others have stated that cuspal patterns should be classified as a tented arch.

Cyanoacrylate Ester (Commonly known as superglue)
A fuming technique used to develop friction ridge detail on nonporous items, but does not interfere with the processing of porous items. The cyanoacrylate ester polymerizes on the components of the latent residue creating a white impression. The value of using cyanoacrylate ester as a latent processing technique was first realized by Fuseo Matsumura in 1977, a trace evidence examiner with the Japanese National Police Agency. Heating cyanoacrylate ester decreases the development time, but heating it above 400 degrees Fahrenheit generates hydrogen cyanide (Identification News, Sept. 1985, "A word of caution"). Humidity and vinegar are both known catalysts to this technique.

Also referred to as superglue, CA, or CAE.

See Colored Superglue and Super-Glue Girl.

Cyclohexane
Solvent used in the preparation of liquid Iodine reagent.
SWGFAST, Glossary - Consolidated 09-09-03 ver. 1.0

D

DAB

Diaminobenzidine. Reagent used to detect / enhance bloody friction ridge detail.
SWGFAST, Glossary - Consolidated 09-09-03 ver. 1.0

A chemical technique used to develop friction ridge detail in blood through oxidation. Can be used on both porous and nonporous items. Found to be very hazardous.

DFO

1,8-Diazafluoren-9-one. The suffix '-one' (pronounced own) refers to the chemical make up, as in acetone or lactone.

Compound that reacts with amino acids to produce friction ridge detail with fluorescent properties when exposed to excitation wavelengths of 352-591 nm.
SWGFAST, Glossary - Consolidated 09-09-03 ver. 1.0

A ninhydrin analog used to develop latent prints on porous items. Optimal viewing is done with an alternate light source (352-591nm) and orange or red goggles.

In 1989, C. A. Pounds, R. Griggs, and T. Monkolanssavaratana with the Department of Chemistry, Belfast, Northern Ireland (per the FBI) introduced the reagent 1, 8-diazafluorenone (DFO), which is commercially available and used in the United Kingdom. Unlike ninhydrin, DFO gives a weakly colored initial print; the main feature of this reagent is its ability to give a fluorescent print without secondary treatment. However, some investigators currently report difficulties with uniform print development using DFO.
New Reagents for Development of Latent Fingerprints. NIJ 1995
http://www.ncjrs.org/txtfiles/finger.txt 06-19-2003

DMAC

See Dimethylaminocinnamaldehyde.

DPR

Dermatopathia Pigmentosa Reticularis. A genetic disorder passed down through the female side of the family. DPR is caused by a gene that mutates during embryonic development resulting in a lack of ridge detail and sweat glands. DPR is just one of several ectodermal dysplasia (ED) syndromes.

Dactiloscopy or Dactiloscopia or Dactiloscopico

The fingerprint classification system developed by Juan Vucetich and used in most areas of South America.

Dactylography
The study of fingerprints as a method of identification.
The American Heritage® Dictionary of the English Language, Fourth Edition Published by Houghton Mifflin Company.
http://dictionary.reference.com/search?q=dactylography 02-27-03

Also the name of the book written in 1905 by Dr. Henry Faulds.

Dactyloscopic Point
A dactyloscopic point is a notable event that occurs in a regular flow of papillary ridges that is subject of analysis. The event is a natural/biological disturbance to the normal parallel system of the ridges (e.g. a ridge stops or starts), and is significant.
http://www.interpol.int/Public/Forensic/fingerprints/WorkingParties/IEEGFI2/default.asp#4

Dactyloscopy
Comparison of fingerprints for identification.
From the Hutchinson Encyclopaedia. Helicon Publishing LTD 2000.
http://www.tiscali.co.uk/reference/dictionaries/difficultwords/data/d0004226.html 04-06-2003

Identification by comparison of fingerprints: also: classification of fingerprints.
Merriam-Webster, Incorporated. © 1997-2000.
http://www.fasthealth.com/dictionary/d/dactyloscopy.php 04-06-2003

Daoud, Ouhnane
See Mayfield, Brandon.

Daubert Court Cases (not a complete list)
Daubert v. Merrell Dow Pharmaceuticals (1993)
General Electric Company v. Joiner (1997)
Kumho Tire Company v. Carmichael (1999)
United States v. Byron Mitchell (1999)
United States v. Plaza (2002)
Commonwealth v. Terry L. Patterson (2005)

Daubert v. Merrell Dow Pharmaceuticals 1993
The Federal Court decision on the admissibility of scientific evidence and testimony in a court of law. The Daubert decision stated on page 597, "….the Rules of Evidence—especially Rule 702—do assign to the trial judge the task of ensuring that an expert's testimony both rests on a reliable foundation and is relevant to the task at hand."

From page 592, "Faced with a proffer of expert scientific testimony, then, the trial judge must determine at the outset, pursuant to Rule 104(a), whether the expert is proposing to testify to (1) scientific knowledge that (2) will assist the trier of fact to understand or determine a fact in issue. This entails a preliminary assessment of whether the reasoning or methodology underlying the testimony is scientifically valid and of whether that reasoning or methodology properly can be applied to the facts in issue."

"Many factors will bear on the inquiry, and we do not presume to set out a definitive checklist or test. But some general observations are appropriate." The observations they mentioned included, "whether the theory or technique in question can be (and has been) tested, whether it has been subjected to peer review and publication, its known or potential error rate and the existence and maintenance of standards controlling its operation, and whether it has attracted widespread acceptance within a relevant scientific community." The acronym GTKPR, which stands for Gatekeeper, was created by Glenn Langenburg in 2001 to help remember these factors. The theories or technique should have:

General Acceptance
Tested (has been)
Known Standards
Peer Review and Publication
Rate of Error (known or potential)

Daubert is considered by some to be a lower criteria than Frye designed to let new scientific evidence into court prior to it being generally accepted. Daubert stated, "General acceptance is not a necessary precondition to the admissibility of scientific evidence under the Federal Rules of Evidence…".

In the Daubert case, Merrell Dow was sued by a mother whose baby had a congenital disorder. That mother had taken Bendectin, an anti-nausea drug made by Merrell Dow, during her pregnancy. Merrell Dow moved for summary judgment, claiming Bendectin had not caused the child's disorder. In the affidavit authored by Dr. Steven H. Lamm, the author testified that he had reviewed multiple published human studies and concluded the use of Bendectin during the first trimester of pregnancy was not supposed to be a health risk. In response to Merrell Dow's affidavit, the plaintiff presented eight affidavits solely based on animal testings, claiming the existence of a link between Bendectin and animal birth defects.

The court granted summary judgment for Merrell Dow and dismissed the case, finding Daubert's experts relied on evidence "not sufficiently established to have general acceptance in the field to which it belongs." The Court held that expert opinion

which is not based on data from the field of epidemiology concerning Bendectin is not admissible to raise an issue regarding causation (in law) to the jury. In addition, the Court also ruled that although Daubert's experts recalculated data obtained from previously published epidemiologic studies, their findings were not considered admissible because they were neither published nor subjected to peer review. The plaintiffs appealed the decision, and, in due course, the case reached the U. S. Supreme Court
The Supreme Court did not apply their new Daubert standard to the case, but rather reversed the decision and remanded the case to the Ninth Circuit court. On remand, the Ninth Circuit applied the Daubert standard and again granted summary judgment for the defendant.
http://en.wikipedia.org/wiki/Daubert_Standard 05-27-2006

See R. v. Mohan (1994) for the Canadian equivalent to this decision.

Daubert Trilogy
The 3 main Daubert cases that set the requirements for admissibility of expert testimony.
Daubert v. Merrell Dow Pharmaceuticals (1993)
General Electric Company v. Joiner (1997)
Kumho Tire Company v. Carmichael (1999)

Deductive Reasoning
Reasoning from the general to the particular
WordNet ® 1.6, © 1997 Princeton University
http://dictionary.reference.com/search?q=deductive%20reasoning 02-27-03

DeForest, Henry Pelouse (AKA Deforrest) (1864-1948)
Pioneered the first systematic use of fingerprints in the United States by the New York Civil Service Commission.
http://www.forensicdna.com/Timeline020702.pdf 03-08-2003

Henry DeForest was the Chief Medical Examiner for New York City. In 1902, he was asked to recommend a method of identification. This was intended as a means of stopping potential employees from hiring others to take the civil service exams for them. The first person was fingerprinted on Dec. 19, 1902. His recommendation of using fingerprints was the first use of fingerprints by a United States government agency and considered the second use of fingerprints in the United States (after Gilbert Thompson). DeForest also invented the dactyloscope, http://rmc.library.cornell.edu/EAD/htmldocs/RMM03214.html.

Degloving
The unintentional separation of the skin from the hands or feet, usually as a whole which resembles a glove. This is the result of a deceased body's prolonged immersion in water.

Delta
The point on a friction ridge at or nearest to the point of divergence of two type lines, and located at or directly in front of the point of divergence.
SWGFAST, Glossary 07-28-2009 ver. 2.0

Classification term for triradius.
Quantitative-Qualitative Friction Ridge Analysis, David R. Ashbaugh 1999 CRC Press

A term introduced by Galton to indicate the small area where 3 folds meet.
Personal Identification, Wentworth and Wilder 1918 pg. 117.

Deposition Pressure
The amount of downward pressure during the deposition of a print.
Quantitative-Qualitative Friction Ridge Analysis, David R. Ashbaugh 1999 CRC Press

Dermabrasion
A technique using chemicals, wire brush, surgery or lasers which can case either temporary or permanent loss of ridge detail.
SWGFAST, Glossary - Consolidated 09-09-03 ver. 1.0

Dermal
Relative to the skin or dermis.
Quantitative-Qualitative Friction Ridge Analysis, David R. Ashbaugh 1999 CRC Press

Dermal Papillae
Peg-like formations on the surface of the dermis.
SWGFAST, Glossary - Consolidated 09-09-03 ver. 1.0

Aka dermal pegs or papillary pegs.

Dermal Papillae increases the surface area between the dermis and the epidermis, allowing for a stronger bond. As a person ages the dermal papillae flattens, which creates less of a bond resulting in loose skin and creating wrinkles and creases. The flattening of the dermal papillae also creates less of a difference in height between the ridges and the furrows.

Dermal Pegs
See Dermal Papillae.

Dermal Ridges
The ridges in the papillary layer of the dermis that connect to the bottom ridges of the epidermis. Also called papillary ridges.

Dermatoglyphics
Study of the surface markings of the skin; friction ridges.

Quantitative-Qualitative Friction Ridge Analysis, David R. Ashbaugh 1999 CRC Press

Cummins and Midlo were professors of Microscopic Anatomy at Tulane University in the United States, and it was they who in fact coined the term 'dermatoglyphics' in 1926 (derma = skin, glyph = carving).
http://users.breathemail.net/chiro/chiro/dermatoglyphics.htm 04-26-03

Usually associated with the study of fingerprint patterns and their association with heredity, race, and medical conditions.

Dermatopathia Pigmentosa Reticularis (DPR)
A genetic disorder passed down through the female side of the family. DPR is caused by a gene that mutates during embryonic development resulting in a lack of ridge detail and sweat glands. DPR is just one of several ectodermal dysplasia (ED) syndromes.

A rare genetic ectodermal dysplasia in which ridge dysplasia is seen. Naegeli – Franceschetti – Jadassohn Syndrome and Hypohidrotic Ectodermal Dysplasia are just two other ectodermal dysplasias where dermatoglyphic aberrations are seen.
Professor Julian Verbov 04-19-08

Dermis
The layer of skin beneath the epidermis.
SWGFAST, Glossary - Consolidated 09-09-03 ver. 1.0

The layer of skin under the epidermis; the true skin.
Quantitative-Qualitative Friction Ridge Analysis, David R. Ashbaugh 1999 CRC Press

The layer of skin beneath the epidermis consisting of two layers, the papillary layer and the reticular layer. The dermis provides nutrients to the epidermis.

Desmosomes
Desmosomes are responsible for lateral cell-to-cell adhesion. The cells in the epidermis are connected with desmosomes. As the cells are pushed to the surface by newly forming cells they eventually break apart and are sloughed off. This is called desquamation.

Desquamation
The separation or shedding of the cuticle or epidermis in the form of flakes or scales; exfoliation, as of bones.
Webster's Revised Unabridged Dictionary, © 1996, 1998 MICRA, Inc.
http://dictionary.reference.com/search?q=desquamation

Determination

To decide or settle authoritatively or conclusively.
Webster's II New Riverside Dictionary, Office Edition. Houghton Mifflin Publishing Co. Copyright 1984, Berkley Addition.

The settling of a question or case by an authoritative decision or pronouncement, especially by a judicial body: The choice of a foster home was left to the determination of the court.
The American Heritage® Dictionary of the English Language, Fourth Edition Copyright © 2000 by Houghton Mifflin Company. Published by Houghton Mifflin Company. All rights reserved.
http://dictionary.reference.com/search?q=determination

Develop
To promote a change in physical attributes, making an item more pronounced or prominent. To enhance. With regard to latent development, examiners change the physical attributes making the original latent more usable.
With regard to fetal friction skin development (or formation), development may insinuate initial creation.

Development Medium
The substance used to develop friction ridge prints, i.e., powder
Quantitative-Qualitative Friction Ridge Analysis, David R. Ashbaugh 1999 CRC Press

Deviation
1. A change in friction ridge path.
2. An alteration or departure from a documented policy or standard procedure.
SWGFAST, Glossary 07-28-2009 ver. 2.0

Dichloromethane
Solvent used in the preparation of liquid Iodine reagent. See Methylene chloride.
SWGFAST, Glossary - Consolidated 09-09-03 ver. 1.0

Diff-Lift™
Specialized lifting tape made for use on textured objects. This product was developed by, and is available through, the Lynn Peavey Company.

Differential Growth
Develops at random without plan.
Quantitative-Qualitative Friction Ridge Analysis, David R. Ashbaugh 1999 CRC Press

See Theory of Differential Growth.

Differentiation
Becoming different, i.e., the cells of an embryo differentiate into organs and parts as it grows; specific friction ridge patterns become unique.
Quantitative-Qualitative Friction Ridge Analysis, David R. Ashbaugh 1999 CRC Press

The process by which cells or tissues undergo a change toward a more specialized form or function, especially during embryonic development.
The American Heritage® Dictionary of the English Language, Fourth Edition Copyright © 2000 by Houghton Mifflin Company. Published by Houghton Mifflin Company. All rights reserved.
http://dictionary.reference.com/search?q=differentiation 03-08-2003

Digit
A toe or finger.
SWGFAST, Glossary - Consolidated 09-09-03 ver. 1.0

Dillinger, John (1903-1934)
Dillinger is noted for trying to elude law enforcement by mutilating his fingerprints. He obliterated the cores and the deltas in all ten of his fingers.

Dimethylaminocinnamaldehyde
Better known as DMAC. A chemical used to develop friction ridge detail on thermal paper. This alternative to using DFO or ninhydrin doesn't turn thermal paper black. Refrigeration is needed to store the treated transfer sheets that are used in this procedure. The developed friction ridge detail has fluorescent properties when exposed to wavelengths of 400-500 nm.

Discrepancy
A difference between two impressions that cannot be attributed to distortion.

The presence of friction ridge detail in one impression that does not exist in the corresponding area of another impression.
SWGFAST, Glossary 07-28-2009 ver. 2.0

See One Discrepancy Rule.

Dissimilar
The appearance of inconsistency between two friction ridge impressions that, based upon further analysis, could be attributed either to distortion or difference.

Dissimilarity
A difference in appearance between two friction ridge impressions.
SWGFAST, Glossary 07-28-2009 ver. 2.0

Dissociated Ridges
1. Disrupted, rather than continuous, friction ridges.
2. An area of friction ridge units that did not form into friction ridges.
SWGFAST, Glossary 07-28-2009 ver. 2.0

An area of ridge units that did not form into friction ridges.
Quantitative-Qualitative Friction Ridge Analysis, David R. Ashbaugh 1999 CRC Press

Distal
1. Farthest away from the center or point of attachment.
2. The direction away from the body.
SWGFAST, Glossary 07-28-2009 ver. 2.0

Away from the center or point of origin.
Quantitative-Qualitative Friction Ridge Analysis, David R. Ashbaugh 1999 CRC Press

Distal Inter-Phalangeal Flexion Crease
The top crease in a finger.

Distal Transverse Crease
The crease above the proximal transverse crease.

Distortion
Variances in the 2-dimensional reproductions of the 3-dimensional friction skin source caused by multiple deposition factors such as pressure, movement, force, or the contact surface.

Variances in the reproduction of friction skin caused by pressure, movement, force, contact surface, and so forth.
SWGFAST, Glossary 07-28-2009 ver. 2.0

Distortion Clues (not a complete list)
Fault line (shadowing where two impressions might meet)
Notch (uneven edges when 2 prints might meet)
Misaligned ridges
Disturbance in ridge flow
Multiple vvv's or multiple bifurcations (may be a sign of twisting)
Overlapping ridges or superimposed ridges (may be a sign of a double tap)

Divergence
The separation of two friction ridges that have been running parallel or nearly parallel.
SWGFAST, Glossary - Consolidated 09-09-03 ver. 1.0

Dizygotic
Derived from two separately fertilized eggs. Used to describe fraternal twins and distinguish them from identical twins (monozygotic).

Doctrine
Belief, what is taught as a group's belief.
Quantitative-Qualitative Friction Ridge Analysis, David R. Ashbaugh 1999 CRC Press

Documentation (amount needed)
Providing documentation is a way to demonstrate correct application of any process. There are generally two forms of documentation. Contemporaneous documentation is useful for physical task that can't be recreated at a later date. Documentation of the justification behind a conclusion is useful for analytical tasks

than can be recreated later. Documentation stating the basis or justification for a conclusion is more desirable when a conclusion isn't clearly apparent to other experts in the field (complex examinations), or when unusual occurrences are present. The amount of documentation depends on the complexity of the data and/or the situation. Documentation of the analytical process isn't required for every comparison but it is a scientific protocol to provide documentation if anyone should ask for it.

Dogma
Statements from an authoritative source that are accepted as being true without having proof.

Dondero, John A. (Nov. 11, 1900-Aug. 1957)
John A. Dondero was a pioneer in the science of investigation and identification. After graduating from college with a degree in Chemical Engineering, John Dondero became interested in this newly developing field. During his life he created many valuable inventions that aided forensic practitioners. In the early 1930's, after seeing his daughter's footprints taken at birth, he developed the first clean and inkless system for taking fingerprints. He also developed the first fingerprint ink and the first commercially available fingerprint powder. At the time most powders were prepared and ground by hand. Around this time he established the Faurot Forensic Company, named after the famous New York Police Department detective. This company is now owned by Sirchie Finger Print Laboratories. One main historical event that Mr. Dondero was involved with was the famous 1944 Hartford Circus fire. He was instrumental in identifying 168 bodies from this tragedy. After World War II, at the request of New York City and Nassau County Police, Mr. Dondero founded a school where he taught classification, latent print development, crime scene investigation and taking and comparing fingerprints. The contributions John Dondero gave to the fingerprint community will forever be remembered. In 1958, the IAI recognized these significant contributions by adopting the IAI John A. Dondero Memorial Award. It is the highest honor an IAI member can receive. It is awarded for the most significant contribution in the area of identification and allied sciences during the calendar year immediately preceding each annual conference. Its first recipient was J. Edgar Hoover. Only 18 people have received this award since inception. The IAI 89th Annual Conference, St. Louis, Missouri, Aug. 27th, 2004, by Marilyn Picard.

Dorsal
The backside of the hand, the non-

palmar side.

Dot
An isolated friction ridge unit whose length approximates its width in size. SWGFAST, Glossary 07-28-2009 ver. 2.0

Double Blind Testing
Double Blind Testing is a valid scientific method of testing a hypothesis. This method implements Blind Testing with the additional element of concealing the fact that the practitioner is part of a test (this information may also be concealed from the person administering the test). The intent behind double blind testing is to eliminate that people may arrive at different conclusions when they know they are being tested. Double Blind Testing tests the reliability of a conclusion (the reproducibility) but it doesn't test the validity of the conclusion (how the conclusion was arrived at), therefore Double Blind Testing isn't considered a valid form of peer review. Restricting information may be beneficial in testing for bias but it may severely impact a conclusion if relevant information is being limited.

Double Blind Verification
A valid scientific method of testing the reliability (reproducibility) of a conclusion by giving the same information to others to independently analyze without being influence by knowing the conclusion of others and not knowing that they are involved in a test. The intent behind double blind verification is to eliminate that people may arrive at different conclusions when they know they are being tested.

Double Impression
A double impression can refer to either overlapping prints (overlays) or double taps.

Double Tap
A subtle double impression where additional friction ridges will coincide or be close to running in the same direction as the existing ridge flow. Double taps are made in close time proximity to the first friction ridge impression. Double Taps are made by the same finger.
Charles Parker 09-06-2006

Dragon's Blood Powder
Dragon's Blood fingerprint powder is made from the resin of the rattan palm. The advantage of using this powder is that you can visualize latent prints on light, dark, and multicolored surfaces.

Dror, Dr. Itiel
Itiel Dror is a cognitive neuroscientist who got his Ph.D. from Harvard University in 1994. He specializes in visual cognition, human performance, expertise and decision making. Dr. Dror's interest and experience is in taking scientific knowledge

about the human brain and mind, and translating them into practical ways to improve and affect human performance and decision making in the workplace. His practical experience is in cognitive aspects involved in fingerprint identification and his research has been funded by a variety of bodies, such as the FBI, NIST, and NIJ. The research and consultancy does not only focus on decision making and perceptual issues, but also pertains to selection and training of fingerprint experts, as well as the use and integration of technology.

Dr. Dror is affiliated with the Institute of Cognitive Neuroscience at University College London (UCL), and researches and consults through Cognitive Consultants International (CCI). His applied research and consultancy has taken place in a variety of countries and has included governmental bodies (such as the UK Passport and Identity Services; the US Air Force; and Police Forces in a variety of countries). Dr. Dror has published more than 75 peer reviewed articles, including a number of leading articles in the forensic science domain. He is an associate editor of the journal Pragmatics and Cognition, and is a member of the NIJ/NIST expert working group in human factors in latent fingerprint examination.

For more details, please see: www.CCI-hq.com

Dry-Benching
Reporting results from tests that were not actually done. Also referred to as Dry-Labbing.

Dry-Labbing
Reporting results from tests that were not actually done. Also referred to as Dry-Benching.

Duct
A tube or canal that delivers secretions or excretions.
SWGFAST, Glossary - Consolidated 09-09-03 ver. 1.0

Duplicate Lift
Taking subsequent lifts from the same area of the same surface with the intention of improving the quality and contrast of the latent print being lifted.

Dysplasia
Ridge units that did not form complete friction ridges due to a genetic cause.
SWGFAST, Glossary - Consolidated 09-09-03 ver. 1.0

Ridge units that did not form friction ridges due to a genetic cause.
Quantitative-Qualitative Friction Ridge Analysis, David R. Ashbaugh 1999 CRC Press

E

ED
Ectodermal dysplasia.

EFPWG
European Fingerprint Working Group.

ENFSI
European Network of Forensic Science Institutes.

ESSO
An AFIS term meaning Enhanced Sending Search to Other, referring to searching another AFIS system from your system.

Eccrine Gland
Any of the numerous small sweat glands distributed over the body's surface that produce a clear aqueous secretion devoid of cytoplasmic constituents and important in regulating body temperature
The American Heritage® Dictionary of the English Language, Fourth Edition Copyright © 2000 by Houghton Mifflin Company. Published by Houghton Mifflin Company. All rights reserved
http://dictionary.reference.com/search?q=eccrine%20gland 02-27-03

Sweat glands that open on all surfaces of the skin.
SWGFAST, Glossary - Consolidated 09-09-03 ver. 1.0

Quantitative-Qualitative Friction Ridge Analysis, David R. Ashbaugh 1999 CRC Press

Eccrine Sweat
The secretion of the eccrine gland. Composed of 99% water, amino acids, sodium chloride and trace amounts of other organic and inorganic elements.

Ectoderm
The outermost of the three primary germ layers of an embryo, from which the epidermis, nervous tissue, and, in vertebrates, sense organs develop.
The American Heritage® Dictionary of the English Language, Fourth Edition Copyright © 2000 by Houghton Mifflin Company. Published by Houghton Mifflin Company. All rights reserved.
http://dictionary.reference.com/search?q=ectoderm

Ectodermal Dysplasia (ED)
Ectodermal dysplasia is a large group of inherited disorders characterised by a primary defect in hair, teeth, nails or sweat gland function, in addition to another abnormality in a tissue of ectodermal origin, e.g. ears, eyes, lips, mucous membranes of the mouth or nose, central ner-

vous system.
The ectoderm is the outermost layer of cells in embryonic development and contributes to the formation of many parts of the body including all those described above. Ectodermal dysplasia occurs when the ectoderm of certain areas fails to develop normally. All ectodermal dysplasias are present from birth and are non-progressive.
http://www.dermnetnz.org/hair-nails-sweat/ectodermal-dysplasia.html 01-28-2007

Ectrodactyly
Congenital absence of all or part of a digit(s).
SWGFAST, Glossary - Consolidated 09-09-03 ver. 1.0

Edgeoscopy
1. Study of the morphological characteristics of friction ridges.
2. Contour or shape of the edges of friction ridges.
SWGFAST, Glossary 07-28-2009 ver. 2.0

Edgeoscopy was established by Sri Salil Kumar Chatterjee of India in 1962.

Elasticity
The ability of skin to recover from stretching, compression, or distortion.
SWGFAST, Glossary - Consolidated 09-09-03 ver. 1.0

Elimination Prints
Exemplars of friction ridge skin detail of persons known to have had legitimate access to an item.
SWGFAST, Glossary 07-28-2009 ver. 2.0

Embryology
A branch of biology that deals with the formation and development of embryos.
Quantitative-Qualitative Friction Ridge Analysis, David R. Ashbaugh 1999 CRC Press

Eminence
A prominence, projection, or elevation.
Quantitative-Qualitative Friction Ridge Analysis, David R. Ashbaugh 1999 CRC Press

Empirical
Relying on or derived from observation or experiment: empirical results that supported the hypothesis. Verifiable or provable by means of observation or experiment: empirical laws
The American Heritage® Dictionary of the English Language, Fourth Edition Copyright © 2000 by Houghton Mifflin Company. Published by Houghton Mifflin Company. All rights reserved.
http://dictionary.reference.com/search?q=empirical 02-27-03

Relating to or based upon direct experience or observation.

Quantitative-Qualitative Friction Ridge Analysis, David R. Ashbaugh 1999 CRC Press

Empirical Probability
Estimating the probability based on long run observations.

See Classical Probability and Subjective Probability.

Enclosure
A single friction ridge that bifurcates and rejoins after a short course and continues as a single friction ridge.
SWGFAST, Glossary 07-28-2009 ver. 2.0

Ending Ridge
A single friction ridge that terminates within the friction ridge structure.
SWGFAST, Glossary 07-28-2009 ver. 2.0

Epidermal Ridges
1. Ridges on the skin, aka friction ridges.
2. Ridges on the bottom of the epidermis corresponding to the surface friction ridges and surface furrows. They are the root system of the surface ridges and furrows. The epidermal ridges that correspond to the friction ridges are referred to as primary ridges and the epidermal ridges that correspond to the surface furrows are referred to as secondary ridges.
3. Epidermal ridges are sometimes referred to as papillary ridges.

Epidermis
The outer layer of the skin.
SWGFAST, Glossary - Consolidated 09-09-03 ver. 1.0

Cuticle or outer layer of the skin.
Quantitative-Qualitative Friction Ridge Analysis, David R. Ashbaugh 1999 CRC Press

The outer layer of skin. Consisting of up to five layers: Stratum Corneum, Stratum Lucidum, Stratum Granulosum, Stratum Spinosum and Stratum Basale (aka Stratum Mucosum, Stratum Malpighi, or Stratum germinatavum). The epidermis is formed from the ectoderm in an embryo.

Epithelial Cells
The millions of cells that line and protect the external and internal surfaces of the body. Epithelial cells form epithelial tissues such as skin and mucous membranes.
American Dietetic Association, Interactive Glossary. Copyright 2003 Jones and Bartlett Publishers.
http://nutrition.jbpub.com/discovering/interactive_glossary_showterm.cfm?term=Epithelial%20cells 02-27-03

All epithelial tissues have the same properties, no blood vessels, frequent cell division, cells are close to each other, and there are cells with nuclei and a basement layer linking it to connective tissue.

Epithelial Tissue
Four kinds of tissue. Simple, stratified, pseudostratified, and transitional. Skin on the fingers is considered stratified epithelium.

Erroneous Exclusion
The incorrect determination that two areas of friction ridge impressions did not originate from the same source.
SWGFAST, Glossary 07-28-2009 ver. 2.0

In logic, an erroneous exclusion is an exclusion without valid justification to support
the conclusion.

Erroneous Exclusions, known cases of:

Mark Miller (suspect) – 2009
Mark Miller was suspected of murdering his ex-girlfriend Helen Bianks on Oct. 31, 2001 in Monroe County, Pennsylvania. His fingerprint had been identified on a gun thought to be the murder weapon. Two retired FBI fingerprint experts, Ivan Futrell and George Wynn, determined that the fingerprints did not match Mr. Miller. In Oct. 2007, Miller pled guilty to third degree murder. In June 2009, the International Association of Identification announced the suspension of certification of the retired FBI examiners for one year, due to a Technical Error. The suspension is being appealed.

Snohomish County Sheriff's Office, Washington State – Feb. 2007
In Feb. 2007, LPE M. Frantzen compared a patent print left in blood at a homicide scene. After comparing the latent print to the suspect and the victim, Ms. Frantzen reported her conclusion as negative. The prosecutor in the case made an inquiry with Ms. Frantzen's supervisor, Ken Christensen, on whether this meant a third person had made the impression. Mr. Christensen reviewed the case and made a tentative identification to the suspect but requested clearer exemplars to make a final conclusion. A discovery hearing was held to determine why more exemplars were needed. Ms. Frantzen's testimony at this hearing indicated that she stood by her results. A latent print examiner from Washington State Patrol verified Mr. Christensen's conclusions and testified to this identification at a subsequent trial. This information was received through a public disclosure request.

Sutherland (suspect) – 2006
On May 26, 2006 "The Scotsman" reported an erroneous identification by the Glasgow Bureau of the Scottish Criminal Record Office

(SCRO). A palm print from a burglary was determined to be erroneous by Allan Bayle and confirmed by John MacLeod and Gary Dempster. Gary Dempster reversed his opinion almost immediately after a more in-depth investigation. The accused was cleared when the prosecution accepted his not guilty plea. The "BBC News" reported the case had been dropped because of reasons other than fingerprint evidence and indicated the original identification was done in February of 2006. "The Scotsman" reported the SCRO stands by its identification.

In June 2006, it was determined that the SCRO identification was correct. Allan Bayle agreed his conclusion was wrong (considered to be an erroneous exclusion). As of July 2007 this case is still being investigated and all of the facts of this case may not be known. The name of the suspect, Sutherland, was published in Strabismus 2007.

Jeremy Bryan Jones (suspect)

Jeremy Bryan Jones was using the name John Paul Chapman. Between October 2003 and June 2004, Jones was arrested 3 times and his fingerprints were sent to the FBI lab in Clarksburg, West Virginia. The FBI's computer failed to match his prints to his real name.

"Had a match been made, authorities would have known Chapman was Jones and he was wanted in Oklahoma for jumping bail in 2000, where he was charged with two counts of rape and two counts of sodomy." http://crime.about.com/od/serial/p/jeremyjones.htm 05-26-2006

Elmer Lee Smith (fingerprint expert)

In February 1994 Elmer Lee Smith, a past president of SCAFO, had his life membership of SCAFO revoked after it was found that he had testified to erroneous exclusions in four separate cases.

http://www.scafo.org/library/100304.html

John Orr (suspect)

In the 1980's a series of arsons swept California. In 1987, another arson took place near an arson investigators conference. A latent print was found but wasn't identified. In 1989 another arson occurred near another arson investigators conference. The Department of Justice compared the latent print against 10 people who attended both conferences and found the latent did not originate from any of these people. In 1991, another fingerprint expert enlarged the print and ran it through an AFIS computer. AFIS produced a possible candidate who had attended both conferences and was one of the previous people the latent was compared to. The latent print was subsequently identified to renowned Fire Captain John Orr. Orr pled guilty to 20 arsons and was also convicted of murder for the 4 people who died in the fires.

Dr. Vassilis C. Morfopoulos (defense expert)
In 1968, Dr. Morfopoulos testified for the defense in People v. Kent. He testified that even though the prints had 12 (some articles say 14) similarities in common, the two prints did not match. Due to this testimony, Richard Stanley Kent was found not guilty of murder. In 1970, the IAI and the FBI refuted Dr. Morfopoulos's claims.

Erroneous Identification
The incorrect determination that two areas of friction ridge impressions originated from the same source. SWGFAST, Glossary 07-28-2009 ver. 2.0

In logic, an erroneous identification is an identification without valid justification to support the conclusion.

Erroneous Identifications and Faulty Evidence (not confirmed):

Dwight Gomas (Suspect) – 2009
Dwight Gomas spent 17 months in jail; accused of robbery, after a fingerprint from the crime scene was identified to him by NYPD Detective Eileen Barrett. Detective Charles Schenkel verified the identification. Detective Daniel Perruzza found the error just prior to Gomas's trial. On Sept. 3, 2009, Gomas accepted a $145,000 settlement.

Derris Lewis (Suspect) – 2009
Derris Lewis spent 18 months in jail, accused of killing his identical twin brother, after a bloody palm print at the scene was identified as being left by him. David Grieve was hired by the defense to review the case and agreed with the identification; however, he wasn't convinced that the print was left in blood. At the recommendation of Mr. Grieve, the prints were tested and found not to have been left in blood. The charges against Derris were dropped on Aug. 6, 2009.

Alysha Wilson (Suspect) – 2009
Miss Wilson was arrested in Dec. 2008 when her fingerprints were found at the scene of a burglary. In July 2009, charges were dropped when it was discovered that the latent prints were labeled by the Greater Manchester Police as coming from a game console box when they were really taken from a wedding card she had given the victim.

Argenis J. Burgos (Suspect) – 2008
Reported by the Associated Press on Oct. 19, 2008 "Teen spends year in jail before charges are dropped" "HARTFORD (AP) — Charges are being dropped against a Hartford teen who spent more than a year behind bars, accused of a 2007 home invasion robbery, because the finger-

print evidence against him is faulty. A judge granted a motion to end the prosecution of Argenis J. Burgos after the initial fingerprint identification in the case proved to be incorrect. And Burgos, now 18, does not fit the victim's description of the robbers. Burgos' lawyer says his client always maintained his innocence and was never near the East Hartford apartment where a 71-year-old woman was robbed at gunpoint. Police initially said they lifted the fingerprint evidence from the base of a cordless phone. But Burgos' lawyer says the print actually came from the getaway car, which was a stolen rental car."
http://www.nhregister.com/articles/2008/10/19/news/a2-fingerprint.txt 07-01-2009

Los Angeles Police Dept.- 2008
In Oct. 2008 it was reported that the LAPD had arrested at least two people due to erroneous fingerprint identifications. Maria Delosange Maldonado was erroneously identified as leaving her fingerprints at the scene of a burglary. It was found that the latent prints were lost when the prints were to be re-examined by the FBI.
In the second case, Latonya McIntyre was extradited from Alabama on burglary charges and the error was found while preparing the evidence for trial. At least one fingerprint analyst was fired and 3 others were suspended.
http://articles.latimes.com/2008/11/18/metro/me-fingerprints18 12-20-2008

Georgia Bureau of Investigation Crime Lab - 2008
Dexter Presnell was jailed from Oct. 2006 until May 2008 due to an error by the Georgia Bureau of Investigation Crime Lab. Dexter Presnell was falsely identified as the person leaving a latent print at the 2005 homicide scene of Regan Wheeler in Dallas, Texas. The examiner in the case mistakenly compared the latent print from the scene to the elimination prints of Wheeler's daughter thinking they were the prints of Dexter Presnell. Presnell wasn't immediately released from jail because other evidence also connected him to the scene. The district attorney said the fingerprint evidence was the main evidence but the error didn't exonerate Prenell.

Certified Examiner Donna Birks - 2007
On May 4, 2007, it was reported that there were some problems with the fingerprint analyses in two cases from a Certified Latent Print Examiner, Donna Birks, from Seminole County, Florida. One of the cases involved a latent print on a wallet in a burglary case, this case was dropped. The other case had an identification of a latent print on a shell casing in

a homicide case. It was determined the latent prints didn't have enough detail to warrant a positive identification.

By June 7, 2007, hundreds of cases had been reviewed. It was found that there was one case that had an erroneous identification and seven others had identifications that should have been inconclusive. Birks resigned, the supervisor of this latent unit was reassigned to supervisor another unit, and another latent examiner (Tara Williamson) was reassigned as a dispatcher. It was reported that Bill McQuay, a retired Certified Examiner, verified the erroneous identification but this hasn't been confirmed.

Sutherland (Suspect) – 2006
On May 26, 2006 "The Scotsman" reported an erroneous identification by the Glasgow Bureau of the Scottish Criminal Record Office (SCRO). A palm print from a burglary was determined to be erroneous by Allan Bayle and confirmed by John MacLeod and Gary Dempster. Gary Dempster reversed his opinion almost immediately after a more in-depth investigation. The accused was cleared when the prosecution accepted his not guilty plea. The "BBC News" reported the case had been dropped because of reasons other than fingerprint evidence and indicated the original identification was done in February of 2006. "The Scotsman" reported the SCRO stands by its identification.
In June 2006, it was determined that the SCRO identification was correct. Allan Bayle agreed his conclusion was wrong (considered to be an erroneous exclusion). As of July 2007 this case is still being investigated and all of the facts of this case may not be known. The name of the suspect, Sutherland, was published in Strabismus 2007.

Brandon Mayfield - 2004
Brandon Mayfield is a U.S. citizen who in May of 2004 was wrongfully arrested as a material witness with regard to a terrorism attack in Spain. His arrest was due to an erroneous fingerprint identification made by three FBI Examiners, Michael Wieners, John T. Massey, Terry Green and one private fingerprint expert, Ken Moses. News reports indicate, "Court records show that retired FBI agent John Massey, who worked on the Madrid case, was reprimanded three times by the FBI between 1969 and 1974 for errors, including twice making false fingerprint identifications. "
http://www.mobmagazine.com/managearticle.asp?C=240&A=7466
In November 2006 Mayfield was awarded a $2 million dollar settlement by the U.S. Justice Department. The settlement also included an apology and an agreement to

destroy communications intercepts conducted by the FBI against Mayfield's home and office during the investigation. The Justice Department added that Mayfield was not targeted because of his Muslim faith.

Stephan Cowans - 2004
In 1997, Stephan Cowans was convicted of shooting a police officer in Boston, Massachusetts. Part of the evidence against him included the identification of a fingerprint on a drinking glass associated with the crime scene. Additional evidence included faulty eyewitness testimony. In 2004, after spending 6 years in prison, Cowans was exonerated with DNA evidence. A mislabeled fingerprint card has been alleged to be the source of the error in the Cowans case. Others have speculated that Cowans may have been framed by members of the Boston Police Dept. Lab technicians Dennis LeBlanc and Rosemary Mclaughlin were put on administrative leave pending an investigation.
In August of 2006, Cowans won a 3.2 million dollar settlement and received $500,000 from the state for the wrongful conviction. On Oct 25, 2007, Cowans was found shot to death in his home.

Roger Benson / Identix computer discrepancy-2004
Miguel Espinoza / Identix computer discrepancy-2004

David Valken-Leduc - 2003
In Aug. 2002 in West Valley, Utah, Certified Latent Print Examiner Scott Spjut testified at a preliminary hearing that a print found at a 1996 murder scene of a motel 6 night clerk belonged to David Jonathan Valken-Leduc. After Spjut's unexpected death in early 2003, his identification was reviewed and found to be erroneous. Valken-Leduc was still convicted of the murder in early 2004.

Mark Sinclair – 2003
In 2003, Mark Sinclair was linked to an Armed Robbery through a fingerprint identification made by the SCRO. This identification has been questioned due to an independent examiners conclusion (Allan Bayle) that the identification was 'unsafe'. Fingerprint experts from Northern Ireland agreed with Allan Bayle's conclusion.

Alan McNamara - 2002
Alan McNamara, a small discount store owner, was arrested in Oct. 1999 for burglary of a house in Rochdale. The only connection in the case between Mr. McNamara and the crime was a disputed thumbprint. The thumbprint lifted by the Greater Manchester Police was alleged to have been taken from a jewelry case in the house owner's bedroom.
Although McNamara maintained his innocence, he was found guilty of the crime and sentenced to 2 ½

years in prison. He was released in Aug. 2002 on good behavior.
In November of the following year, McNamara won the right to appeal his conviction.
At trial, examiners Allan Bayle and Pat Wertheim testified that the print was that of Mr. McNamara, but that the print was lifted off a different surface than the jewelry case. It appeared that the print was lifted off a smooth curved surface, which could have been touched by Mr. McNamara quite innocently during his day to day business.
In Dec. 2004, the appeal was heard at The Royal Courts of Justice and McNamara's conviction stood. It was determined that since McNamara's prints were found on an item with the home owners prints on the same item, he must have been the burglar. McNamara hopes to take the case to the Criminal Case Review Commission, an independent body set up by the government to look at alleged cases of miscarriage of justice.

Kathleen Hatfield - 2002
In 2002, Kathleen Hatfield was identified as the victim of a homicide after an erroneous fingerprint identification by the Las Vegas Metropolitan Police Department. The error may have been due to the body being badly decomposed, similar tattoos, and the fact that Kathleen Hatfield was listed as a missing person.

Richard Jackson - 2000
In 1998, Rick Jackson was convicted of murdering his friend Alvin David and given a life sentence in Delaware County, Pennsylvania based on an erroneous fingerprint identification. Two local police officers, Anthony Paparo and Upper Darby Police Superintendent Vincent Ficchi, made the erroneous identification and it was verified by an out of state Certified Examiner. Retired FBI examiner George Wynn was the first examiner to discover the mistake, Vernon McCloud, another former FBI examiner, verified Wynn's conclusion just days before Jackson's trial. Even with this testimony, Jackson was found guilty. The International Association of Identification reviewed the identification and agreed that it was erroneous. In 2000, after the FBI concurred with these results, Jackson was released from prison. The Certified Examiner was decertified and lost his job. The Upper Darby Police and Anthony Paparo stand by the identification.
MSNBC "When Forensics Fail" Oct. 25, 2007

Danny McNamee - 1998
In 1986, Danny McNamee was sentenced for conspiracy to cause explosions in London and found guilty of being "The Hyde Park Bomber". In 1998 his charges were quashed. 14 experts analyzed the latent prints and couldn't find more than 11 char-

acteristics in common (in a country that required 16 to make a positive identification).

Shirley McKie - 1997

In 1997, Shirley McKie, a detective with the Strathclyde Police in Scotland, was charged with perjury after denying that she had left a fingerprint at the murder scene of Marion Ross. David Asbury was convicted of this murder based on other fingerprint evidence. Later both charges were overturned while the SCRO, who performed the fingerprint analysis, stood by their identifications. On February 7, 2006, just prior to Shirley McKie's civil hearing, The Scottish Ministers settled out of court for the full amount Ms. McKie was suing for, while not admitting to any errors.

Over 10 years after the murder the identifications were still under dispute and a resolution seemed impossible. In April 2007, the examiners involved in this case were asked to resign. Four of the six examiners (Robert McKenzie, Allan Dunbar, Hugh McPherson and Charlie Stewart) took a redundancy package. One examiner, Tony McKenna, agreed to be redeployed to Strathclyde Police. Fiona McBride refused to accept another job at 1/3 of her salary and was fired on May 1, 2007. Fiona McBride is pursuing legal action.

Manuel Quinta Guerra - 1996

Manuel Quinta Guerra served 4 months in jail due to an erroneous identification by the Houston Police Department. In July of 1996, two fingerprint analysts identified a latent print on a fork from the homicide scene of Lawrence Perham to Guerra. Guerra and Perham were roommates. In December 1996, the identification was reviewed by the FBI and found to be an error. Rafael Saldivar was reprimanded for the error in 1997. This was reported on July 18, 2010 by the Houston Chronicle.

Andrew Chiory - 1996

In 1996, Andrew Chiory served 2 months in prison due to an erroneous identification done by Scotland Yard. This was claimed to be the first mistaken identification by Scotland Yard since the bureau's inception in 1901 (Cole, "Suspect Identities" 2001). Simon Harris initially made the erroneous identification (Daily Mall, April 10, 1997) which led to the arrest of Andrew Chiory for the 1995 home burglary of well-known writer and broadcaster Dr. Miriam Stoppard. The identification was said to be triple checked by Scotland Yard. Ron Cook was one of the examiners that re-examined the evidence and determined it to be erroneous. In defense motions, this case is commonly referred to by a newspaper article by Stephen Grey, "Yard in Fingerprint Blunder", April 1997.

David Asbury – 1996
David Asbury was linked to the murder of Marion Ross after his fingerprint was identified on a gift tag in her home and a latent print found on a candy tin in David Asbury's home was identified as that of Marion Ross. During the trial, the identification of a latent print from a door frame was identified as belonging to Detective Shirley McKie. Ms. McKie insisted this identification was erroneous. Subsequently, the previous identifications were questioned and the identification of the print on the candy tin was declared to be erroneous. Despite the uncertainty of the fingerprint evidence, David Asbury was found guilty of murder and sentenced to life. In 2000, after spending 3 years in jail, Asbury won an appeal and his conviction was eventually overturned. The SCRO, who made the identifications, stands by their conclusions. In January 2006 it was reported that a 3rd erroneous ID was made on a banknote linking Asbury to the murder. This was later reported as false information.
Over 10 years after the murder the identifications were still under dispute and a resolution seemed impossible. In April 2007, the examiners involved in this case were asked to resign. 4 of the 6 examiners (Robert McKenzie, Allan Dunbar, Hugh McPherson and Charlie Stewart) took a redundancy package. One examiner, Tony McKenna, agreed to be redeployed to Strathclyde Police. Fiona McBride refused to accept another job at 1/3 of her salary and was fired on May 1, 2007. Fiona McBride is pursuing legal action.

Clapham - 1993
On Nov.9, 1993 the South Wales Argus reported the erroneous identification in the "Newport betting shop murder" trial. The victim of the murder was 24 year old Sian Collier, manager of the betting shop. William Ervin, a New Scotland Yard fingerprint bureau expert, blamed his erroneous identification of Clapham on an inability to see properly. When he re-examined the evidence during the trial (Oct. 28, 1993), he noticed his mistake but didn't immediately notify the courts.

Neville Lee - 1991
In 1991, based on fingerprint evidence, Nottinghamshire police arrested Neville Lee for raping an 11-year old girl. He was released only after someone else confessed to the crime.

Barry Bowden and Mike Barrett - 1988
In North Carolina, officials had to reconsider 159 criminal cases because local authorities discovered questionable fingerprint identifications. [FN110] The fingerprint misidentification resulted in two murder charges being dropped by the district

attorney's office.
[FN110]. Barry Bowden and Mike Barrett, Fingerprint Errors Raise Questions on Local Convictions, FAYETTEVILLE TIMES, Jan. 15, 1988, at 1A.
http://www.law-forensic.com/expert_malpractice_1.htm 01-19-2005

Michael Cooper - 1986
In 1986, Michael Cooper was wrongfully arrested as the Prime Time Rapist, when his fingerprints were erroneously identified by the Tucson Police Department as those from the Prime Time Rapist crime scenes. Within one day of his arrest it was found that the prints did not match.
http://michaeljbloom.lawoffice.com/CustomPage_3.shtml 08-07-2004

Bruce Basden - 1986
In June 1985 Bruce Basden was arrested and indicted for the murders of Remus and Blanche Adams in Fayetteville North Caroliana on the basis of a fingerprint found in the decedents' home. [FN113] Basden's*53 attorney requested funds to have the fingerprint evidence reappraised and filed a motion to discover the physical evidence in the possession of the state. [FN114] "At this point the state's fingerprint expert made enlargements of the prints from which he had made an identification of Basden as the intruder .... The state's expert admitted that he found unexplained dissimilarities along with similarities in the prints." [FN115] These discrepancies caused him to change his mind. The state subsequently dismissed all charges against Basden, who had been incarcerated in the local jail for thirteen months. [FN116]
http://www.law-forensic.com/expert_malpractice_1.htm#FN;F4 08-07-2004

Roger Caldwell - 1981
In 1977, Caldwell was convicted of 2 counts of murder partly based on latent print evidence from an envelope. The latent prints in question were developed and identified by Steven Sedlacek. A defense expert, Ronald Welbaum, agreed with the identification. During the trial of a co-defendant (Caldwell's wife), it was discovered that the original latent had faded and another fingerprint expert testified that the images on the negatives were very poor but his opinion was that they did not match Caldwell's prints. In 1981 or 1982, the Minnesota Supreme Court granted Caldwell a new trial. In a plea agreement Caldwell plead guilty in exchange for time served. In 1988, Caldwell committed suicide still proclaiming his innocence. Steven Sedlacek's and Ronald Welbaum's IAI certifications were revoked over this incident along with another certified examiner named Claude Cook. Cook was decertified for submitting communication in support of the

erroneous identification (Cole, "Suspect Identities" 2001). In 2003, DNA testing was done on the envelope and it was determined that the DNA on the adhesive portion of the envelope did belong to Caldwell.

William Stevens - 1926
In 1926, Stevens was one of several suspects in a double murder case known as the Hall-Mills murders (New Jersey 1922). Retired Deputy Police Commissioner Joseph Faurot, along with Lieutenant Fred Drewen and Edward H. Schwartz, erroneously identified a latent print on key evidence to William Stevens. J.H. Taylor and Gerhardt Kuhne (brother of Frederick Kuhne) testified for the defense in this trial. William Stevens and the other suspects were acquitted and the double murder was never solved.

Also see Fabricated Latent Prints, known cases of.

Error
a) An incorrect conclusion was arrived at.
b) A correct conclusion was arrived at through unacceptable justification.
c) A correct conclusion was arrived at but justification could not be demonstrated.

Error Rate
The rate at which errors occur. The error rate of fingerprint comparisons is constantly changing. The exact rate can never be known but it can be estimated.

Error Rate Studies
-Peterson and Markham (1995) – "Crime Laboratory Proficiency Test Results"
-Dror, Peron, Hind, and Charlton (2005) – "When emotions get the better of us: The effect of contextual top-down processing on matching fingerprints"
-Dror, Charlton, and Peron (2006) – "Contextual information renders experts vulnerable to making erroneous identifications"
-Wertheim, Langenburg, and Moenssens (2006) – "A Report of Latent Print Examiner Accuracy During Comparison Training Exercises"

Errors (types of)
a) Erroneous Individualization, aka a false positive or type 1 error.
b) False negative, aka false exclusion or a type 2 error.
c) Erroneous Verification.
d) Clerical Errors.
e) Missed Individualization.

Etched Print
The result of a chemical reaction between fingerprint residue and a substrate. The acids in fingerprint residue deteriorate the substrate that was touched leaving an impression of friction ridge detail. This usually

occurs with metals and leathers.

Ethanol
Solvent used in preparation of reagents, dye stains and rinses (ethyl alcohol).
SWGFAST, Glossary - Consolidated 09-09-03 ver. 1.0

Ethyl Acetate
Solvent used in the preparation of reagents and dye stains.
SWGFAST, Glossary - Consolidated 09-09-03 ver. 1.0

European Network of Forensic Science Institutes.
Informally started in March of 1993 and formally founded in Oct. 1995, the ENFSI is the European equivalent of the American Society of Crime Laboratory Directors (ASCLD).

Evaluation
The third step of the ACE-V method where an examiner assesses the value of the details observed during the analysis and the comparison steps and reaches a conclusion.
SWGFAST, Glossary 07-28-2009 ver. 2.0

The process of examining a system or system component to determine the extent to which specified properties are present.
The Free On-line Dictionary of Computing, © 1993-2004 Denis Howe
http://dictionary.reference.com/search?q=evaluation 01-05-2005

More definitions listed under ACE-V.

Evans, Edward A.
Son of Captain Michael Evans. One of Ferrier's nine fingerprint students taught in 1904 during the World's Fair. Superintendent of the National Bureau of Identification.

Evans, Captain Emmett A. (?-Dec. 23, 1953)
Son of Captain Michael Evans. One of Ferrier's nine fingerprint students taught in 1904 during the World's Fair. Chief Identification Inspector for the Chicago Police Department.

Evans, Captain Michael P. (?-Oct. 7, 1931)
Implemented the Bertillon system in 1888 at the Chicago Police Department and implemented the fingerprint system in 1905 while he was the Chief of the Identity Bureau. Testified in "People vs. Jennings".

Evans, William M.
Son of Captain Michael Evans. Testified in "People vs. Jennings". Head of the Chicago Police Department Bureau of Identification.

Evans, Captain William K.
In 1916, as a retired Captain of the U.S. Army Intelligence Service, Capt. Evans along with T.G. Cooke found-

ed the first home study course in fingerprint identification. Located in Chicago, Illinois and originally named "Evans University", the name was changed one year later to the "University of Applied Science". Around 1929 the name was again changed to the "Institute of Applied Science". Evans connection with the school only lasted one year. In 1917, Evans was called back to active duty to serve in World War I.

Evans University
See Institute of Applied Science.

Evett – Williams Study
In 1989 (published in 1996) I. W. Evett and R.L. Williams did a review of the 16 point standard used in England and Wales (the 16-point standard was abandoned by England and Wales in 2001). Their review included the historical aspects, statistical aspects, visits to different agencies, and a review of practitioners comparisons (practitioners conducted 10 comparisons). By the end of their review they determined there was no need for the 16 point standard.

While conducting their study they found that examiners had a high variation in how many points they stated were in common while conducting comparisons. Evett and Williams concluded that "....decision making in relation to individual points of comparison is highly subjective."

The variation in the results may have been due to how the questions were phrased. On the answer sheet of this study practitioners were asked to count 'ridge characteristics in agreement' and in another part of the study they asked for "..the number of points of similarity" (pg 16 of the study results). There seems to be a wide variation between how practitioners view 'points' and 'characteristics'. The term 'points' generally refers to bifurcations and ending ridges while the term 'characteristics' can refer to large pores, incipient ridges, dots, scars, etc. It's possible that the variation between practitioners in this study was due to a lack of clarity in the directions.

Exact Science
Historically, this expression comes from Aristotle. He used the phrase to describe sciences that demonstrate precise conclusions from known principles; philosophy, arithmetic, geometry, astronomy, and harmonics. Ptolemy argued that philosophy was less precise and was not based from known principles. In the 17th century, the meaning of this expression began to change. Mathematics no longer appeared to be a science, but the language of or an assistant to science. Physics is now regarded as an exact science.

Exchange Principle
See Locard's Principle of Exchange.

Exclusion
The determination by an examiner that there is sufficient quality and quantity of detail in disagreement to conclude that two areas of friction ridge impressions did not originate from the same source.
SWGFAST, Glossary 07-28-2009 ver. 2.0

Extrusion Marks
Marks that are made when casting metals or plastics. These marks can resemble friction ridge detail by replication ridges with bifurcations and ending ridges. These marks typically appear with a wavy motion and have no signs of pores or ridge edges. These marks have been called sprue marks and/or false ridge detail.

Exemplar
The known prints of an individual, recorded electronically, photographically, by ink, or by another medium.
SWGFAST, Glossary 07-28-2009 ver. 2.0

Expert
Person with much skill who knows a great deal about some special thing; has an in-depth understanding of a subject.
Quantitative-Qualitative Friction Ridge Analysis, David R. Ashbaugh 1999 CRC Press

A person with great knowledge, skill or experience in a specific subject.
Webster's II New Riverside Dictionary, Office Edition. Houghton Mifflin Publishing Co. Copyright 1984, Berkley Addition.

Explainable Differences (in friction ridge identifications)
Differences in appearance that don't interfere with the identification process. These differences can include such things as size, thickness of ridges, distortion and level 3 characteristics being absent in one impression. Typically these differences are a result of one of the "Latent Print Recovery Conditions".

F

FBI / Lockheed-Martin 50k x 50k Study (1999)
A statistical study done to support the uniqueness theory of fingerprints. This study was used in Daubert hearings to justify biological uniqueness and to validate fingerprint methodology. The 50k x 50k study was never published and therefore many claim that it is not a scientifically sound study and should not be used as supporting evidence.

FEPAC
Forensic Science Education Programs Accreditation Commission.

FER
Fluorescence Excitation Radiometry. A new forensic light source introduced in 2005 by Light Diagnostics.

FFS
Fellow of The Fingerprint Society.

FLS
Forensic Light Source. Common term for all light sources including lasers used in forensic examinations.
SWGFAST, Glossary - Consolidated 09-09-03 ver. 1.0

FQS
Forensic Quality Services.

FSAB
Forensic Specialties Accreditation Board.

Fabricated Latent Print
"A "fabricated" latent print is a representation of print that never existed on the surface from which it purportedly came." "A fabricated print is fabricated evidence produced by a police employee in order to bolster a case or frame a person."
George Bonebrake, 1976, presentation to the International Association for Identification.
http://www.geocities.com/cfpdlab/fabrica.htm 02-07-04

See Forged Latent Print.

Fabricated Latent Prints, known cases of:

Fred van der Vyver (South Africa)
In March 2005 Fred van der Vyver was the main suspect in the murder of his girlfriend, Inge Lotz. Crucial evidence against him was a fingerprint identification labeled as being lifted from a DVD cover. The identification of the print was never in question. The question was whether or not the fingerprint was actually lifted from the DVD cover or from some other substrate. Fred van der Vyver maintained his innocence and provided an air tight alibi while the State denied any possibility of a mistake. The first person to suggest that

the fingerprints were from a different surface was Mr. Nico Kotze. Several other fingerprint experts, including Dr. David Klatzow, Mike Grace, Daan Bekker, Pat Wertheim and Arie Zeelenberg, reviewed the case. Daan Bekker was the first person to state that the latent print was lifted from a drinking glass. In December 2006, due to the experts' findings, the South African Police Department announced that they were not going to pursue the fingerprint evidence. When the trail began, the fingerprint evidence was admitted as part of the evidence (along with other evidence that was suspected of being fabricated). Mike Grimm, Bill Bodziak and Paul Ryder were the footwear experts in this case. On Nov. 29, 2007 the judge, accepting that the latent print evidence did not come from a DVD cover, found Fred van der Vyver not guilty of the charges against him. One article about this case claimed that the judge also slammed the testimony of several police witnesses who had given evidence on key forensic evidence, calling their evidence "untrustworthy", "unreliable" and "dishonest".
http://www.iol.co.za/index.php?set_id=1&click_id=15&art_id=vn20071201112945223C761205
12-01-07

Diana Boyd Monahan (Texas)
Indicted in 2000 on 13 counts of falsifying fingerprint reports on evidence she never tested. She pled guilty and received 5 years probation.

New York State Police
In 1992 an investigator with the New York State Police, David L. Harding, was arrested for fabricating evidence in a murder trial. Subsequently, 4 other employees (Robert M. Lishansky, Craig D. Harvey, David M. Beers, and Patrick O'Hara) were charged with fabricating fingerprint evidence in other cases. The total number of cases is estimated to be as high as 40 cases.
In 1993, Shirley Kinge, one of the victims of fingerprint fabrication, sued the New York State Police. In Feb. 2008, Judge Midey Jr. found that Kinge was the victim of malicious prosecution and negligent supervision of the investigator who planted the phony evidence implicating her in the crime. Senior Investigator David McElligott, the supervisor of the Troopers involved, was forced to retire due to this scandal.

Deputy Sheriff Jesus Durazo
In 1992, the Arizona crime lab found that Jesus Durazo had fabricated fingerprint evidence against a drug suspect. Despite his claims of innocence, when he was offered to resign and no prosecution would occur, Durazo accepted.

James Bakken, Buena Park, California
In a 1967 bank robbery (some sources say 1969), James Bakken from Buena Park, California fabricated evidence that resulted in William DePalma being found guilty and sentenced to 15 years. DePalma began serving his sentence in 1971. Bakken testified that the latent print was found at the bank but it was really an exact replica of a print from a previous arrest. After Orange County investigated the claims, DePalma was released after serving 3 years in prison. Bakken served 1 year on an unrelated charge. He could not be prosecuted for the DePalma case because the statute of limitations had expired.
Dec. 1975 / Aug. 1976 Identification News

Det. Herman Wiggins, San Diego Police Department
In the 1970's, Det. Herman Wiggins was found to have fabricated latent print evidence in up to 40 cases. It is believed he had people touch the hood of his car and then he would lift the prints and saved them for other cases. Officer Wiggins was arrested and faced several counts of falsifying evidence. When the authenticity of the latent lift cards were questioned, Officer Wiggins claimed that he had several lift cards together and they may have gotten mixed up when he dropped his briefcase. In Dec. of 1974 he was found guilty and sentenced to two years in custody.
Information provided by Rachelle Babler.

Capt. James Barker
James Barker was one of the primary investigators in the 1943 Sir Harry Oakes Case. Maurice O'Neill filed charges with the IAI against Barker for fabricating evidence in this case. In a very unpopular decision, the IAI cleared Barker of any wrongdoing.

Also see Erroneous Identifications, known cases of.

Falsifiable
There must be a way to prove the theory wrong. If we can't prove it wrong, it is not a scientific theory. This idea of a theory being falsifiable is one of the most important aspects of science. The theory, "Beyond Earth there is intelligent life in the universe", may be true, but it is not a scientific theory since there is no way to prove it false.
http://home.earthlink.net/~johnh55/science/whatisscience.html 02-27-03

Faulds, Dr. Henry (June 1, 1843-Mar. 24, 1930)
Dr. Henry Faulds was a Scottish physician and a medical missionary in Japan. Dr. Faulds is credited with doing many experiments to prove permanence and uniqueness. The earliest article on using fingerprints as a means of identification was

written by Faulds. Nature Magazine published this article, "On the Skin-Furrows of the Hand", on Oct. 28, 1880. Herschel replied in Nature Magazine on Nov. 25, 1880 stating he had been using fingerprints as a means of identification for over 20 years. Faulds is credited for being the first European to suggest that fingerprints could assist in criminal investigations. Additionally, he is noted as being the first person to use a latent fingerprint to eliminate someone as a suspect and he was the person who recommended using printer's ink to record fingerprints. In 1905 (as stated in "A Manual of Practical Dactylography" page 60), Dr. Faulds published "Guide to Finger- Print Identification". In 1912 he published "Dactylography, The Study of Finger-Prints" (noted in "A Manual of Practical Dactylography" page 10) and in approx. 1915 he published "A Manual of Practical Dactylography". Although Dr. Faulds greatly contributed to the science of fingerprint identification, he was never given full credit for this during his lifetime.

Fault Line
Shadowing in an impression in the form of a curved line. A fault line is a visual clue that some sort of distortion may exist.

Faurot, Joseph A. (Oct. 14, 1872-Nov. 20 1942)

In 1906, N.Y.P.D. Police Commissioner McAdoo sent Det. Sgt. Joseph Faurot to London to obtain information of the process of fingerprinting, where it had been in use for several years. Det. Sgt. Faurot returned with samples of the first fingerprint cards, at which time the Department began to implement this new crime fighting technique. In 1908, a murder case was the first case solved by the N.Y.P.D. utilizing this technology. http://www.nycpolicemuseum.org/html/faq.html#fingerprint

Joseph A. Faurot retired from the New York Police Department as a Deputy Police Commissioner in 1926. http://www.findagrave.com/cgi-bin/famousSearch.cgi?mode=county&FScountyid=2013 10-08-2004

Faurot was involved in many historical trials. One of the most well known trials was the case of Caesar Cella in People v Crispi 1911. Remarkably, Retired Deputy Police Commissioner Joseph Faurot was also involved in the trial that involved the first erroneous identification. In the 1926 Hall-Mills double murder trial (New Jersey), Joseph Faurot along with Lieutenant Fred Drewen and Edward H. Schwartz erroneously identified a latent print on key evidence to one of the suspects, William Stevens. J.H. Taylor and Gerhardt Kuhne (brother of Frederick Kuhne) testified for the defense in this trial. William Stevens and the other suspects were acquitted. The double murder, which actually happened in 1922, was never solved.

Features

As of November 2004 the National Fingerprint Board of England and Wales determined:

1. The Third Level Detail Working Group acknowledges that within the international fingerprint community, the terminologies 1st, 2nd and 3rd Level detail is used. This group recommends that because of the holistic nature of fingerprint identification, there is no need for the use of these terms within the comparison process. ALL information assisting with establishing the identification of an area of friction ridge detail will be termed, 'features'.

2. ALL visible features employed within the identification process may be used without regard to the information falling within any particular category.

3. Consequently, there is no justification for treating any type, or group of features separately and no requirement for a Third Level Detail Working group as such, and this group recommends that the national Fingerprint Board considers retaining the existing members as the 'Identification Working Group.' (this group has been re-named as the, 'Bureaux Practitioners' Group).

Ferric Nitrate

Chemical used in Physical Developer and Multimetal Deposition solutions. SWGFAST, Glossary - Consolidated 09-09-03 ver. 1.0

Ferrier, John Kenneth

Ferrier worked for the fingerprint branch of Scotland Yard. In 1904, he was assigned to guard the British Crown Jewels at the World's Fair in St. Louis, Missouri. The American police officials became interested in fingerprinting through Ferrier and for seven months he taught nine individuals about fingerprints and the Henry System (Edward A. Evans, Emmett A. Evans, Edward Brennan, John Shea, Mr. Ryan, Mary Holland, George Koestle, Edward Foster, and Albert G. Perrott). During this time Ferrier also gave instruction to many others who were interested. He is considered to be the first fingerprint instructor in the United States. Although fingerprints had been used sporadically in the United States prior to Ferrier's arrival, Ferrier is credited with being the driving force behind the use of fingerprints in the U.S.

Ferrous Ammonium Sulfate

Chemical used in Physical Developer and Multimetal Deposition solutions. SWGFAST, Glossary - Consolidated

09-09-03 ver. 1.0

Fetus
For the human species, the unborn individual from about the end of the second month of development until birth. Earlier stages are termed embryo.
SWGFAST, Glossary - Consolidated 09-09-03 ver. 1.0

An embryo during latter stages of development in the womb, after three months.
Quantitative-Qualitative Friction Ridge Analysis, David R. Ashbaugh 1999 CRC Press

Fibula
The smaller of the two bones in the lower leg on the little toe side.
SWGFAST, Glossary - Consolidated 09-09-03 ver. 1.0

The shorter of the two bones in the lower leg on the little toe side.

Fibular Area
The plantar area situated on the little toe side of the foot.
SWGFAST, Glossary - Consolidated 09-09-03 ver. 1.0

Final
A numerical value that is derived from the ridge count of a little finger, usually the right.
SWGFAST, Glossary - Consolidated 09-09-03 ver. 1.0

Finger
See Phalange.
SWGFAST, Glossary - Consolidated 09-09-03 ver. 1.0

Finger Print and Identification Magazine
Originally named "Finger Print Magazine", it was a monthly publication put out by the Institute of Applied Science. This magazine was published from 1919-1978 and was considered to be a vital part of knowledge to the identification industry.

Fingerprint
An impression of the friction ridges of all or any part of the finger.
SWGFAST, Glossary 07-28-2009 ver. 2.0

A fingerprint is the unique pattern that is created by the friction ridges on the fingers. This pattern may be transferred from the fingers to other items in the form of a known print, a latent print or a patent print.

Fingerprint Identification (AKA Friction Ridge Identification or Friction Skin Identification)
The applied science of identification by friction skin based on the Theory of Differential Growth and the Theory of Permanence.

Fingerprint Powders
Powders used to visualize friction

ridge detail. Can be magnetic, nonmagnetic, fluorescent, bichromatic, or a variety of monochromatic types. SWGFAST, Glossary - Consolidated 09-09-03 ver. 1.0

The Fingerprint Society
The Fingerprint Society was first conceived of in 1974 by Martin J. Leadbetter, Stephen E. Haylock, David R. Brooker, and Nicolas J. Hall while working for the Hertfordshire Constabulary in England. Martin J. Leadbetter and Stephen E. Haylock officially formed their organization in 1975 under the name the 'National Society of Fingerprint Officers' (NSFO). The name was later changed to "The Fingerprint Society". This educational organization publishes a quarterly journal called "Fingerprint Whorld". The first issue was published in July 1975.

First Level Detail (also see Level 1 Detail)
General overall pattern shape, i.e., circular, looping, arching, or straight. Quantitative-Qualitative Friction Ridge Analysis, David R. Ashbaugh 1999 CRC Press

Flame Technique
Many common materials (e.g., camphor, magnesium, masking tape, nito-cellulose, pine tar, titanium tetrachloride) burned to produce soot for detection of friction ridge detail. SWGFAST, Glossary - Consolidated 09-09-03 ver. 1.0

See Hot Flame Method.

Flavin(e)
A yellow dye used as an ingredient in many reagents that are used to stain friction ridge detail.

Flexion Crease
Creases that are formed during friction ridge formation, completely lacking of any ridge detail. Flexion creases are unique and permanent.

See Creases, White Lines, Tension Creases and Occasional Features.

Fluorescein
Fluorescent reagent used to develop bloody friction ridge detail. SWGFAST, Glossary - Consolidated 09-09-03 ver. 1.0

Fluorescence
Emission of light, resulting from the absorption of radiation from another source. SWGFAST, Glossary - Consolidated 09-09-03 ver. 1.0

The emission of light caused by the absorption of radiant energy from an external source or stimulus, such as a lamp, a laser, or an ALS. The emission of light continues only as long as the stimulus continues (as opposed to phosphorescence).

Fluorescence Excitation Radiometry

A new forensic light source introduced in 2005 by Light Diagnostics.

Focal Points

1. A group of specific features used to limit search parameters. Focal points may include a delta, core, creases, scars, or the flow of friction ridge detail (as with a recurve). Focal points may be used for searching but not necessarily be used in arriving at a conclusion during the ACE-V process. The search parameters are increased for prints with limited or no focal points.
2. In the Henry Classification, focal points refer specifically to the core and deltas areas.
3. The term focal point is occasionally used to refer to a target group.

1. In classification, those areas that are enclosed within the pattern area of loops and whorls. They are also known as the core and the delta.
2. In ACE-V, the areas selected for comparison purposes.
SWGFAST, Glossary 07-28-2009 ver. 2.0

Folien

Another name for a gel lifter. Used to lift and preserve latent fingerprints.

Footprint

An impression left by the friction ridge skin from a plantar surface.

Forensic

Relating to, used in, or appropriate for courts of law or for public discussion or argumentation.
Of, relating to, or used in debate or argument; rhetorical.
Relating to the use of science or technology in the investigation and establishment of facts or evidence in a court of law: a forensic laboratory.
The American Heritage® Dictionary of the English Language, Fourth Edition Copyright © 2000 by Houghton Mifflin Company. Published by Houghton Mifflin Company. All rights reserved.
http://dictionary.reference.com/search?q=forensic 02-27-03

Forensic Light Source (FLS)

Common term for all light sources including lasers used in forensic examinations.
SWGFAST, Glossary - Consolidated 09-09-03 ver. 1.0

Forged Latent Print

"A "forged" latent print is one which actually exists on a surface, but was not left by the person whose fingerprint it represents." "A forged print would be a latent planted at a crime scene by the true criminal in order to fool the police." "In those terms, forgery of latent print evidence is virtually nonexistent."
George Bonebrake, 1976, presentation to the International Association for Identification.
http://www.geocities.com/cfpdlab/

fabrica.htm 02-07-04

See Fabricated Latent Print.

Forgeot, Rene Dr.
A French criminologist at the Laboratoire D'Anthropologie Criminale, Lyon, France (Laboratory of Criminal Anthropology) who researched latent developmental techniques in approx. 1891. He is credited with using ink to recover latent prints on paper, using hydrofluoric acid to recover latent prints on glass and osmic acid fuming to oxidize sebaceous matter.

Forking Ridge
Another term for a bifurcating ridge.

Form Blindness
The inability to see minute differences in form regarding shapes, curves, angles and size. First referenced to forensic science by Albert Osborn in his 1910 book, "Questioned documents".
Form Blindness: What do you see?, Jon S. Byrd

Form Perception
The ability to see minute differences in angles, forms, and size. Form perception or recognition takes place in the visual cortex of the brain, not the eye.
Form Blindness: What do you see?, Jon S. Byrd

Foster, Edward (Aka Thomas Alfred Edward Foster) (Nov. 14, 1863-Jan. 21, 1956)
A Constable with the Dominion Police in Canada. Credited with bringing fingerprint identification to Canada after meeting Ferrier at the 1904 World's Fair. Foster, along with Mary Holland , William M. Evans and Michael P. Evans, was one of the four fingerprint experts who testified in the historic trial "People vs. Jennings". This was the first time Foster testified as a fingerprint expert.
http://www.rcmp.ca/pdfs/foster_e.pdf 08-12-2003

Fox, Albert Ebenezer and Ebenezer Albert (1857-19??)
The Story of the Fox twins is the English equivalent to the William and Will West story in the United States. The Fox twins were born in St. Ippolytes, England and recognized as poachers and petty thieves who accumulated over 220 convictions between them. Sgt. John Ferrier is said to have used this case as an example at the 1904 World's Fair to show how the Bertillon system wasn't sufficient for identification but the Fingerprint System prevailed. Sir Edward Henry is also said to have used this case of incorrect identification of the twins to throw out the Bertillon system and fully adopt the Fingerprint System at the Yard in 1901. Articles regarding this case are "Ferrier of the Yard" by John Berry, Fingerprint Whorld,

12:46 (Oct 1986) and "A Sly Pair" by D.R. Brooker, Fingerprint Whorld, 3:11 (Jan 1978). Although this story is related to events in 1901 and 1904, it is interesting to note that the fingerprint cards in the above articles are dated Sept. 7, 1913.

Friction Ridge
A raised portion of the epidermis on the palmar or plantar skin, consisting of one or more connected ridge units.
SWGFAST, Glossary 07-28-2009 ver. 2.0

Sometimes referred to as ruga or rugae.

Friction Ridge Detail (morphology)
An area comprised of the combination of ridge flow, ridge characteristics, and ridge structure.
SWGFAST, Glossary 07-28-2009 ver. 2.0

Friction Ridge Examiner
An examiner that analyzes, compares, evaluates and verifies friction ridge impressions for the purpose of identification or exclusion. Examinations can be one-to-one or one-to-many and can range from simple to complex.
A) Tenprint examiner: Examines intentionally recorded impression(s).
B) Latent print examiner: Examines unintentionally recorded and developed or captured impression(s).

Friction Ridge Flow
The flow or curvature of the friction ridges. Also referred to as Level 1 detail or 1st level detail.

Friction Ridge Identification
See Individualization.
SWGFAST, Glossary - Consolidated 09-09-03 ver. 1.0

See Fingerprint Identification

Friction Ridge Identification Philosophy
See Philosophy of Friction Ridge Identification.

Friction Ridge Path
The paths or deviations of a friction ridge (endings and bifurcations). Also referred to as Level 2 details or 2nd level details.

Friction Ridge Shapes
The shapes (width and contour) of the ridges. Also referred to as Level 3 details or 3rd level details.

Friction Ridge Unit
A single section of ridge containing one pore.
SWGFAST, Glossary 07-28-2009 ver. 2.0

Friction Skin
Corrugated skin on the volar areas

that enhances friction of the surface. Quantitative-Qualitative Friction Ridge Analysis, David R. Ashbaugh 1999 CRC Press

Also known as thick skin, compared to the skin on the rest of the body, which is thin skin.

Friction Skin Formation, stages of:
(Current Hypothesis)
Swelling of the volar pads.
The volar pads start to regress.
Primary ridges form.
Sweat glands develop.
Secondary ridges develop.
Anastomoses form.
Dermal papillae are created.

Frye vs. US 1923
The court decision which states that a science can be testified to as long as the discipline is generally accepted in the field which it belongs.

The Frye standard dates back to 1923. The Frye case involved a criminal conviction in which the defense proposed that an expert instruct the jury by administering a systolic blood pressure test as a means of establishing Frye's innocence. The trial court ruled this testimony inadmissible. The appellate court upheld the trial court's decision, stating that the expert witness testimony lacked "general acceptance" in its particular field, thereby establishing the Frye standard.
http://www.aaos.org/wordhtml/bulletin/oct04/fline2.htm 05-27-2006

The court opinion was the systolic blood pressure test hadn't crossed the line between experimental and demonstrable.

Fulcrum Area
The area between the thumb and index finger on the palm.
SWGFAST, Glossary - Consolidated 09-09-03 ver. 1.0

Funnel
A term popularized by Ron Smith to describe the ridge pattern in the hypothenar area of the palm. The ridges start on the outer edge of the palm and turn upward converging to the center of the palm.

Furrow Folds
Folds on the underside of the epidermis that correspond to the surface furrows. Aka Secondary ridges.

Furrows
Valleys or depressions between friction ridges.
SWGFAST, Glossary 07-28-2009 ver. 2.0

Also referred to a sulcus (plural: sulci).

G

GTKPR
An acronym, which stands for Gatekeeper, created by Glenn Langenburg in 2001 to help remember the suggested Daubert criteria. The theories or technique should have:

General Acceptance
Tested (has been)
Known Standards
Peer Review and Publication
Rate of Error (known or potential)

Galton Details
Term referring to friction ridge characteristics attributed to the research of English fingerprint pioneer, Sir Francis Galton.
SWGFAST, Glossary 07-28-2009 ver. 2.0

Galton, Sir Francis (Feb. 16, 1822-Jan 17, 1911)
Early fingerprint pioneer. Credited with naming the original details found in a fingerprint. In his 1892 book "Finger Prints", Galton refers to them as forking ridges, beginning or ending ridges, islands and enclosures (pg. 90).

Garson, Dr. John George
Dr. Garson learned about anthropometry directly from Alphonse Bertillon. He was a staunch supporter of the Anthropometry System in the late 1800's and early 1900's. During the 1890's, he headed the Scotland Yard Anthropometric Office. In 1894, when the Troup Committee recommended adding fingerprints to Bertillon cards, Garson implemented a system of classification that was used in conjunction with the anthropometry system but it doesn't appear that the fingerprints were used for identification purposes for some time after this. In 1900, he presented his system to the British Association for the Advancement of Science at Bradford and subsequently wrote a book explaining it, titled "A System of Classification of Finger Impressions" (1900). In the same year Dr. Garson testified in front of the Bepler Committee against using fingerprints as a form of identification. Garson's name appears in some well-known identification cases. His name comes up as being involved in Adolph Beck's 1895 erroneous identification due to personal recognition and he is known for testifying for the defense in the 1905 Stratton Brothers case.

General Electric Co. vs. Joiner (1997)
In a unanimous decision, the court overturned part of the lower court's decision, ruling that trial judges can specify the kind of scientific testimony that juries can hear.
http://www.washingtonpost.com/

wp-srv/national/longterm/supcourt/1997-98/genelec.htm 02-27-03

Some people have interpreted this court decision to mean that the courts can determine if the science was applied reliably (which is different that Daubert which determines if the science is reliable).

See Daubert and Kumho Tire Co.

Generating Layer of Epidermis
See Stratum Basale.

Genetics
Having to do with origin and natural growth or the genes.
Quantitative-Qualitative Friction Ridge Analysis, David R. Ashbaugh 1999 CRC Press

Genipin
A reagent used to develop friction ridge detail on porous items producing dark blue images. Genipin can be visualized with or without fluorescence.
J Forensic Sci, Mar. 2004, Vol. 49, No. 2

Gentian Violet
Violet stain used to develop or enhance friction ridge detail, which can be viewed by either fluorescence or nonfluorescence. Also known as Crystal Violet.
SWGFAST, Glossary - Consolidated 09-09-03 ver. 1.0
A stain that dyes the fats, greases and oils that are sebaceous sweat. Usually used on the adhesive side of tape.

George, Marc Terrance
On Sept. 24, 2005 Marc Terrance George tried to enter the United States illegally. In the process it was determined George had altered his fingerprints by having surgery to switch the skin on his hands and feet. On May 3, 2006, George was sentenced to 13 months in jail for money laundering and drug trafficking.

In May 2007, the doctor who performed the surgery, Dr. José L. Covarrubias, was arrested trying to enter the United States. Dr. Covarrubias was charged with conspiring to distribute marijuana. In Nov. 2007, he plead guilty to a federal charge of harboring and concealing a fugitive. On Feb. 12, 2008, he was sentenced to 18 months in prison. 6 months were taken off of his sentence for his cooperation during the investigation.

German, Edward Raymond
Ed German is considered to be one of the most prominent and influential examiners in the latent print community. He began his career with the FBI in 1971 and has since been involved in every aspect of latent print work, including research, training, and setting industry standards. He has been a distinguished representative of many fingerprint

organizations - he held various leadership roles in the IAI, is a Fellow in The Fingerprint Society, an active member of ASCLD, a charter member of the Japan Identification Society, and is currently a member and Committee Chairman for SWGFAST. Early on he was involved in many research projects, the most notable resulting in his invention of Redwop in 1986. In addition, he was responsible for the introduction of cyanoacrylate fuming, potassium thiocyanate, and RUVIS to many English-speaking countries. He was the first Examiner to testify to visualization of latent prints using lasers (Sierra Vista, AZ, Oct. 1981), and was a key witness in the first Daubert Hearing (US v. Mitchell, 1999). He has also been a contributor to many authoritative books and publications, which include "Scott's Fingerprint Mechanics", "Advances of Fingerprint Technology" and McGraw Hill "Encyclopedia of Science and Technology" as well as being the primary author of the Boy Scouts of America's "Fingerprinting Merit Badge Pamphlet". Besides his fingerprint expertise, he is also an expert in many other areas of forensic science including footwear, tire, and fabric impression evidence. This is only a brief summary of the contributions and accomplishments Ed German has brought to the latent print community. He has received numerous awards and honors for his significant efforts and is recognized as one of the leading experts in his field.

Germinating Layer of Epidermis
See Stratum Basal.

Giglio v. United States (1972)
An extension of the Brady decision which states that the prosecutor is obligated to disclose impeachment material to the defense. Impeachment material can include honesty, integrity, impartiality, and credibility.

See Brady and United States v Henthorn.

Glacial Acetic Acid
Chemical used in the preparation of reagents and dye stains.
SWGFAST, Glossary - Consolidated 09-09-03 ver. 1.0

Glandular Folds
Folds on the underside of the epidermis that correspond to the friction ridges, aka primary ridges.

Glycine
Glycine is the simplest amino acid and the second most common amino acid found in proteins, occurring at a rate of approximately 7.5%. Since amino acids are one of the organic components of eccrine sweat, glycine is often used to test latent print chemicals for an amino acid reaction.

Gold Chloride
A metal salt used in the multimetal process for developing latent prints. SWGFAST, Glossary - Consolidated 09-09-03 ver. 1.0

Gold Tetrachloride / Colloidal Gold
Initial suspension used in the Multimetal Deposition Process. SWGFAST, Glossary - Consolidated 09-09-03 ver. 1.0

Granular Layer of Epidermis
See Stratum Granulosum.

Grew, Dr. Nehemiah (September 26, 1641-March 25, 1712)
Dr. Nehemiah Grew was an English scientist and physician who microscopically studied cells, tissues, and organs of plants. He was born in Mancetter Parish, Warwickshire 1641 and died in 1712 in London. In 1684 he described the patterns on the hands in great detail. Besides the ridges, he also noted pores. Dr. Grew's writings are some of the earliest writing found on the subject of fingerprints, subsequent to Marcello Malpighi.

Grieve, David L.
David Grieve began his fingerprint career in 1965 with the Portland Police Bureau, Portland, Oregon. In 1974, Mr. Grieve became the technical supervisor of the Washington State Patrol's Identification Section in Olympia, Washington, helping to resurrect a state bureau that had been dormant for 13 years . Mr. Grieve accepted a position with the Illinois State Police in 1982 at their Maywood Laboratory as a forensic scientist. In 1984, Mr. Grieve assumed the responsibility of training coordinator in the Illinois State Police Forensic Sciences Command, and has since then trained over 65 forensic scientists in the mysteries and nuances of latent print examination. Mr. Grieve was editor of the Journal of Forensic Identification from 1990 to 2001, and has been a member of the FBI-sponsored Scientific Working Group on Friction Ridge Analysis, Study and Technology since 1996. Mr. Grieve was selected by the US Attorney's Office in Philadelphia to be part of the government's team in the first Daubert challenge to fingerprints, US v Mitchell, in 1999. Also that same year, Mr. Grieve testified for the defense in High Court, Glasgow, Scotland, related to an incorrect fingerprint identification in which a police officer was charged with perjury and subsequently acquitted. In addition, Mr. Grieve was the chief delegate to the International Forensic Science Symposium in Taiwan, a moderator at the International Symposium on Fingerprint Detection and Identification in Israel, invited speaker to fingerprint conferences in the UK, and participated in a forensic science exchange program in Moscow, Russia. On Nov. 30, 2007, David Grieve re-

tired from the Illinois State Police Department.

Gun Blueing
A solution consisting of acetic acid, selenious acid and cupric salt, used to develop friction ridge detail on metal surfaces.
SWGFAST, Glossary - Consolidated 09-09-03 ver. 1.0

H

HFE 7100 ®
A commercial solvent by 3M used as carrier in reagents such as ninhydrin, DFO, and Indanedione.
SWGFAST, Glossary - Consolidated 09-09-03 ver. 1.0

Hale, Dr. Alfred R. (1952)
A fingerprint researcher from Tulane University noted for his research into friction ridge formation and the uniqueness of fingerprints. Hale believed that prior to primary ridges forming, cells proliferate forming clusters or units. These clusters fuse together forming primary ridges. So far there is no evidence that supports this hypothesis. The current data shows that fiction ridges develop as a whole. They may indeed develop from clusters, but so far there is no visual scientific evidence of this.

Credited with the definitive treatise on the development of fingerprints: Morphogenesis of Volar Skin in the Human Fetus, American Journal of Anatomy 91:147-173, 1952.
http://www.handanalysis.net/library/derm_history.htm

Hall-Mills Case (1922)(Trial, Nov. 1926)
On Sept. 14, 1922 the Reverend Edward W. Hall and Mrs. Eleanor Mills were murdered in Somerville, New Jersey. This quickly became one of the most sensational investigations and trials in American crime. The case involved sex, scandal, dramatic players, a bungled investigation and a million dollar defense. Although numerous articles and books have been written about this case, its significance to the fingerprint community seems to have gone by unnoticed. This is the case of the first known erroneous identification. Retired Deputy Police Commissioner Joseph Faurot (NYPD) along with Lieutenant Fred Drewen and Edward H. Schwartz erroneously identified a latent print on key evidence to one of the suspects, William Stevens. J.H. Taylor and Gerhardt Kuhne (brother of Frederick Kuhne) testified for the defense in this trial. All suspects were acquitted and this case remains unsolved today.

Hallucal
A region which corresponds to the distal thenar and first interdigital region on the palm.
SWGFAST, Glossary - Consolidated 09-09-03 ver. 1.0

Another opinion:
The region around the hallux (big toe) on the sole of the foot.

Hallux
Big toe.

Quantitative-Qualitative Friction Ridge Analysis, David R. Ashbaugh 1999 CRC Press

Hamm, Ernest D.
Ernest D. (Ernie) Hamm is recognized as an expert in latent print, footwear and tire track examinations. He began his career as a military police patrol officer and worked as a Special Agent-Criminal Investigator in the Army Criminal Investigation Command where he continued his career as a forensic examiner in the US Army and the Florida Department of Law Enforcement. He became an IAI Certified Latent Print Examiner in 1978. For over 30 years he has been an instrumental part of the forensic community. Not only is Mr. Hamm a leading practitioner and remarkable historian, he's also a renowned educator. Mr. Hamm instructed examiners worldwide, conducting presentations, training seminars, classes, and workshops and has participated in numerous educational conferences. He has received instructor certification from the Arkansas and Florida Commissions on Law Enforcement Standards and Training and the South Carolina Criminal Justice Academy. His participation in several professional organizations spans decades long and include numerous articles, lectures and presentations. He has been associated with the CID Agents Association, Florida Division of the IAI, Forensic Science Society of England, Canadian Identification Society (CIS), International Association for Identification (IAI), The Fingerprint Society (England) and American Academy of Forensic Sciences (AAFS). He is a Life Member of the CIS, a Life and Distinguished Member of the IAI, Fellow of the Fingerprint Society and a Fellow of the American Academy of Forensic Sciences. Mr. Hamm was also a certified inspector of the ASCLD Laboratory Accreditation Board.

In addition, Mr. Hamm was instrumental in a revision of the current IAI logo. He enhanced the fingerprint image of Sir Francis Galton, which was the central focus of the logo. The enhancement version was first introduced at the 1985 IAI Conference and the details regarding the enhancement were presented at the 1991 IAI Conference. The revised and enhanced logo was adopted by the IAI for use on the cover of the Journal of Forensic Identification in 1992.

Haque, Azizul (1800's)
Aka Azizul Haque, Azizul Hacque, or Khan Bahadur Azizul Huq.
One of the Indian Police Officers in Bengal who worked for Sir Edward Richard Henry and helped him develop the Henry System of Classification. Haque devised a mathematical formula to supplement Henry's idea of sorting slips in 1024 pigeon holes,

based on fingerprint patterns. http://www.jpgmonline.com/article.asp?issn=0022-3859;year=2000;volume=46;issue=4;spage=303;epage=8;aulast=Tewari 02-15-2004

Hayden, Eric
See State of Washington vs. Eric Hayden.

Heel
The lowest part of a foot print or the portion furthest from the toes.

Heidenhain, Martin (1864-1949)
Pathologist & histologist who researched the relationship between the dermis and the epidermis. Alfred R. Hale describes him by saying, "The true anatomical relationship of epidermis to dermis was not realized until the classic article of Heidenhain appeared in 1906. The older investigators with the exception of Blaschko (1887) believed the epidermis to send into the substance of the dermis peg-like projections (epidermal papillae, Hautpapillen)."
Morphogensis of volar skin in the human fetus, Alfred R. Hale, 1952.

Hemidesmosome (Hemi-desmosome)
The cells in the basal layer are connected to the basement membrane by hemidesmosomes.

Henry Classification
A system of fingerprint classification named for Sir Edward Richard Henry (1850 - 1931).
SWGFAST, Glossary 07-28-2009 ver. 2.0

Henry, Sir Edward Richard (July 26, 1850-Feb. 19, 1931)
Henry was in India when he and 2 Bengali police officers (Haque and Bose) came up with the classification system that was adopted by the British in 1897. This classification system, bearing his name, became the most widely used classification system worldwide for the next 100 years. In 1900, Henry devised a statistical model to determine the probability of two fingerprints from different fingers having the same series of Galton points. In 1901, Henry was appointed Assistant Commissioner at Scotland Yard where he implemented the first fingerprint bureau that regularly took fingerprints of inmates.

Henthorn Decision (1991)
See United States v Henthorn.

Hepburn, Dr. David
Dr. David Hepburn was one of the original researchers of friction skin. It doesn't appear that he was interested in individuality but rather the development and function of friction skin. Dr. Hepburn studied the ridges of six species of monkeys. Dr. Wilder credits Hepburn with the first to suggest that there is a mechani-

cal function to ridges in addition to sensitivity, i.e. gripping. Wilder also credits Hepburn with naming two of the eminences on the hand, the thenar and the hypothenar. Hepburn wrote "The Papillary Ridges on the Hands and Feet of Monkeys and Men" in 1895.

Heptane
Solvent used in the preparation of reagents.
SWGFAST, Glossary - Consolidated 09-09-03 ver. 1.0

Herschel, Sir William James (Jan. 9, 1833-1917 or 1918)
Credited with being the first European to recognize the value of fingerprints for identification. He recognized that fingerprints were unique and permanent. Herschel documented his own fingerprints over his lifetime to prove permanence. He was also credited with being the first person to used fingerprints in a practical manner. As early as the 1850's, working as a British officer for the Indian Civil Service, he started putting fingerprints on contracts.

Hexane
Solvent used in the preparation of reagents.
SWGFAST, Glossary - Consolidated 09-09-03 ver. 1.0

Hinge Lifter
The adhesive used to lift a latent print hinged to the backing that it would be secured to.

Histology
The branch of biology that studies the microscopic structure of animal or plant tissues.
WordNet ® 1.6, © 1997 Princeton University
http://dictionary.reference.com/search?q=histology

Holland, Mary E. (Feb. 25, 1868-Mar 27, 1915)
Mary and Phil Holland operated the Holland Detective Agency in the early 1900's. In 1904, they met Ferrier at the World's Fair in St. Louis. Ferrier instructed Mary Holland and eight others on fingerprints and how to use the Henry System. In 1907, Mary Holland was hired by the US Navy as a fingerprint instructor. She is considered to be the second American fingerprint instructor in the United States (second to Parke) but the first woman fingerprint instructor. Her teachings promoted the Henry System throughout the United States. Mary Holland is also credited as one of the fingerprint experts (along with Edward Foster, William M. Evans and Michael P. Evans) to testify in the trial "People vs. Jennings".

Holt, Sarah B.
Assistant of L. S. Penrose. Noted for her research into the association between dermal ridges and various

diseases and the statistical distribution of dermal patterns. She wrote "Significance of Dermatoglyphics in Medicine" in 1949 and "The Genetics of Dermal Ridges" in 1968.

Holy Grail Reference Library
The Holy Grail Reference Library is a collection of 149 hard to find articles, books, presentations, and court decisions related to friction skin. These documents, dating back to 1892, are essential resources for latent print examiners. Glenn Langenburg, from the Minnesota Bureau of Criminal Apprehension, (with the help of others) has compiled and distributes this reference material on compact disk.

Horny Layer of Epidermis
See Stratum Corneum.

Horseshoe
A form of documentation used to show that an impression has some form of value. This is done by putting a horseshoe marking around the impression. Multiple horseshoes can be used to document simultaneous impressions.

Hot Breath Method or Technique (aka Huffing)
Breathing on a latent print either to visualize the print or to infuse moisture back into an older latent print.

Hot Flame Method
Aka the Flame Technique. The hot flame method is a process used to develop friction ridge detail on non-porous items. A substance, such as camphor, masking tape, or pine tar is burned to produce heavy soot. While the substance is burning, an object is placed in the smoke until a thick coat of soot is formed on the object. The extra soot is then brushed away with a fingerprint brush leaving soot on the friction ridge detail.

See Flame Technique.

Huber, Assistant Commissioner Roy A. (July 1921- September 28, 2005)
Retired Assistant Commissioner Roy A. Huber, RCMP, Ottawa, Ontario, Canada, is credited as being the person who formulated Analysis, Comparison, Evaluation in the 1950's, now known as ACE-V. Inspector Huber wrote the articles "Expert Witness" in 1959 and "The Philosophy of Identification" in 1972 where he explains the comparison process and "...the process of identification regardless of the subject matter". Additionally, he wrote the book "Handwriting Identification: Facts & Fundamentals" in 1999 with Alfred Headrick.

Hudson, Dr. Erastus Mead (1930's)
Credited with the discovery of the silver nitrate processing method for obtaining latent prints from unpainted wood. This process became well known after Dr. Hudson developed

latent prints on the ladder involved in the Lindbergh kidnapping case (1932). Others had experimented with silver nitrate prior to Dr. Hudson, but historically he is given the recognition. Dr. Hudson also did research in using silver nitrate to develop latent prints on other items, such as cloth and gloves.
Finger Print and Identification Magazine, Vol. 17, No. 3, September 1935.

Huffing (aka The Hot Breath Technique)
Breathing on a latent print either to visualize the print or to infuse moisture back into an older latent print.

Hungarian Red
A red protein stain used to visualize bloody friction ridge detail.
SWGFAST, Glossary - Consolidated 09-09-03 ver. 1.0

Also known as Acid Fuchsin.

Hyalin Layer of Epidermis
See Stratum Lucidum.

Hydrochloric Acid
A chemical used to process thermal paper to develop friction ridge detail. Also known as Muriatic Acid.

Hydrofluoric Acid (Hydrogen Fluoride)
A latent developmental technique, discovered by Dr. Rene Forgeot in 1891, used for recovering latent friction ridge detail on glass. The hydrofluoric acid vapors deteriorate the glass around a latent image. This method is very dangerous to use and is no longer needed due to more advanced methods of latent print recovery.

Hydrogen Peroxide
Chemical used in friction ridge development reagents.
SWGFAST, Glossary - Consolidated 09-09-03 ver. 1.0

Hyperdactyly
See Polydactyly.
SWGFAST, Glossary - Consolidated 09-09-03 ver. 1.0

Birth defect (in humans) characterized by the presence of more than the normal number of fingers or toes
Synonyms: polydactyly
Source: WordNet ® 1.7, © 2001 Princeton University

Hypohidrosis
See Anhidrosis.

Hypothenar Area
The friction ridge skin on the palm, below the interdigital area on the ulnar side of the palm.
SWGFAST, Glossary - Consolidated 09-09-03 ver. 1.0

Ulnar side of the palm between the little finger and wrist.
Quantitative-Qualitative Friction

Ridge Analysis, David R. Ashbaugh
1999 CRC Press

Hypothesis
A tentative explanation for an observation, phenomenon, or scientific problem that can be tested by further investigation.
The American Heritage® Dictionary of the English Language, Fourth Edition
http://dictionary.reference.com/search?q=hypothesis 02-27-03

Hypothesis testing
A valid scientific technique to show others that you have observations to support your theory. (Inductive reasoning)
Question
Gather data - all data, not only data that supports your conclusion.
Conclusion - testable, repeatable or reproducible, falsifiable, and explainable.
Peer review / Publication - insures objectivity and unbiasedness, does not insure accurate results or conclusions.

I

IAFIS

The FBI's Integrated Automated Fingerprint Identification System.

IAFS

International Association of Forensic Sciences.

IAI

International Association for Identification.
The IAI was founded by Harry Caldwell in 1915 in Oakland, California as the "International Association for Criminal Identification". The name was changed in 1918 to reflect the noncriminal work done by the identification bureaus. The IAI has put out many publications since its inception including the 'International Identification Outlook', 'Sparks from the Anvil', 'Identification News' and the 'Journal of Forensic Identification'.

IAI Resolutions

Resolution 1973 – Minimum Number of Characteristics (revised in 2009)
In 1973, The IAI Standardization Committee released the results of a three-year study. They recommended and adopted that "no valid basis exists at this time for requiring that a pre-determined minimum number of friction ridge characteristics must be present in two impressions in order to establish positive identification." This was based on the fact that each print has a unique set of circumstances.
http://www.latent-prints.com/iai_standardization_committee.htm
03-21-2003

Resolution 1979 VII (revised in 1980)
"THEREFORE BE IT RESOLVED that any member, officer or certified latent print examiner who provides oral or written reports, or gives testimony of possible, probable or likely friction ridge identification shall be deemed to be engaged in conduct unbecoming such member, officer or certified latent print examiner as described in Article XVII, Section 5, of the constitution of the International Association for Identification, and charges may be brought under such conditions set forth in Article XVI, Section 5, of the constitution. If such member be a certified latent print examiner, his conduct and status shall be reconsidered by the Latent Print Certification Board..."
www.clpex.com detail 78 Feb.3 2003

Resolution, 1980-V, the amended version of Resolution VII, 1979:
"Now therefore be it resolved that any member, officer or certified latent print examiner who initiates or volunteers oral or written reports or testimony of possible, probable

or likely friction ridge identification, or who, when required in a judicial proceeding to provide such reports or testimony, does not qualify it with a statement that the print in question could be that of someone else, shall be deemed to be engaged in conduct unbecoming such member,.....”
http://www.latent-prints.com/realizing_the_full_value_of_late.htm

Resolution 2009-10
RESOLVED, that the International Association for Identification recognizes that Tenprint Identification (individualization) and Latent Print Identification (individualization) utilize the same scientific methodology when practiced by a person trained to competency.

Resolution 2009-18, the amended version of the 1973 Resolution
RESOLVED, the official position of the I.A.I., effective August 21, 2009, is as follows:
“There currently exists no scientific basis for requiring a minimum amount of corresponding friction ridge detail information between two impressions to arrive at an opinion of single source attribution.”

IEEGFI I and IEEGFI II
The Interpol European Expert Group on Fingerprint Identification. The IEEGFI I was adopted by the 29th European Regional Conference, held in Reykjavik, Iceland. The IEEGFI II was formed in May 2000 and was a progression of the IEEGFI II. The goals of this group are ‘To explore, define and establish common terminology concerning the content of the fingerprint identification process and the general application of this process to the detection, validation and comparison of ridge detail, so as to provide basis for communication and promote uniformity’ and ‘To define and establish recognised principles concerning the application of this process so that it can be standardised, controlled and made objective. This may cover aspects such as definitions, norms, standards, rules, guidelines and rules of thumb’.
http://www.interpol.int/Public/Forensic/fingerprints/WorkingParties/IEEGFI2/default.asp#4

INC
The common abbreviation for an ‘inconclusive’ determination, meaning that a conclusive determination could not be arrived at.

INC is also used to indicate ‘incomplete’, meaning that a full comparison could not be completed.

ISO
International Organization for Standardization.

Icnofalangometric or Icnofalangometria
The original name of the classifica-

tion system developed by Juan Vucetich. This name was later changed to 'Dactiloscopico' or 'Dactiloscopy'.

Identakey
A system of classification developed in the 1930's by G. Tyler Mairs. The aim of this classification system was to unite the morphology described by Wilder and Whipple and judicial identification. Fingerprints were broken down into classes, families, orders, genus, species and subspecies. This system never caught on.
Suspect Identities, Simon A. Cole 2001 Harvard University Press

Identification
1. In some forensic disciplines, this term denotes the similarity of class characteristics.
2. See Individualization.
SWGFAST, Glossary 07-28-2009 ver. 2.0

The act or process of identifying; prove to be the same.
Quantitative-Qualitative Friction Ridge Analysis, David R. Ashbaugh 1999 CRC Press

Establishing an association with a group or individual item.

Identification News
A magazine produced by the IAI and published from 1951-1957. In 2008, the IAI began publishing Identification News again starting with Vol. 38 No.1.

Ideology
A set of doctrines or beliefs that form the basis of a political, economic, or other system.
The American Heritage® Dictionary of the English Language, Fourth Edition Copyright © 2000 by Houghton Mifflin Company. Published by Houghton Mifflin Company. All rights reserved
http://dictionary.reference.com/search?q=ideology 02-27-03

Image Reversal
An Image Reversal is when the friction ridges in a latent print are reversed from the standard direction. This typically occurs in unintentional transferred prints and on latents lifted with rubber lifters.

Impressed Print
See Plastic Print.

Incipient
Beginning; coming into existence; immature.
Quantitative-Qualitative Friction Ridge Analysis, David R. Ashbaugh 1999 CRC Press

Beginning to exist or appear.
The American Heritage® Dictionary of the English Language, Fourth Edition Copyright © 2000 by Houghton Mifflin Company. Published by Houghton Mifflin

Company.
http://dictionary.reference.com/search?q=incipient 05-13-03

Incipient Ridge
A friction ridge not fully developed that may appear shorter and thinner than fully developed friction ridges.
SWGFAST, Glossary 07-28-2009 ver. 2.0

An incipient ridge is an immature friction ridge. There are two kinds of ridges both described by the word incipient.
1) An 'incipient ridge' may describe a ridge that is thinner and shallower than the surrounding ridges. These incipient ridges may have immature pores associated with them. They may not appear in all representations but are permanent and repeatable friction ridge characteristics. (Ashbaugh, 1999)
2) An 'incipient ridge' may describe a ridge that is thinner and shallower than the surrounding ridges. These ridges do not have pores associated with them. Generally, they are not visible the first few years of life. They do not appear in all representations, but once visible they are permanent and repeatable. They may be considered occasional print features.

Inclusion
A latent image concurs with the exemplar but there is not enough to individualize.

Inconclusive
During Evaluation, the conclusion reached that neither sufficient agreement exists to individualize nor sufficient disagreement exists to exclude.
SWGFAST, Glossary 07-28-2009 ver. 2.0

1, 2-Indanedione (pronounced in-dane-die-on)
Compound that reacts with the amino acids present in print residue, producing a fluorescent product when exposed to excitation wavelengths of 352-591 nm.
SWGFAST, Glossary - Consolidated 09-09-03 ver. 1.0

A chemical process used to find latent prints on porous items. The chemical reacts with the amino acids in fingerprint residue and fluoresces under certain wavelengths. Optimal viewing is done at 515nm-570nm with orange or red goggles. This chemical process is an alternative to DFO reportedly resulting in similar quality prints at a lower cost and easier to prepare.
Research by Jon Stimac of the Oregon State Police showed that the HFE-7100 formulation published by Wiesner (JFS 2001) can be used on thermal papers.
http://www.bvda.com/EN/prdctinf/en_ind_1.html 06-25-2003

The use of 1, 2-Indanedione for visualizing latent fingerprints on porous items was discovered by Professor Madeleine Joullié and her graduate students, Drs. Diane Hauze and Olga Petrovskaia, from the University of Pennsylvania.

Independent
Free from external influence, guidance, control, or constraint.

Individual Characteristics
Individual characteristics are those features that separate one item from another, as opposed to class characteristics. When referring to fingerprints, level 2 and level 3 details are considered to be individual characteristics.

Individualization
The state of being individualized.
Quantitative-Qualitative Friction Ridge Analysis, David R. Ashbaugh 1999 CRC Press

The determination of an examiner that there is sufficient quality and quantity of detail in agreement to conclude that two friction ridge impressions originated from the same source.
SWGFAST, Glossary 07-28-2009 ver. 2.0

Individualize
Differentiate from other individuals; distinctive.
Quantitative-Qualitative Friction Ridge Analysis, David R. Ashbaugh 1999 CRC Press

Inductive Reasoning
Reasoning from detailed facts to general principles
WordNet ® 1.6, © 1997 Princeton
http://dictionary.reference.com/search?q=inductive%20reasoning
02-27-03

Infrared
Light wavelengths longer than the visible spectrum, 700- 1,000,000 nm.
SWGFAST, Glossary - Consolidated 09-09-03 ver. 1.0

Inherent Luminescence
Luminescence resulting from selected wavelength illumination without chemical treatment.
SWGFAST, Glossary - Consolidated 09-09-03 ver. 1.0

Inked Print (Finger, Palm, Foot)
See Exemplar.
See Known Print.
SWGFAST, Glossary - Consolidated 09-09-03 ver. 1.0

Inner Terminus
See Core.
SWGFAST, Glossary - Consolidated 09-09-03 ver. 1.0

Institute of Applied Science
The Institute of Applied Science was founded in Chicago, Illinois in 1916 by Captain William K. Evans, of the United States Military Intelligence

Agency, and T. G. Cooke. The original name was "Evans University". One year after it was established Captain Evans was recalled to military service for World War I. At this time he severed his connections with the school and the name was changed to "The University of Applied Science". Around 1929, the name was again changed to "The Institute of Applied Science". The IAS started as a correspondence school specializing in all aspects of identification work. In 1919, they began publishing a monthly newsletter called "Finger Print Magazine" which was later changed to "Finger Print and Identification Magazine". In 1952, T.G. Cooke died and his sons T. Dickerson Cooke and Donald Cooke took over running the institution. They retired in 1975 and Sirchie took over ownership of the school. Their magazine stopped being published around 1978. The IAS was, and continues to be, an instrumental part of training experts in the identification field.
Finger Print and Identification Magazine Oct. 1938
Journal of Forensic Identification 40 (1) 1994

Interdigital
Palmar area below the fingers and above the thenar and hypothenar areas.
SWGFAST, Glossary - Consolidated 09-09-03 ver. 1.0
Between the digits; an area at the base of the digits.
Quantitative-Qualitative Friction Ridge Analysis, David R. Ashbaugh 1999 CRC Press

In some countries, such as Portugal, this area of the palm is known as the superior region instead of the interdigital region.

Interdigital Delta's
The deltas in the interdigital region of the palm have been referred to as the clean delta, the snow cones, and the side cone.

International Association of Forensic Sciences
The International Association of Forensic Sciences was inaugurated in 1957. This organization holds world meetings every 3 years.

International Association for Identification
See IAI.

International Identification Outlook
The International Identification Outlook was the first periodical published by the IAI. It began in 1916 and was only published for a short time.

Interstitial
Relating to or situated in the small, narrow spaces between tissues or

parts of an organ.
The American Heritage® Dictionary of the English Language, Fourth Edition Copyright © 2000 by Houghton Mifflin Company. Published by Houghton Mifflin Company.
http://dictionary.reference.com/search?q=interstitial07-01-2003

SWGFAST refers to incipient ridges as Interstitial.

Alfred R. Hale refers to interstitial ridges as Secondary ridges in his paper "Morphogenesis of Volar Skin in the Human Fetus" 1952.

Inter-Subjectively Tested
Subjective conclusions that are independently tested by others. This eliminates individual biases for a more objective conclusion.
Karl Popper contends that we never know the truth but we get closer to it each time a single observation is inter-subjectively tested. The more times people independently replicate a conclusion, the more confident we can be in that conclusion.

Intervening Ridges
The number of friction ridges between two characteristics.
SWGFAST, Glossary - Consolidated 09-09-03 ver. 1.0

Intuition
The act or faculty of knowing or sensing without the use of rational processes; immediate cognition.
Knowledge gained by the use of this faculty; a perceptive insight.
A sense of something not evident or deducible; an impression.
The American Heritage® Dictionary of the English Language, Fourth Edition Copyright © 2000 by Houghton Mifflin Company. Published by Houghton Mifflin Company. All rights reserved.
http://dictionary.reference.com/search?q=intuition 03-18-2003

Instinctive knowing (without the use of rational processes) 2: an impression that something might be the case.
WordNet ® 1.6, © 1997 Princeton University
http://dictionary.reference.com/search?q=intuition 03-18-2003

Inverted Ridges
See Tonal Reversal.

Iodine
Element used as either a vapor or solution; binds with fats and oils to visualize friction ridge detail.
SWGFAST, Glossary - Consolidated 09-09-03 ver. 1.0

Iodine vapors are best used on porous surfaces. They color the fats and oils present in sebaceous residue and as the iodine evaporates, the color fades. It has been found that iodine works best on latents that are freshly deposited. Due to the hazards associated with it and the advances of other processing techniques, iodine is seldom used.

Iodine-Silver Transfer Method
A method for recovering friction ridge detail. Developed by John McMorris and presented at the IAI California Division Conference in 1936.

Islands
Friction ridges of varying lengths.
Quantitative-Qualitative Friction Ridge Analysis, David R. Ashbaugh 1999 CRC Press

Isopropanol (Isopropyl Alcohol)
Solvent used in the preparation of reagents.
SWGFAST, Glossary - Consolidated 09-09-03 ver. 1.0

J

JFI
See Journal of Forensic Identification.

JFS
Journal of Forensic Sciences. Published by the American Academy of Forensic Sciences.

Jennings (People vs. Jennings, Illinois, 1910)
The first State Supreme Court case to uphold the admissibility of fingerprint evidence. Dec. 21, 1911, The Illinois State Supreme Court upheld the admissibility of fingerprint evidence concluding that fingerprints are a reliable form of identification.

Jennings, Thomas
Thomas Jennings was the first person to be convicted of murder in the United States based on fingerprint evidence. In 1911, Jennings appealed his conviction to the Illinois Supreme Court, questioning the admissibility of fingerprint evidence. The Illinois Supreme Court upheld his conviction concluding that fingerprint evidence is admissible and a reliable form of identification. Thomas Jennings was sentenced to death and executed on Feb. 16, 1912 for the murder of Clarence B. Hiller. Mary Holland, Michael P. Evans, William M. Evans, and Edward Foster were the four fingerprint experts that testified at Jennings original trial.

Jennings, William Nicholson (1860-1946)
William Jennings is credited with being the first person in the United States to record his own palm prints years apart to test their persistency. After hearing a lecture at the Franklin Institute in Philadelphia in 1887 he recorded his prints. In 1937 he again recorded his prints and saw they did not change. Jennings did not publish either of the recordings until 1939. An interesting side note is that this was Jennings only connection to the fingerprint industry. Jennings was an internationally known photographer famous for being the first person to photograph lightning.

Joiner
See General Electric Co.

Joint
The hinged area where two bones are joined together.

Journal of Forensic Identification
A peer review journal produced by the International Association of Identification and published from 1988 until the present.

Justification
Good justification behind a conclusion strengthens the integrity of the conclusion which in turn improves the weight of a conclusion.

K

Kelly Rule (California, 1976)
See People v. Kelly.

Kelly v. State 824 S.W.2d (Texas, 1992)
The admissibility requirements for scientific evidence in Texas criminal courts. Kelly recognized that reliability was more important than the Frye requirement of general acceptance. Kelly has 3 factors; "(a) [that] the underlying scientific technique [is] valid; (b) [that] the technique applying the theory [is] valid; and (c) [that] the technique [has] been properly applied on the occasion in question."
From the court document THE STATE COURT OF CRIMINAL APPEALS OF TEXAS, NO. 1919-02, THE STATE OF TEXAS, Appellant v. MATTHEW MEDRANO, Appellee 09-10-2008

Kent-Morfopoulos Case
See People v. Kent.

Keratinocyte
A cell which is found in our skin. It is the major constituent of the epidermis. In their process of maturation keratinocytes die and eventually become the horny protective layer of our skin.
http://skincancer.dermis.net/glossary/

Keratinocytes differentiate as they progress from the basal layer to the skin surface. Keratinocytes are stratified, squamous, epithelial cells which comprise skin and mucosa, including oral, esophageal, corneal, conjunctival, and genital epithelia. Keratinocyte stem cells reside in the basal layer. These cells have a low rate of mitosis and give rise to a population of transient amplifying cells. The major proteins formed within keratinocytes are keratins.
http://www.aad.org/education/keratinocytes.htm 03-08-2003

Keratins
Group of highly insoluble fibrous proteins (of high ⊠ -helical content) which are found as constituents of the outer layer of vertebrate skin and of skin-related structures such as hair, wool, hoof and horn, claws, beaks and feathers. Extracellular keratins are derived from cytokeratins, a large and diverse group of intermediate filament proteins.
John Edwards
http://www.mblab.gla.ac.uk/~julian/dict2.cgi?3456

Key
A numerical value derived from the ridge count of the first loop beginning with the right thumb exclusive of the little fingers.

SWGFAST, Glossary - Consolidated 09-09-03 ver. 1.0

Kingston, Charles R.
Charles Kingston did several statistical studies on the uniqueness of fingerprints. In 1964, he finished his dissertation at the University of California Berkley titled, "Probabilistic Analysis of Partial Fingerprint Patterns".

Kirk, Paul Leland (1902-1970)
Along with Vollmer, Kirk established criminology and criminalistics as an academic discipline. In 1950 the University of California Berkeley began offering criminal justice degrees. In 1953, Kirk authored "Crime Investigation", one of the first crime scene investigation books to include not only practical information, but also included theory. Kirk went on to work with C.R. Kingston to analyze the statistical aspect of fingerprint identification.

Klaatsch, Dr. Hermann (1863-1916)
Dr. Hermann Klaatsch was a Professor of Anatomy and as well as an evolutionist. He is sometimes referred to in fingerprint books for his early studies on friction skin development. Dr. Klaatsch researched the volar pads association with the epidermal patterns, grouping the volar pads of humans and primates together. Subsequent to Kollmann, Klaatsch also gave names to the different volar pads (1888).

Known Print (Finger, Palm, Foot)
A recording of an individual's friction ridges with black ink, electronic imaging, photography, or other medium on a contrasting background. SWGFAST, Glossary 07-28-2009 ver. 2.0

Koehler, Jonathan Jay Ph. D.
Jonathan Koehler is a Professor of Behavioral Decision Making at McCombs School of Business, University of Texas at Austin. He's considered to be a critic of forensic sciences. His main criticisms are:

-Examiners should undergo mandatory testing by external agencies. This testing should be done frequently, blind, and represent latents that mirror those found in actual case work.

-Fingerprints haven't been able to satisfy the Daubert conditions but courts have been reluctant to exclude fingerprint evidence so they offer some sort of unscientific reasoning for admitting them. As an example, has a sufficient amount of testing been done? Some judges have determined that 100 years worth of court use counts as testing.

-Experts describe by exaggeration (100% match, no possibility of error).

-Dr. Koehler admits that fingerprints are not junk science, it has probative value, but how much? Dr. Koehler believes the probative value of a fingerprint that reportedly matches a source should be based on two considerations: (1) the frequency with which the match profile occurs in the relevant population, and (2) the rate at which false match errors occur. He also believes that in the special cases where the false match error rate is several orders of magnitude larger than the coincidental match rate (which it probably is in fingerprinting), the false match error rate controls the probative value of the evidence.

-"The assumption of discernible uniqueness that resides at the core of these fields is weakened by evidence of errors in proficiency testing and actual cases."

-"...data from a well-known forensic testing program contradict industry boasts of perfect, or even near-perfect, agreement (30). Since 1995, about one-fourth of examiners failed to correctly identify all latent prints in this test (which includes 9 to 12 latent prints and palm prints). About 4 to 5% of examiners committed false-positive errors on at least one latent."

-"Although lacking theoretical or empirical foundations, the assumption of discernible uniqueness offers important practical benefits to the traditional forensic sciences. It enables forensic sciences to draw bold, definitive conclusions that can make or break cases. It excuses the forensic sciences from developing measures of object attributes, collecting population data on the frequencies of variations in those attributes, testing attribute independence, or calculating and explaining the probability that different objects share a common set of observable attributes. Without the discernible uniqueness assumption, far more scientific work would be needed, and criminalists would need to offer more tempered opinions in court."

All items in quotes are from: Michael J. Saks and Jonathan J. Koehler, "The Coming Paradigm Shift in Forensic Identification Science". Science, Vol 309, Issue 5736, 892-895 , 5 August 2005

Kolliker, Rudolph Albert Von (AKA Kolliker, Albert Von) (1817-1905) Swiss anatomist and physiologist, wrote a prominent textbook on cell theory, Handbuch der Gewebelehre (Manual of Histology), (1852). He added great contributions to many aspects of science, namely histology. Alfred R. Hale describes him as the first to study the embryogenesis of the skin (1848-1849).

Kollmann, Arthur (18??-1941)
In the late 1800's (1883, 1885), Kollmann of Hamburg Germany, was the first researcher to address the formation of friction ridges on the fetus and the random physical stresses and tensions which may have played a part in their growth.
http://www.ridgesandfurrows.homestead.com/scientific_researchers.html 03-08-2003

Arthur Kollmann may have been the first researcher to study the development of friction ridges. He not only grouped the volar pads of humans but also grouped the volar pads of many primates. Dr. Wilder credits Kollmann with establishing and naming ten volar pads in humans and the first to study epidermic markings in different races. Alfred R. Hale describes him as the first researcher (1883) to suggest that mechanical stresses inherent in growth may influence the ultimate dermatoglyphic configuration.

Konai, Rajyadhar
Rajyadhar Konai was one of the first people Herschel fingerprinted as a means of identification. This is noted as the first practical uses of fingerprints. On July 28, 1858, Herschel obtained the entire hand impression of Rajyadhar Konai as a signature on a contract.

Kuhl, Ben
Ben Kuhl was the defendant in what may have been the first palm print case to be tried in the United States. He was accused of murdering the driver of a stagecoach and this case has become known as "the story of the last horse drawn stage robbery in the U.S.A.". It's also said to be "the first palm print ever to be testified to in U.S. Courts". The murder happened in Dec. 1916, and the trial date is unknown. Others have said the first palm print case may have been the Betts case of Ohio (brought to trial in 1917).

See State of Nevada v. Kuhl 1918.

Kuhne, Frederick
Author of the first textbook on fingerprints in the United States. "The Finger Print Instructor" was published in 1916.

Kumho Tire Company v. Carmichael (1999)
This ruling extended Daubert to include all types of expert testimony. Including technical and other specialized knowledge.

L

LCV
Leucocrystal Violet. Reagent used to detect / enhance bloody friction ridge detail by either fluorescent or nonfluorescent staining.
SWGFAST, Glossary - Consolidated 09-09-03 ver. 1.0

Langenburg, Glenn
Glenn Langenburg is currently employed by the Minnesota Bureau of Criminal Apprehension as a Certified Latent Print Examiner and Crime Scene Investigator. Glenn earned a BS in Forensic Science from Michigan State University in 1993 and a MS in Analytical Chemistry in 1999 from the University of Minnesota. Currently he is a PHD candidate in the Forensic Science program at the University of Lausanne, Switzerland, under the direction of Professor Christophe Champod. His thesis research involves the statistical analysis of fingerprint comparison methodology. He is also privileged to serve on SWGFAST. In addition to his duties as a forensic scientist, Glenn is an adjunct professor at two universities in Minnesota: Hamline University and Metropolitan State University.

Langerhans Cells
Cells in the stratum spinosum layer of the epidermis designed to process foreign antibodies to the immune system.

Langill Decision (2007)
See State of New Hampshire v. Richard Langill.

Laser
Light Amplification by Stimulated Emission of Radiation. A device that produces a coherent wavelength(s) of light. See FLS.
SWGFAST, Glossary - Consolidated 09-09-03 ver. 1.0

First used for viewing latent prints by a team of Canadian researchers in 1976. These researchers were E. Roland Menzel of Texas Tech University, Brian E. Dalrymple of the Ontario Provincial Police, and J.M. Duff of the Xerox Research Centre of Canada.
J. Forensic Sci. 22, (1), 106 (1977).
A special lens is used to expand the laser beam to the entire viewing area. The first testimony in the United States regarding this method of visualization was in 1981 in Sierra Vista, Arizona by Ed German.

Latent Print
A transferred impression of friction ridge detail that is not readily visible to the naked eye; A generic term used for a friction ridge impression that was not intentionally recorded.

1. Transferred impression of friction ridge detail not readily visible.
2. Generic term used for questioned friction ridge detail.
SWGFAST, Glossary 07-28-2009 ver. 2.0

A fingerprint that is not apparent to the eye but can be made sufficiently visible, as by dusting or fuming, for use in identification.
The American Heritage® Dictionary of the English Language, Fourth Edition Copyright © 2000 by Houghton Mifflin Company. Published by Houghton Mifflin Company. All rights reserved
http://dictionary.reference.com/search?q=latent&r=3 02-27-03

Latent Print Recovery Conditions
Whether or not a latent is recovered is dependant on:
1. The surface (substrate):
a) Its physical composition,
b) Its texture,
c) Condition,
d) and cleanliness.
2. The person touching the item:
a) The condition of their ridges (which could be affected by medical condition or occupation),
b) how much they sweat (which is dependant on age, diet, temperature, emotional state, medical condition and the recent amount of physical exertion),
c) And the pressure they apply.
3. Whether or not there is a transferable substance on the friction skin other than sweat.
4. Post transfer conditions:
a) The environment (heat or rain will deteriorate a latent),
b) How it's handled (handling and packaging may destroy a latent)
c) and the developing medium.

Latzina, Dr. Francisco
A fingerprint pioneer that is credited with influencing Vucetich to change the name of his classification system from Icnofalangometria to Dactiloscopy.

Laws
Generalizations about what has happened, from which we can generalize about what we expect to happen. They pertain to observational data. The ability of the ancients to predict eclipses had nothing to do with whether they knew just how they happened; they had a law but not a theory.
http://www.madsci.org/posts/archives/oct99/940942724.Sh.r.html 02-27-03

States an observation without any attempt to explain it (law of gravity).

Law of Biological Uniqueness
The Scientific Law that states that all items in nature are unique.

Leadbetter, Martin FFS, RFP, Bachleor of Arts + Honours

Martin Leadbetter was employed within the Fingerprint Branch at New Scotland Yard from 1966/72. During this period he was also responsible for attending crime scenes in Central London as a Divisional Fingerprint Officer. Having qualified as a Fingerprint Expert in 1972, he transferred to the Gloucestershire Constabulary where he remained employed for just over two years, after which he took up the post of Deputy Head of the Fingerprint Bureau for Hertfordshire Constabulary, just north of London.

In 1988 he was seconded to the Home Office as part of the team investigating implementation of a national AFIS for England and Wales. This secondment lasted until 1991 and during this time he assisted in the writing of the Detailed Operation Requirement for a national AFIS and made several visits with the bench-marking team to the USA and France where systems produced by Printrak, NEC, Morpho Systèmes (now Sagem) and ISS were all tested.

From January 1991/August 1995 he was employed by Sagem SA as Fingerprint Expert and Consultant. During this period he visited the police departments of more than thirty countries worldwide, including two visits to Siberia, South American countries, South Africa, numerous visits to the USA, Russia and most European countries.

In September 1995 he took up his present post as Head of the Fingerprint Bureau for Cambridgeshire Constabulary, based in the East Anglian region of the UK.

He has been a member of IAI since 1978, a Distinguished Member since 1988 and achieved Life Membership in 2003. He is a Founder, Fellow and Life Member of The Fingerprint Society and was its first Secretary and Assistant Editor of the Society's journal, Fingerprint Whorld for just on fifteen years. Today, Mr. Leadbetter is a serving member of The Fingerprint Society Committee. Recently, he has acted in a consultative position in Bosnia, assisting the European Union Police to implement a national AFIS for that country. He has addressed several conferences, both at home and abroad, in particular at the Humboldt University, East Berlin, Surgut, Siberia and most recently, in October 2004 at the Centenary Conference in Budapest, which celebrated the first hundred years of the fingerprint system in Hungary.

At home he is now very active holding several important national posts. He is a member of the National Fingerprint Board of England and Wales, Chairman of the Bureau Practitioners' Sub-Group and a member of the Standards Working Group. Until recently he chaired the Third Level Detail Sub-Group, which had been instigated by the Association of Chief Police Officers to investigate the potential use of so-called 'third level detail' within the identification process. He also sits on the IAI's International Committee and is a member of the Journal of Forensic Identification's Editorial Board.

He is a Registered Forensic Practitioner with the Council for the registration of Forensic Practitioners and Member of the British Academy of Forensic Sciences and holds the degree of Bachelor of Arts with Honours.

Throughout his long career within the fingerprint discipline he has been a constant contributor to forensic and scientific journals. He strongly holds the view that fingerprint identification is not a science, but a technique that requires considerable skill, but is prepared to compromise and accept that it has a scientific, albeit a rather nebulous 'scientific' basis.

In his spare time Martin Leadbetter enjoys gourmet cooking, wine and is a composer having written three symphonies, numerous works for chamber and instrumental ensembles, more than fifty songs, and works for choir, band and orchestra. He is also a Member of the Corporation of the Royal Albert Hall, London. As an author he has just completed his first full-length novel, Deep and Crisp and Evil, which gives an uncompromising insight into the working of the modern police service and forensic discipline.
11-24-2004

Martin Leadbetter retired from the Cambridgeshire Constabulary on Aug. 12, 2005. He remains an active participant in the fingerprint industry.

Leuco Rhodamine 6G
A reagent that reacts with the heme moiety of the hemoglobin of red cells in blood to visualize friction ridge detail left in blood. The sulfosalicylic acid in this solution fixes the blood so no pretreatment is necessary.
Luo Yapping and Wang Yue. Journal of Forensic Identification Vol. 54, No. 5, 2004

Leucocrystal Violet
A colorless or reduced form of gentian violet (per the FBI) used to stain blood residue (through oxidation) on both porous and nonporous items. Aka LCV.

Leucomalachite Green
Reagent used to detect / enhance bloody friction ridge detail.
SWGFAST, Glossary - Consolidated 09-09-03 ver. 1.0

LeuR6G

See Leuco rhodamine 6G.

Level 1 detail
Friction ridge flow and general morphological information.
SWGFAST, Glossary 07-28-2009 ver. 2.0

General overall pattern shape, i.e., circular, looping, arching, or straight.
Quantitative-Qualitative Friction Ridge Analysis, David R. Ashbaugh 1999 CRC Press

In Nov. 2004, the Third Level Detail working group (from the Standards Sub-Group of the National Fingerprint Board of England and Wales) determined that it was not necessary to subdivide the features used in friction ridge identifications. In England and Wales these terms are no longer recognized and it has been established that they should not be used. See Features.

Level 2 detail
Individual friction ridge paths and friction ridge events (e.g., bifurcations, ending ridges, and dots).
SWGFAST, Glossary 07-28-2009 ver. 2.0

Ridge path, major ridge path deviations, and paths caused by damage such as scars.
Quantitative-Qualitative Friction Ridge Analysis, David R. Ashbaugh 1999 CRC Press

In Nov. 2004, the Third Level Detail working group (from the Standards Sub-Group of the National Fingerprint Board of England and Wales) determined that it was not necessary to subdivide the features used in friction ridge identifications. In England and Wales these terms are no longer recognized and it has been established that they should not be used. See Features.

Level 3 detail
Friction ridge dimensional attributes (e.g., width, edge shapes, and pores).
SWGFAST, Glossary 07-28-2009 ver. 2.0

Ridge shape, relative pore location, and some accidental details.
Quantitative-Qualitative Friction Ridge Analysis, David R. Ashbaugh 1999 CRC Press

In Nov. 2004, the Third Level Detail working group (from the Standards Sub-Group of the National Fingerprint Board of England and Wales) determined that it was not necessary to subdivide the features used in friction ridge identifications. In England and Wales these terms are no longer recognized and it has been established that they should not be used. See Features.

Lift
An adhesive or other medium on which recovered friction ridge detail

is preserved.
SWGFAST, Glossary 07-28-2009 ver. 2.0

Light Wavelengths
Ultraviolet light wavelengths approx. 10nm-400nm
UV-C wavelengths approx. 200nm-280nm (dangerous)
UV-B wavelengths approx. 280nm-315nm (hazardous)
UV-A wavelengths approx. 315nm-400nm
Black light wavelengths approx. 345nm-400nm

Visible light wavelengths approx. 400nm-700nm
Purple wavelengths approx. 410nm
Blue wavelengths approx. 475nm
Green wavelengths approx. 510nm
Yellow wavelengths approx. 570nm
Orange wavelengths approx. 590nm
Red wavelengths approx. 650-700nm

Infrared light wavelengths approx. 700nm-1,000,000 nm

Visible light is sometimes referred to as white light. Technically speaking, white light is a combination of all the colors in the visible light spectrum.

Lighting Techniques
Ambient, oblique or direct lighting are the most common types used in this field.

Ligroine
See Petroleum ether.
SWGFAST, Glossary - Consolidated 09-09-03 ver. 1.0

Likelihood Ratios
A mathematical model to assess the likelihood that the corresponding features between two fingerprints have the same donor. Tools currently under development use minutia (ridge endings and bifurcations) and generate Likelihood Ratios. The main people involved in this type of model include Christophe Champod, Paul Chamberlain, Glenn Langenburg, and Cedric Nuemann.

Lipids
Fats or fat-like substances that are insoluble in water.
Quantitative-Qualitative Friction Ridge Analysis, David R. Ashbaugh 1999 CRC Press

The major component of sebaceous sweat, which includes fats, oils and waxes.

Liquid Nitrogen
An element used in its liquid state (-195 degree C)for the separation of adhesive surfaces, as well as to enhance the fluorescence of Zinc Chlo-

ride and Zinc Nitrate treated prints for visualization and photography.
SWGFAST, Glossary - Consolidated 09-09-03 ver. 1.0

Liqui-drox
Fluorescent yellow solution used to develop friction ridge detail on the adhesive and non-adhesive sides of dark colored tape.
SWGFAST, Glossary - Consolidated 09-09-03 ver. 1.0

Liqui-nox ®
Detergent used in a solution to develop friction ridge detail on adhesive and non-adhesive sides of tape; cleaning agent.
SWGFAST, Glossary - Consolidated 09-09-03 ver. 1.0

Locard, Edmond (1877-1966)
A major contributor in criminalistics in the early 1900's. Locard trained as a medical doctor in Lyon and did a thesis with Lacassagne. Lyon was at that time one of the best places for forensic medicine in Europe (under the guidance of Lacassagne).

In 1910, while successor to Lacassagne as Professor of Forensic Medicine at the University of Lyon, France, Locard established the first police crime laboratory.
In 1912, Locard established Poroscopy.
In the early 1910's, Edmond Locard published his Tripartite Rule stating how many Galton points were needed to make a positive fingerprint identification. Locard's rule appears to have been based on his own work as well as the work of others (Galton, Balthazard, etc.)
Due to some of Locard's writings from the 1920's and 30's, the concept of the unintentional transfer of different minute materials between objects became known as Locard's Exchange Principle (aka Locard's Principle of Exchange). Locard wasn't the only person to recognize and publish this information but he did articulate in better than others.

Locard's Principle of Exchange (aka Locards Exchange Principle)
Edmond Locard's Principle of Exchange states that when any two objects come into contact, there is always transference of material from each object onto the other.
http://www.computing.surrey.ac.uk/ai/impress/ 06-19-2003

Lockheed-Martin 50k x 50k Study (1999)
See FBI / Lockheed-Martin 50k x 50k Study (1999).

Loop - Radial
A type of pattern in which one or more friction ridges enter upon either side, recurve, touch or pass an imaginary line between delta and core and flow out, or tend to flow out, on the same side the friction ridges

entered. The flow of the pattern runs in the direction of the radius bone of the forearm (toward the thumb).
SWGFAST, Glossary 07-28-2009 ver. 2.0

Loop - Ulnar
A type of pattern in which one or more friction ridges enter upon either side, recurve, touch or pass an imaginary line between delta and core and flow out, or tend to flow out, on the same side the friction ridges entered. The flow of the pattern runs in the direction of the ulna bone of the forearm (toward the little finger).
SWGFAST, Glossary 07-28-2009 ver. 2.0

Lophoscopy
The study of the development, the classification, and the identification of the prints left by the papillary ridges of the skin.
http://users.tpg.com.au/kjw18/fingerprints/Referen/Fpterm/LTERM.HTM 11-12-2005

Loupe
A small magnifying glass.

Luminescence
Emission of light by energy from non-thermal sources (i.e., chemical, biochemical, electrical), including both fluorescence and phosphorescence.
SWGFAST, Glossary - Consolidated 09-09-03 ver. 1.0
Any form of light that produces 'cool light' (vs. hot light) as with fluorescence or phosphorescence. Often this term is used in situations where the term phosphorescence is more appropriate.

Luminol
Luminol is a chemical that glows greenish-blue when it comes into contact with blood (and some other items)— even traces that are years old. To be exact, it reacts to hemoglobin, an oxygen-carrying protein in red-blood cells. Luminol is so sensitive, it can detect blood at 1 part per million. In other words, if there is one drop of blood within a container of 999,999 drops of water, luminol will glow.
http://dsc.discovery.com/fansites/onthecase/toolbox/tool_01.html

MBD

7-(P-Methoxybenzlamino-4Notro-benz-2-Oxa-1,3-Diazile). Yellow dye which produces a fluorescent product when exposed to selected wavelengths of light; used to visualize cyanoacrylate fumed friction ridge detail.
SWGFAST, Glossary - Consolidated 09-09-03 ver. 1.0

A fluorescent dye stain used with an alternate light source to visualize cyanoacrylate ester fumed friction ridge detail. Optimum viewing is done with an alternate light source (435nm-535nm) and orange or red goggles.

MCP's

Major Case Prints.

MMD

Multimetal Deposition. Two step process using a colloidal gold and a modified Physical Developer solution to visualize friction ridge detail.
SWGFAST, Glossary - Consolidated 09-09-03 ver. 1.0

MRM-10

Combination of Basic Yellow 40, Rhodamine 6G and MBD dyes which produce fluorescence when exposed to selected wavelengths of light; used to visualize cyanoacrylate fumed friction ridge detail.
SWGFAST, Glossary - Consolidated 09-09-03 ver. 1.0

MSDS

Material Safety Data Sheet. Manufacturers' information concerning the handling and use of a chemical.
SWGFAST, Glossary - Consolidated 09-09-03 ver. 1.0

5-MTN

Methylthioninhydrin. A reagent that reacts with amino acids to develop friction ridge detail on porous items.

MXRF

Micro-X-ray Fluorescence. A new fingerprint visualization technique developed by University of California scientists working at Los Alamos National Laboratory. MXRF is a noninvasive method that uses X-rays to detect elements like sodium, potassium and chlorine. This technique was described at the 229th national meeting of the American Chemical Society in March 2005.

Maceo, Alice V.

Alice Maceo is currently the Forensic Laboratory Manager for the Latent Print Detail of the Las Vegas Metropolitan Police Department Forensic Laboratory. She has worked in the latent print discipline since 1997 and achieved latent print certification by the International Association for Identification in 2001. Alice is an active speaker at forensic conferences in the United States, Canada, and Europe. She has published articles in the Journal of Forensic Identification and Fingerprint Whorld. Alice also serves on the Scientific Working Group on Friction Ridge Analysis, Study, and Technology and the General Forensic Technical Working Group, both sponsored by the National Institute of Justice. In 2004, Alice was awarded Distinguished Membership with the International Association for Identification.

Macrodactyly
Congenitally abnormal largeness of fingers or toes.
SWGFAST, Glossary - Consolidated 09-09-03 ver. 1.0

Magnetic Powder (aka Magna Powder)
Available since the early 1960's, magnetic powder is used to process an object with the purpose of visualizing friction ridge detail. Magnetic powder looks similar to regular black powder but contains iron to establish a magnetic affect. It is commonly black but is available in a wide range of colors. Magnetic powder is best used on paper, plastic, glass, and vinyl objects (any nonmagnetic surface) and is applied by using a magnetic powder applicator. The advantage of using a magnetic powder instead of a regular latent print powder is that with magnetic powder the brush never touches the latent print, avoiding possible damage to the latent print. Also, magnetic powder doesn't become airborne as easily as regular latent print powders, resulting in less powder being inhaled by the user.
http://www.crimeandclues.com/magneticpowder.htm 07-11-2004

The magnetic powder process was developed by Herbert McDonnell.

See Fingerprint Powders.

Major
A value derived from the pattern types of the thumbs.
SWGFAST, Glossary - Consolidated 09-09-03 ver. 1.0

Major Case Prints
1. A systematic recording of the friction ridge detail appearing on the palmar sides of the hands. This includes the extreme sides of the palms; and joints, tips, and sides of the fingers.
2. See Complete Friction Ridge Exemplars.
SWGFAST, Glossary 07-28-2009 ver. 2.0

See Complete Friction Ridge Exemplars.

Maleic Acid
Weak acid used in an aqueous solution as a pre-wash step for the Physical Developer Process.
SWGFAST, Glossary - Consolidated 09-09-03 ver. 1.0

Malpighi, Marcello (1628-1694)
Pronounced Mal-pee-gee.
An Italian anatomist who worked as a Professor of Anatomy at the University of Bologna. He described the patterns on the fingers while doing an overall study of the skin but never mentioned their value for identification. He is credited as being the first person to study fingerprints under a microscope. A layer of skin is named after him, known as the "Malpighian Layer". Malpighi described ridges and pores in De Externo Tactus Organo, first published in Naples 1665 and then later in London in 1686.

See Stratum Germinativum.

Mark
1. Term commonly used in the United Kingdom and some Commonwealth countries to designate a latent impression.
2. See Latent Print.
SWGFAST, Glossary 07-28-2009 ver. 2.0

Matrix
The substance that is deposited or removed by the friction ridge skin when making an impression.
SWGFAST, Glossary 07-28-2009 ver. 2.0
The formative part of a fingerprint; the substance that is actually deposited by the finger and eventually developed, i.e., sweat, foreign material, sebaceous oils, blood, etc.
Quantitative-Qualitative Friction Ridge Analysis, David R. Ashbaugh 1999 CRC Press

Maxilon Flavone 10GFF
See Basic Yellow 40. See Panacryl Brilliant Flavone 10GFF.
SWGFAST, Glossary - Consolidated 09-09-03 ver. 1.0

Mayer, J.C.A. (1788)
During the 1700's, Mayer was the first to recognize that although specific friction ridge arrangements may be similar, they are never duplicated.
http://www.ridgesandfurrows.homestead.com/scientific_researchers.html 03-08-2003

Mayfield, Brandon
Brandon Mayfield is a U.S. citizen who in May of 2004 was wrongfully arrested as a material witness with regard to a terrorism attack in Spain. His arrest was due to an erroneous fingerprint identification made by 3 FBI Examiners and 1 private fingerprint expert. The fingerprint was later identified to Algerian national Ouhnane Daoud. In November 2006 Mayfield was awarded a $2 million dollar settlement by the U.S. Justice

Department. The settlement also included an apology and an agreement to destroy communications intercepts conducted by the FBI against Mayfield's home and office during the investigation. The Justice Department added that Mayfield was not targeted because of his Muslim faith.

McClaughry, Major Robert Wilson
(1839-1920)
McClaughry is acknowledged as the person responsible for implementing the Bertillon system in the United States. In 1887, he implemented this system while working as the Warden of the Illinois State Penitentiary at Joliet. In 1899, McClaughry became the Warden of Leavenworth Prison. After hearing a lecture from Ferrier in 1904, McClaughry implemented a fingerprint system at Leavenworth. In 1923-1924 this collection of fingerprint cards along with those from the International Association of Chiefs of Police's were merged together to form the Identification Unit of the FBI in Washington DC.

McClaughry, Matthew Wilson
(6/19/1871-3/14/1922)
The son of R. W. McClaughry and the records clerk at Leavenworth Prison during the implementation of its fingerprint system.

McKie Case
Pronounced McKee.
See Erroneous Identifications.

McMorris, John
John McMorris developed the fuming pipe used in conjunction with iodine to develop friction ridge detail on porous items. For a short time it was known as the McMorris Fuming Pipe. He also developed the iodine-silver plate transfer method used for recovering latent prints. He presented this process at the IAI California Division Conference in 1936.
http://www.scafo.org/About_SCAFO/scafo_history.html 10-12-2004

McRoberts, Alan
Alan McRoberts is recognized as one of the most prominent and well-respected latent print experts working in the United States. In 1971, he began his career with the Los Angeles Sheriff's Department and remained there until his retirement in 2002. His duties included every aspect of latent print work including investigating, comparing, instructing, creating training and procedural manuals, and supervising. During his career, he has been extremely active in educational organizations. He has been a member of the IAI for more than 23 years, spending 10 years on the IAI Editorial Review Board and the last 7 years as the editor of the Journal of Forensic Identification (2002-2010). In 1991, he was the president of SCAFO, and in 1999/2000, he was

the president of the California division of the IAI. He's a Fellow of the Fingerprint Society and a member of the American Academy of Forensic Sciences. He was also one of the organizers of the Southern California Laser Study Group. He has written and presented more than 25 educational papers and articles. Mr. McRoberts has been extremely active in setting industry standards, including being a member of SWGFAST since 1995. He was the SWGFAST Chairperson (2000-2006).
In recognition of his commitment, dedication, and contributions to our industry, Alan McRoberts has been presented with many prestigious awards including the SCAFO Distinguished Member Award, SCAFO's Charles Wolford Award, the Los Angeles Sheriff's Department's Distinguished Service Award, and the Los Angeles Sheriff's Department's Exemplary Service Award. This is a brief summary of the contributions he has made to the fingerprint community. Currently, he manages "McRobert's Forensic Investigations", which he founded in 2001, a company that specializes in fingerprint services.

Medial
At or near the center.
SWGFAST, Glossary 07-28-2009 ver. 2.0

Medial Interphalangeal Flexion Crease
The middle crease on a finger.

Melanocyte
Skin cell that is able to produce melanin and can be found in the basal layer of the epidermis.
http://skincancer.dermis.net/glossary/index_html?query_start=51

Melendez-Diaz v. Massachusetts
See Supreme Court of the United States, Melendez-Diaz v. Massachusetts.

Merbromin
Reagent used to detect / enhance bloody friction ridge detail; produces a fluorescent product when exposed to excitation at selected wavelengths.
SWGFAST, Glossary - Consolidated 09-09-03 ver. 1.0

Mercuric Nitrate
Chemical used as a clearing agent for silver staining.
SWGFAST, Glossary - Consolidated 09-09-03 ver. 1.0

Merkel Cells
Sensory receptor cells located in the basal layer of the epidermis.

Mesenchyme
The part of the embryonic mesoderm, consisting of loosely packed, unspecialized cells set in a gelatinous ground substance, from which con-

nective tissue, bone, cartilage, and the circulatory and lymphatic systems develop.
The American Heritage® Dictionary of the English Language, Fourth Edition Copyright © 2000 by Houghton Mifflin Company. Published by Houghton Mifflin Company. All rights reserved
http://dictionary.reference.com/search?q=mesenchyme

The bone and the dermis are formed from mesenchyme, which is derived from the mesoderm in an embryo.

Mesoderm
The middle embryonic germ layer, lying between the ectoderm and the endoderm, from which connective tissue, muscle, bone, and the urogenital and circulatory systems develop.
The American Heritage® Dictionary of the English Language, Fourth Edition Copyright © 2000 by Houghton Mifflin Company. Published by Houghton Mifflin Company
http://dictionary.reference.com/search?q=mesoderm 05-30-2003

Metacarpo-phalangeal Crease
Creases that divide the fingers from the palm.

Metal Etching
Technique utilizing acidic solutions or vapors in the development of friction ridge detail on select metal surfaces.
SWGFAST, Glossary - Consolidated 09-09-03 ver. 1.0

Metal Salt
Secondary treatment of ninhydrin developed friction ridge detail for visualization (e.g., /zinc Chloride, Zinc Nitrate, or Cadmuum Chloride); produces a fluorescent product when exposed to selected wavelengths of light.
SWGFAST, Glossary - Consolidated 09-09-03 ver. 1.0

Methanol (Methyl Alcohol)
Solvent used as a carrier in reagents, dyes, stains, and rinses; also used as a cleaning agent.
SWGFAST, Glossary - Consolidated 09-09-03 ver. 1.0

Methodology
A body of practices, procedures, and rules used by those who work in a discipline or engage in an inquiry; a set of working methods
The American Heritage® Dictionary of the English Language, Fourth Edition Copyright © 2000 by Houghton Mifflin Company. Published by Houghton Mifflin Company. All rights reserved
http://dictionary.reference.com/search?q=methodology 02-27-03

A system of methods or procedures used in any field.
Quantitative-Qualitative Friction

Ridge Analysis, David R. Ashbaugh 1999 CRC Press

Methylene Chloride
Solvent used in the preparation of liquid iodine. See Dichloromethane. SWGFAST, Glossary - Consolidated 09-09-03 ver. 1.0

Methylthioninhydrin
See 5-MTN.

Microburst Method
A specialized form of the Cyanoacrylate method for developing latent prints on nonporous items. This method was developed by the FBI and is currently unpublished (Jan. 2004). This method is designed to expose a nonporous item to a large amount of fumes for a small amount of time. It involves adding glue to a heat source of over 300 degrees. Once the chamber is filled with fumes, the nonporous item is placed in the chamber for 30-45 seconds.

Micro-X-ray Fluorescence
See MXRF.

Midlo, Dr. Charles
A professor of microscopic anatomy at Tulane University. Known for his research with Harold Cummins on dermatoglyphics associated with Down's Syndrome. He, along with Harold Cummins, coined the term dermatoglyphics and wrote the book "Fingerprints, Palms and Soles" in 1943.

Mikrosil ™
A silicone-casting agent developed by Kjell Carlsson of Sweden. This product is useful for lifting latent prints from textured or curved surfaces. It also works well in recovering prints from the deceased.

Minimum Number of Characteristics
In 1973, The IAI Standardization Committee released the results of a three-year study. They recommended and adopted that "no valid basis exists at this time for requiring that a pre-determined minimum number of friction ridge characteristics must be present in two impressions in order to establish positive identification." This was based on the fact that each print has a unique set of circumstances.
http://www.latent-prints.com/iai_standardization_committee.htm
03-21-2003

In 1995, the Ne'urim Declaration was adopted. It stated, "No scientific basis exists for requiring that a pre-determined minimum number of friction ridge features must be present in two impressions in order to establish a positive identification." This was a slight change from the 1973 IAI Resolution on the minimum number of characteristics needed to make an identification.

On June 11, 2001, after a 4 year study, the ACPO Fingerprint Evidence Project Board abolished the use of the 16 point standard used in England, Wales, and Northern Ireland.

Minshall, Lewis Q.P.M. (19??-1980)
In the 1970's, Detective Superintendent Lewis Minshall was in charge of the Essex Police Fingerprint Bureau. He was a working fingerprint technician, not merely a department figurehead, and was awarded The Queens Police Medal for his meritorious services to fingerprints. The National Society of Fingerprint Officers (later re-named The Fingerprint Society) was initiated in Hertfordshire by the so-called Four Founders in 1974. They were civilian technicians, and expected fingerprint staff from all British police forces to join the society. During the seventies, many British fingerprint employees were police officers, and there appeared to be "unofficial" suggestions from certain sources that they should not join what was alleged to be a civilian organization, perhaps campaigning for wage equality and conditions of service, with the potential for strike action. The Hertfordshire 'founders' wished the society to solely concerned with fingerprint matters and the circulation of new techniques in the journal, and the facility for members all over the world to be able to communicate with fellow technicians to everyone's advantage. Mr. Minshall, being a senior police officer, joined the society, realizing the potential of a worldwide exchange of information, and he successfully encouraged many police officers to join the society. After his death it was revealed that he had allocated monies to be used annually for the presentation of The Lewis Minshall Award for outstanding contributions to the discipline.

Minutiae
Small details.
Quantitative-Qualitative Friction Ridge Analysis, David R. Ashbaugh 1999 CRC Press

See Characteristics.
SWGFAST, Glossary 07-28-2009 ver. 2.0

Missed Identification
The failure to make an identification when an identification could have been made.

The failure to make an identification (individualization) when, in fact, both friction ridge impressions are from the same source.
SWGFAST, Glossary 07-28-2009 ver. 2.0

Mitchell, Byron
See United States vs. Byron Mitchell.

Mitosis
Cell segmentation during which

chromosomes are split longitudinally and duplicated.
http://skincancer.dermis.net/glossary/index_html?query_start=51

Moenssens, Andre A. J.D., LL.M. Andre Moenssens is a forensic consultant and retired law professor. He started his training and study in fingerprints in 1950 in Belgium under the tutelage of the late Major Georges E. Defawe. He joined the International Association for Identification (IAI) in 1953, emigrated to the U.S. in 1956 and became a lawyer in this country in 1966 after receiving the Juris Doctor (JD) degree with Honors in 1966 at Illinois Institute of Technology-Chicago Kent College of Law. The following year he earned the Master of Laws (LL.M.) degree at Northwestern University.

He was head instructor in fingerprint identification (1960-1967) at the Institute of Applied Science in Chicago when T. Dickerson Cooke was its director, and associate editor of the Finger Print and Identification Magazine (1960 to 1968). In 1967, he began his service as a law professor, has been tenured since 1968 successively at: Chicago-Kent College of Law (1967-1973), the University of Richmond, Virginia (1973-1995), and the University of Missouri at Kansas City (UMKC) (1996-2002) where he held the Douglas Stripp Professorship in Law and was also a member of the doctoral faculty. After retiring from UMKC and being elected an emeritus professor, West Virginia University College of Law invited him to be a visiting professor in 2004, 2005, and again in 2006. He had served on that factury as visiting professor during 1993-1995 in the William J. Maier Jr. Chair.

After retiring from UMKC at the end of 2002, he became a resident of Indiana, where he lives at Shriner Lake, near Fort Wayne. In 2004, he was elected to membership in SWGFAST.

He has testified as an expert in several states for the prosecution and the defense and has been consulted by lawyers, governmental agencies, and news media on forensic issues in the U.S. and abroad. He is the author of Fingerprint Techniques (1971) and Fingerprints and the Law (1969), and the senior co-author of Scientific Evidence in Civil and Criminal Cases, of which the 5th edition is due to be published in 2006. He has written dozens of other books, book chapters and articles on topics in the forensic evidence and criminal justice fields. His Criminal Law casebook is in its seventh edition and is used in law schools throughout the country. He is one of the two Editors'-in-Chief of the Wiley Encyclopedia of Forensic Science, to be published in 2007. He has been the editor of the Illinois Law Enforcement Officers

Law Bulletin since 1972-and retired from that position in 2006. In addition to membership in the IAI, and a member of the editorial board of its Journal of Forensic Identification, he has been a Fellow of the American Academy of Forensic Sciences since 1966, and served two terms as the Academy's secretary-treasurer as well as in a number of other leadership functions. In 2005 he was named a Distinguished Fellow of the AAFS. He is also a member of the Canadian Identification Society, The Forensic Science Society (U.K.), and a number of legal organizations. He is a member of the Indiana Division of the IAI and was previously a member of the Chesapeake Bay Division of the IAI when he lived in Virginia.

His website is www.forensic-evidence.com .

Molded Print
See Plastic Print.

Molybdenum Disulfide
Chemical used in the preparation of Small Particle Reagent (SPR).
SWGFAST, Glossary - Consolidated 09-09-03 ver. 1.0

Monozygotic
Derived from a single fertilized egg. Used to describe identical twins and distinguish them from fraternal twins (dizygotic).

Morfopoulos, Dr. Vassilis C.
See People v. Kent.

Mottled Skin
Ridge detail is present, but is dissociated due to trauma or genetic causes. It lacks any continuous pattern flow.
SWGFAST, Glossary - Consolidated 09-09-03 ver. 1.0

Mulvihill, John J. MD
Wrote "The Genesis of Dermatoglyphics" with David W. Smith MD for the Journal of Pediatrics, Oct. 1969 issue. It is said to be one of the most thorough discussions of fingerprint formation. Their findings were:
6-8 weeks after conception volar pads form
10-12 weeks volar pads begin to recede
13th week skin ridges begin to appear
21st week after conception fingerprint patters are complete
http://www.handanalysis.net/library/derm_history.htm 02-27-03

Muriatic Acid
A chemical used to process thermal paper to develop friction ridge detail. Also known as Hydrochloric Acid.

Mutilation
See Perez, George, Dillinger, Pitts, and Roquerre.

N

N-Dodecylamine Acetate
Chemical used in the preparation of the detergent solution in Physical Developer.
SWGFAST, Glossary - Consolidated 09-09-03 ver. 1.0

NAS Report
In 2005, the CFSO requested federal funds become available to support a variety of forensic disciples. Congress asked the National Academy of Sciences (NAS) to research the needs of these forensic disciples to determine if the funds were needed. On Feb 18, 2009, the NAS published its finding in a report titled "Strengthening Forensic Science in the United States – A Path Forward". These findings became known as the NAS report.

NCIC
National Crime Information Center.

NCIC Classification
An alpha/numeric system of fingerprint classification.
SWGFAST, Glossary - Consolidated 09-09-03 ver. 1.0

NFB
National Fingerprint Board (of England and Wales). An adjunct to the ACPO.

NGI
Next Generation Identification. The updated version of IAFIS, the FBI's national computerized fingerprint system.

NIST
National Institute of Standards and Technology.

NV
The common abbreviation for 'No Value', usually indication that an impression has no value for identification purposes.

NSFO
The National Society of Fingerprint Officers was an organization that started in 1975. This organization was later renamed 'The Fingerprint Society'.

Nanometer
A metric unit of measurement equal to 1 billionth of a meter. Commonly used to measure light.

Nanoparticle Powder
A new fluorescent fingerprint powder designed in 2003 by Professor Fred Rowell of the University of Sunderland, England, for latent print recovery. This new powder is comprised of glass like nanoparticles imbedded with fluorescent material. Since this powder involves nanotechnology, it

adheres better than standard powders to older latent prints and produces a much better resolution with both old and new latent prints. With this technology smaller characteristics in a latent print may be able to be seen making smaller partial images more usable. This product is still in the experimental testing phase (Dec. 2004) but is expected to be released soon.
Previous research has been conducted by such agencies as the University of Texas with regard to a magnetic nanoparticle powder but the results didn't provide good contrast between the substrate and the matrix.

Naphthalene Black
See Amido Black
SWGFAST, Glossary - Consolidated 09-09-03 ver. 1.0

Nascent
Coming into existence.
The American Heritage® Dictionary of the English Language, Fourth Edition Copyright © 2000 by Houghton Mifflin Company. Published by Houghton Mifflin Company.
http://dictionary.reference.com/search?q=nascent

Refers to an incipient ridge.

National Bureau of Identification
See Bureau of Criminal Identification.

National Society of Fingerprint Officers
See NSFO.

Negative Impression (Negative Print)
See Take Away Print.

Neumann, Cedric
Cedric Neumann was awarded his MS in Forensic Science in 1998 and completed his PhD in 2008. During this time he worked as a research assistant and lecturer at the University of Lausanne in Switzerland. He joined the UK Forensic Science Service as a Senior Forensic Scientist to work on fingerprint interpretation research. He then managed the Statistics and Interpretation research group of the FSS. He is involved in a number of projects relating to fingerprints including the development of peer review procedures and training. His main area of research is currently the validation and implementation of an operational evaluation tool based on a mathematical model for the assessment of fingerprint evidence for use in Probability Based Fingerprint Evidence (PBFE). In January 2007, "Computation of Likelihood Ratios in Fingerprint Identification for Configurations of Any Number of Minutiæ", was published in the Journal of Forensic Science, Vol. 52 No. 1. In 2009, Cedric Neumann won the Emerging Forensic Scientist Award.

Ne'urim Declaration
In 1995, at the International Symposium on Fingerprints, a resolution was adopted. It stated, "No scientific basis exists for requiring that a pre-determined minimum number of friction ridge features must be present in two impressions in order to establish a positive identification." This was a slight change from the 1973 IAI Resolution on the minimum number of characteristics needed to make an identification.

Nile Red
A fluorescent dye stain used to visualize cyanoacrylate ester fumed friction ridge detail. Optimum viewing is done with an alternate light source (450-560nm) and orange or red goggles.

Ninhydrin
1,2,3-triketohydrindine hydrate. Reagent that reacts with amino acids to develop friction ridge detail.
SWGFAST, Glossary - Consolidated 09-09-03 ver. 1.0

Ninhydrin was first prepared in 1910 by the English chemist, Siegfried Ruhemann, who also investigated the formation of the violet compound (Ruhemann's Purple, or RP) produced by ninhydrin's reaction with amino acids. The significance of this discovery to forensic science went unnoticed until 1954, when Oden and von Hoffsten reported the use of ninhydrin as a fingerprint developing reagent that reacts with amino acids secreted from sweat glands. Although the content of amino acids in a fingerprint residue is low (compared to the content of salts and fatty acids), the RP produced from the reaction of these amino acids with ninhydrin is deeply colored, and the developed fingerprints are usually highly visible. Thus, ninhydrin has long been known as one of the most affordable and useful reagents for visualization of latent fingerprints on porous surfaces (such as paper, wood, and walls). In cases where the developed fingerprints are weak, secondary treatment with an aqueous zinc chloride solution can improve the print's line resolution quality. Zinc chloride-treated prints can be observed as "glowing" (fluorescent) when
illuminated with light of a certain wavelength.
"New Reagents for Development of Latent Fingerprints", NIJ 1995
http://www.ncjrs.org/txtfiles/finger.txt 06-19-2003

Nitric Acid
Acid used in a fuming technique to visualize friction ridge detail on select metal surfaces.
SWGFAST, Glossary - Consolidated 09-09-03 ver. 1.0

Non-identification
See Exclusion.
SWGFAST, Glossary - Consolidated 09-09-03 ver. 1.0

Another opinion: A latent print that has not been individualized due to an exclusion or missed identification. Or not being able to establishing an association with a group or individual item.

Non-Porous
Non-absorbent.
SWGFAST, Glossary - Consolidated 09-09-03 ver. 1.0

Non-secretor
See Secretor.

Notch
A visual observance that the outer edges of a latent print is uneven or inconsistent, i.e. a notch exists. This could be a distortional clue that this is two impressions and not just one.

Nutant Loop
Also referred to as a lazy loop or a drooping loop. When the core of a loop droops over toward the delta. This usually occurs in the opposite hand as the slant, especially in the index fingers.

ORO
Oil Red O.

Oakes, Sir Harry Case (Trial, Oct. 1943)
The most sensational unsolved murder that happened during WWII. On July 8, 1943, Sir Harry Oakes, one of the wealthiest people in the British Empire, was found dead in his home in the Bahamas. The list of suspects included Edward VIII, Charles Lucky Luciano, and his son-in-law Freddie de Marigny, among others. This case became known as one of the biggest botched investigations of all times. The Govenor, the Duke of Windsor, sidestepped local authorities and called two experts from the Miami Police Department. This was the beginning of events that drew suspicion. The investigators, Capt. James Barker and Capt. Edward Melchen, found a latent print on a Chinese screen and a bloody print on the wall, but the evidence wasn't preserved as well as it could have been. They were highly criticized for their actions in the case. Prominent people were allowed access to the crime scene prior to finishing the investigation. The photographs of the bloody handprint were destroyed by light exposure prior to development. Barker's lifts from the screen also came into question and many people believed that the latent lifts were really lifted from a different object, like a glass. Harry Oakes son-in-law was charged with the murder due to his fingerprints being identified on the screen. During the trial, Barker's testimony severely damaged the prosecutions case, and Freddie de Marigny was found not guilty. Maurice O'neill filed charges against James Barker with the IAI for fabricating evidence. The IAI cleared Barker of any wrongdoing. This was an extremely unpopular decision among IAI members.

Objective
Uninfluenced by emotions or personal prejudices
The American Heritage® Dictionary of the English Language, Fourth Edition Copyright © 2000 by Houghton Mifflin Company. Published by Houghton Mifflin Company. All rights reserved.
http://dictionary.reference.com/search?q=objective 02-27-03

Something real and observable.
Quantitative-Qualitative Friction Ridge Analysis, David R. Ashbaugh 1999 CRC Press

Oblique Lighting
A lighting technique used to visualize latent friction ridge impressions where the light is directed on an ob-

ject in a sloping direction.

Occasional Print Features
Scarring and tension creases (or white lines) are occasional features. They do not appear in all representations, but they are permanent and repeatable.

Oil Gland
The sebaceous gland is considered an oil gland, as opposed to the eccrine and apocrine glands which are sweat glands.

Oil Red O Stain
A stain used in histology to stain lipoid deposits. Suggested as a processing method to develop latent prints in 2004 by Alexandre Beaudoin of Québec, Canada. ORO is a safe alternative to the Physical Developer processing method for porous items that may have been saturated by water.

Okajima, Michio
Michio Okajima is a Japanese scientist who's done thorough research regarding the skin. In 1976 he wrote "Dermal and Epidermal Structure of the Volar Skin" in which he describes the two rows of dermal papillae. The historical relevance of this research was confirming that the incipient ridges are permanent friction ridge structures. Some of the other articles he's written include:
"Development of Dermal Ridges in the Fetus". Journal of Medical Genetics, 1975, Vol 12, 243-250.
"A Methodological Approach to the Development of Epidermal Ridges Viewed on the Dermal Surface of Fetuses". Progress in Dermatoglyphic Reasearch, 1982, p. 175-188.
"Nonprimate Mammalian Dermatoglyphics as Models for Genetic and Embrylogic Studies: Comparative and Methodologic Aspects". Birth Defects: Orig. Artic., 1991, Ser. 27:131–149.

Oligodactyly
Fewer than the normal number of fingers or toes. Oligo- is from the Greek "oligos" (few or scanty) + -dactyly from the Greek "dactylos" (finger) = few fingers. Oligodactyly is the opposite of polydactyly which means too many fingers or toes. http://www.medterms.com/script/main/art.asp?articlekey=6668 06-18-2003

Oloriz Classification System
The fingerprint classification system developed by Dr. Federico Oloriz (Aguillera or Aguilera). This classifications system was the primary classification system used in Portugal and Spain prior to the use of computer filing systems, such as AFIS.

Oloriz, Dr. Federico 1855-1912 (Dr. Federico Oloriz Aguillera or Aguilera)
A Professor of Anatomy at the Ma-

drid University who developed the primary fingerprint classification system used in Spain and Portugal throughout the 20th Century. Dr. Oloriz established and named 10 fingerprint characteristics.

Olsen, Robert D. Sr. (May 15, 1934-1989)
Special Agent Robert Olsen, with the US Army Criminal Investigation Laboratory, was instrumental in creating professional standards and training curriculums for the USACIL. These standards and curriculums were so influential they were adopted by many civilian agencies. He stressed practical applications and techniques, research, training, testing and professional standards. Robert Olsen was most known for revising Walter Scott's 1951 book "Fingerprint Mechanics". It was published in 1978 titled "Scott's Fingerprint Mechanics". To date, this book is considered one of the most comprehensive fingerprint books worldwide. He encouraged active participation in professional organizations, research and publication. He was extremely active in the IAI, a Fellow of the AAFS and a Fellow of the Fingerprint Society. He wrote many articles and gave numerous presentations during his career. Robert Olsen retired from the Army Crime Lab in 1978 and continued his career with the Kansas Bureau of Investigation until his death in 1989. Robert Olson's friends remember him as someone who always had time and respect for everyone as well as someone who lead by example.

One Discrepancy Rule
A quality assurance guideline of some agencies. The one discrepancy rule is not a rule that governs the friction ridge discipline. Examiners conclusions are made by considering several factors including dissimilarity, distortion, and discrepancies. The examiner decides if these factors are within acceptable limits. No scientific conclusion should ever be based on a single event or a single test.

The "one discrepancy rule" under which a single difference in appearance between a latent fingerprint and a known fingerprint must rule out an identification unless the examiner has a valid explanation for the difference.
http://www.usdoj.gov/oig/special/s0603/ 05-27-2006

"Let us acknowledge that the one-dissimilarity doctrine has never been demonstrated to have originated from a firm scientific basis. Once we recognize this, we will not be forced to guess the manner of occurrence of unexplained differences. In view of a preponderance of matching characteristics, one dissimilarity isn't important."
John I. Thronton, "The One-Dissim-

ilarity Doctrine in Fingerprint Identification", International Criminal Police Review, No. 306, March 1977.

One Dissimilarity Doctrine
See One Discrepancy Rule.

Ontogenetic
Of or relating to the origin and development of individual organisms.
WordNet ® 1.6, © 1997 Princeton University
http://dictionary.reference.com/search?q=ontogenetic 03-08-2003

Ontogenetic Theory of ridge development suggests that ridge units fuse together to form ridges.

Opinion
A belief held with confidence but not substantiated by positive knowledge.
A conclusion based on special knowledge.
Webster's II New Riverside Dictionary, Office Edition. Houghton Mifflin Publishing Co. Copyright 1984, Berkley Addition.

Open to dispute.

See Conclusion and Determination.

Original Image
An accurate replica (bit-for-bit value) of the primary image.
SWGFAST, Glossary 07-28-2009 ver. 2.0

See Primary Image.

Orientation
The location and direction of an area of friction ridge detail.

Orthodactyly
Fingers and toes cannot be flexed.
SWGFAST, Glossary - Consolidated 09-09-03 ver. 1.0

Ortho-Tolidine
A chemical that is a presumptive test for blood and has also been used to develop friction ridge detail on human skin. Aka O-Tolidine.

Osborn Grid Method
This involves preparing photographic enlargements of the latent and inked fingerprints. A grid of equally-sized squares is then superimposed on each, with the squares of each grid occupying identical positions on each print. The forensic scientist examines both imprints square by square looking for identical characteristics.
http://www.rsc.org/lap/educatio/eic/2002/sodhi_jul02.htm

Os calcis
A bone in the foot.
Quantitative-Qualitative Friction Ridge Analysis, David R. Ashbaugh 1999 CRC Press

Osmium Tetroxide (Osmic Acid Fuming)
A fuming technique used to process items for latent fingerprints. This process was developed in 1891 by Dr. Rene Forgeot. When a latent print is exposed to the vapors, oxidation of sebaceous matter occurs. This method has been found to be extremely hazardous and expensive is seldom, if ever, used.

Osterburg, James William
Former head of the Department of criminal justice at the University of Illinois at Chicago, a former New York Police Officer for 20 years, where he assisted in the investigation of thousands of serious crimes. Past President of the American Academy of Forensic Science. He also is a frequent participant in educational symposia discussing criminal investigation, criminalistics, fingerprint characteristics and scientific evidence. The author of books on criminalistics and scientific investigations. He has been a consultant to the State Department, the Department of Justice and the Stanford Research Institute.
http://www.angelfire.com/sc/Centner/jamesw.html

In 1977, Osterburg developed a statistical model to calculate the probability of two fingerprints being alike. His model was one of the first to consider empty space and the first to consider the frequency of occurrence of different minutia.

O-Tolidine
See Ortho-Tolidine.

Outer Terminus
See Delta.
SWGFAST, Glossary - Consolidated 09-09-03 ver. 1.0

Overlay
A double impression where additional friction ridges overlap an existing friction ridge image. Overlays will not coincide with ridge flow and may exhibit some type of checkering. Overlays are not immediate double impressions of ridge detail. Overlays may or may not be the same finger impression or made by the same person.
Charles Parker 09-06-2006

Overall Pattern
Overall pattern shape used during identification; first level detail.
Quantitative-Qualitative Friction Ridge Analysis, David R. Ashbaugh 1999 CRC Press

P

PBFE
Probability Based Fingerprint Evidence.

PDMAC
Para-dimethylaminocinnamaldehyde. Reagent that reacts with urea, amines and their salts to develop friction ridge detail with fluorescent properties when exposed to selected wavelengths of light.
SWGFAST, Glossary - Consolidated 09-09-03 ver. 1.0

PZ Code
See Palmar Exemplar & Latent Zone Codes.

Palm (Palmar Area)
The friction ridge skin area on the side and underside of the hand.
SWGFAST, Glossary - Consolidated 09-09-03 ver. 1.0

Concerning the palm of the hand.
Quantitative-Qualitative Friction Ridge Analysis, David R. Ashbaugh 1999 CRC Press

Palm Print Court Cases
See State vs Kuhn (1918).
See Betts Case (1917).

Palmar Exemplar & Latent Zone Codes (PZ Codes)
An alpha-numeric system developed in 2003 by Craig Coppock as a communication tool to refer to specific areas of the fingers and palms. In this system each hand is divided into 28 regions and given an alphanumeric identifier. This system offers a quick and efficient means of distinguishing a particular area in the hand to those familiar and unfamiliar with scientific terminology.

Palmar Zone
The interdigital area of the palm.
SWGFAST, Glossary - Consolidated 09-09-03 ver. 1.0

Panacryl Brilliant Flavone 10GFF
See Basic Yellow 40.
SWGFAST, Glossary - Consolidated 09-09-03 ver. 1.0

Papillae (Papilla)
Peg-like structures of the dermis.
SWGFAST, Glossary - Consolidated 09-09-03 ver. 1.0

A small nipple-like protuberance or elevation.
Quantitative-Qualitative Friction Ridge Analysis, David R. Ashbaugh 1999 CRC Press

Papillary Layer
One of the two layers of the dermis.

The superficial layer of the dermis raised into papillae that fit into cor-

responding depressions on the inner surface of the epidermis.
Published under license with Merriam-Webster, Incorporated. © 1997-2000
http://www.fasthealth.com/dictionary/p/papillary_layer.php

Papillary Pegs
See Dermal Papillae.

Papillary Ridges
Orderly rows of eccrine glands positioned along the path of the friction ridge.
SWGFAST, Glossary - Consolidated 09-09-03 ver. 1.0

The term 'papillary ridge' can be used to describe many different areas in the skin. It is not important to discern whether one is right or wrong, just to understand the area that is being referred to. How this term is used will also effect how the terms 'primary ridges' and 'secondary ridges' are used.
1) From Hale: Ridges on the bottom of the epidermis corresponding to the surface friction ridges and surface furrows. They are the root system of the surface ridges and furrows. The papillary ridges that correspond to the friction ridges are referred to as primary ridges and the papillary ridges that correspond to the surface furrows are referred to as secondary ridges. Aka Epidermal Ridges.
2) Papillary ridges may refer to the ridges in the papillary layer of the dermis that connect to the bottom ridges of the epidermis. In this description, the connecting ridges of the epidermis are referred to grooves (primary and secondary). This definition is referred to in "Bloom and Fawcett's Concise Histology". Aka Dermal Ridges.
3) In many books and articles papillary ridges refer to friction ridges.

Parke, Edward
Son of fingerprint pioneer Capt. James H. Parke. Edward Parke seems to have studied fingerprints simultaneously with his father. He is sometimes credited with developing the 8 x 8 standard fingerprint card in 1913 that his father initially suggested. But it appears that Michael P. Evans used an 8 x 8 fingerprint card as early as 1905. Like his father, Edward Parke also worked for the New York State Prison Department and in 1913 was transferred to work with the fingerprints his father had started accumulating years earlier.

Parke, Capt. James H. (1848-?)
Capt. James H. Parke was the bookkeeper at the headquarters of the New York State Department of Prisons at Albany. He was given the responsibility of setting up a fingerprint file for the prison department. In 1903, he began fingerprinting the inmates and used his own classification system to file his cards. His

classification system (The American System of Fingerprint Classification) was a modified version of the English Henry Classification System. Parke presented his system at the 1904 World's Fair in St. Louis along side Ferrier who presented the Henry System. Although Parke influenced other organizations to use fingerprints as their main form of identification, the New York prison system continued to use the Bertillon Identification method as their primary system for many years. Parke's system was primarily used by New England states. Parke's use of fingerprints was the first use for criminal identification in the United States and considered the third use of fingerprints in the United States overall (after Thompson and DeForest). Parke is also credited as being the first American fingerprint instructor, 1904.

Patent Print
Friction ridge impression of unknown origin, visible without development.
SWGFAST, Glossary - Consolidated 09-09-03 ver. 1.0

Pathology
The study of causes, nature, and effects of diseases, trauma, and other abnormalities.
SWGFAST, Glossary - Consolidated 09-09-03 ver. 1.0

Pattern Area (Classification)
In the distal phalange of the fingers, the configuration of friction ridges that are utilized in classification.
SWGFAST, Glossary - Consolidated 09-09-03 ver. 1.0

Pattern Formations
Friction ridge skin arrangements formed as early as the third month of gestation.
SWGFAST, Glossary - Consolidated 09-09-03 ver. 1.0

Patterns
The designation of friction ridge skin into basic categories of general shapes.
SWGFAST, Glossary - Consolidated 09-09-03 ver. 1.0

Patterson, Terry L.
See State of Massachusetts v. Patterson, officially called Commonwealth (of Massachusetts) v. Terry L. Patterson.

Peer Review
Peer Review is the process that scientific knowledge undergoes prior to publication in a scientific journal. It involves reviewing the theoretical correctness behind the information as well as the reliability of the conclusions given.

Specific scientific conclusions can also undergo this type of complete review to ensure quality results.

Reviewing the process, as well as replicating the result, ensures that judgments are not based on flawed reasoning and leads to the most accurate result. For specific scientific conclusions, this process is referred to as 'scientific scrutiny' or 'scientific review' or a 'technical review'.

Peer Review Journal
A peer-reviewed journal is an academic periodical that has some sort of peer review process to ensure its accuracy. This often involves having several people read the article without knowledge of its author before accepting it, as well as a rigorous editing and fact-checking process. Peer-reviewed journals are generally considered the most reliable academic sources.
http://en.wikipedia.org/wiki/Peer-reviewed_journal 10-14-2005

Pelmatoscopy
The science which studies the friction ridges of the soles.

Penrose, LS (Lionel Sharples) (1898-1972)
A British geneticist who studied the genetic aspect of fingerprints and an early form of dermatoglyphics. He studied the relationship between fingerprints and Down's Syndrome as well as their relationship to congenital mental defects. He wrote in "The Lancet" in 1931.

Pentadactylous
Having five fingers on each limb.
Quantitative-Qualitative Friction Ridge Analysis, David R. Ashbaugh 1999 CRC Press

Pentadactyly
The occurrence of five fingers or toes on a hand or foot.
SWGFAST, Glossary - Consolidated 09-09-03 ver. 1.0

People v. Crispi (New York, 1911)
Charles Crispi, aka Cesare J. Cella, was the defendant in this case, which is noted as being the first case that fingerprint evidence was the sole evidence. Fingerprint expert Joseph Faurot testified to the identification process. After hearing Faurot's testimony, Crispi pled guilty. The judge asked Crispi for a full confession, insuring him that no additional charges would be filed. The judge wanted to insure that the scientific evidence that was testified to was indeed correct.

People v. Jennings (Illinois, 1910)
See Jennings. See Jennings, Thomas.

People v. Kelly (California, 1976)
The court case that lead to the Kelly rule for the admissibility of new, novel and experimental techniques. Several admissibility hearing for fingerprint evidence have determined that fingerprint evidence is not new or novel and a Kelly hearing was

denied.

People v. Kent (New York, 1968)
Perhaps the first trial that a defense expert testified that although the identification had 12 (some articles say 14) points of similarity, the prints were not identical. Richard Stanley Kent was charged with murdering Joseph Murphy, a retired New York City Policeman. The key evidence against Kent, a latent print on a bed board, seemed to be irrefutable. William J. Ciolko, Dutchess County Public Defender, hired Dr. Vassilis C. Morfopoulos, director of the American Standards Testing Bureau, to look at the identification. Dr. Morfopoulos analyzed the identification using a 25x microscope. He testified that he found 3 differences, "One distinct and crucial difference destroys the validity of an identification", he said. Richard Kent was found not guilty of the murder. In 1970, the FBI and the IAI refuted Dr. Morfopoulos's analysis and sided with Wilfred Holick, the original examiner in this case. The defense attorney and the defense expert gave a presentation of this case at the 55th IAI Conference.

There were two significant points to this case. This was the first time 'the prints are not identical' was used in court as a defense strategy, and the defense claimed that this case broke down the apparent ironclad status of fingerprints.

People v. Les (Michigan, 1934)
In People v. Les, (255 NW 407) the defendant's palm print was recovered from the windowsill at the point of entry of a breaking and entering scene. Before trial, the defendant contended that palm prints were not sufficient to sustain a conviction. The court ruled that the evidence was insufficient to hold the defendant for trial, quashed the information, and ordered the discharge of the defendant. The Government appealed that the trial court was in error in their ruling regarding the palm print evidence, and the Supreme Court of Michigan (1934) agreed that fingerprints and palm prints are both "considered physical characteristics" and therefore were "sufficient evidence to go to trial." The trial judge was directed to reinstate the information. http://www.clpex.com/Articles/TheDetail/TheDetail82.htm 10-20-2004

Perceptual Set
A tendency to see what we expect to see.
http://psy1.clarion.edu/mm/General/GlossaryA.html#Perception 02-27-03

A non-intentional mental predisposition that influences how we perceive visual and non-visual information. When a person is given only partial data their brain fills in what it expects the missing information to be.

Perez, Gerald
On Feb 07, 2008 Gerald Perez was arrested on drug charges using the name Edgardo Tirado. While officials were taking his fingerprints they realized he altered his fingerprints in an attempt to conceal his identity but Perez claimed he had been in a fight when his fingers were cut. His true identity was revealed when someone recognized him as Gerald Perez, which was later confirmed. Perez had his fingers cut lengthwise and then stitched back together. Some believe this surgery took place in the Dominican Republic in order to conceal his criminal record and avoid possible deportation.

Performance Check
An experiment to assess the ability of a technique to perform as desired.

See Validation Study.

Periderm
A superficial layer of cells that covers the developing epidermis. Periderm is replaced by stratum corneum.

Persistent
Having lasting qualities; remaining the same; nonchanging.
Quantitative-Qualitative Friction Ridge Analysis, David R. Ashbaugh 1999 CRC Press

Petroleum Ether
Solvent used as a carrier in reagents; also as a rinse or cleaning agent.
SWGFAST, Glossary - Consolidated 09-09-03 ver. 1.0

Phalange (Phalanx)
Any bone in the fingers or toes.
Quantitative-Qualitative Friction Ridge Analysis, David R. Ashbaugh 1999 CRC Press

Any bone in a finger or toe is referred to as a phalanx (or phalange). The fingers each having 3; the distal phalanx, the medial or middle phalanx, and the proximal phalanx. The thumb has two; the distal phalanx and the proximal phalanx. Phalanx is more frequently used for the singular form of the word and phalanges is more frequently used for the plural form of the word, but phalange or phalanxes can be substituted.

Some people refer to the segments of the fingers as the proximal phalange, the medial phalange, and the distal phalange since there is a connection between the bones and the finger segments. This connection is closer in medial and distal segments of the fingers than in the proximal segment. The proximal phalange bone incorporates a finger segment as well as part of the interdigital area.

Phalangeal
Of the bones in the fingers and toes.

Quantitative-Qualitative Friction Ridge Analysis, David R. Ashbaugh 1999 CRC Press

Philosophy

The principles of a particular subject or field.

Quantitative-Qualitative Friction Ridge Analysis, David R. Ashbaugh 1999 CRC Press

Investigation of the nature, causes, or principles of reality, knowledge, or values, based on logical reasoning rather than empirical methods.

The American Heritage® Dictionary of the English Language, Fourth Edition http://dictionary.reference.com/search?q=philosophy

Philosophy of Friction Ridge Identification

Friction ridge identification is established through the agreement of friction

ridge formations, in sequence, having sufficient uniqueness to individualize.

Quantitative-Qualitative Friction Ridge Analysis, David R. Ashbaugh 1999 CRC Press

Phloxine B

Phloxine B is a protein stain which develops a reddish-orange colored print. Phloxine B is particularly good when used to develop latents on dark-colored or multicolored backgrounds.

http://www.evidentcrimescenc.com/cata/chem/chem.html 10-06-2004

Phosphorescence

The emission of light caused by the absorption of radiant energy from an external source or stimulus, such as a lamp, a laser, or an ALS. The emission of light continues after the stimulus has stopped (as opposed to fluorescence).

Photo-Flo ™

Surfactant developed by Kodak, used in powder suspension techniques for the development of friction ridge detail.

SWGFAST, Glossary - Consolidated 09-09-03 ver. 1.0

Phylogenic (Phylogenetic)

The evolutionary development and history of a species or higher taxonomic grouping of organisms. Also called phylogenesis.

The evolutionary development of an organ or other part of an organism.

The American Heritage® Dictionary of the English Language, Fourth Edition http://dictionary.reference.com/search?q=phylogenic 03-08-2003

Inez Whipple wrote about the phylogenic theory of fingerprint development. She suggested that early mammals were completely covered with hair, but there was an evolutionary change on the palm and soles due to surface use.

Physical Developer
Silver physical development process which reacts with some components of friction ridge secretions, as well as fatty or oily contaminants.
SWGFAST, Glossary - Consolidated 09-09-03 ver. 1.0

A chemical processing technique created in the early 1970's by Atomic Weapons Research Establishment (AWRE), per the FBI, to develop latent prints on porous items. PD reacts with the lipids in a latent print and is used after the ninhydrin process. It should not be used in conjunction with the silver nitrate process because these two processes compete against each other.

Pincushion Method
Also known as the Constellation Method. An obsolete method used in the first half of the 20th century to confirm an identification. In this method enlargements of the latent and known prints are used. Pins are pushed through the enlargement at each ridge characteristic. The holes on the reverse side are joined together and the designs are compared. This method is published in the April 1956 Fingerprint and Identification Magazine.

Pitts, Robert J. (Known as Roscoe Pitts)
A career criminal noted for altering his fingerprints in 1941. He had a doctor remove the skin from his first joints and replace it with skin from his chest.

Plantar Area
The friction ridge skin area on the side and underside of the foot.
SWGFAST, Glossary - Consolidated 09-09-03 ver. 1.0

Concerning the sole of the foot.
Quantitative-Qualitative Friction Ridge Analysis, David R. Ashbaugh 1999 CRC Press

Plastic Print
A fingerprint image left in a soft pliable surface, such as clay or wax. Also referred to as a molded print or an impressed print.

Plaza Court Decision
See United States vs. Plaza.

Podoscopy
A term coined by Wentworth and Wilder as a possible word, if ever needed, referring to the study of the soles.

Points/ Points of Identification
(Fingerprints) Ridge characteristics. Quantitative-Qualitative Friction Ridge Analysis, David R. Ashbaugh 1999 CRC Press

See Characteristics.
SWGFAST, Glossary - Consolidated 09-09-03 ver. 1.0

Another opinion:
The term 'points' was initially referring to Galton points. As it was recognized that more than just Galton points were used to make an identification, the term became synonymous with 'characteristics'.

See Dactyloscopic Points.

Pollak, Louis Federal Judge
See United States vs. Plaza.

Polydactyly
A hand or foot having more than the normal number of fingers or toes.
SWGFAST, Glossary - Consolidated 09-09-03 ver. 1.0

Synonymous with hyperdactyly.

Polyethylene Lifting Tape (Poly Tape)
Specialized lifting tape made for use on curved objects. This tape is thicker than normal tape and stretches to prevent tape creases from damaging the lift. Poly tape can also works well on textured objects.

Polylight
A forensic light source used to visualize items unseen under normal lighting conditions.

Polymerization
Chaining together many simple molecules to form a more complex molecule with different physical properties.
SWGFAST, Glossary - Consolidated 09-09-03 ver. 1.0

Polymerization is a chemical reaction where small molecules (monomers) are bound together to form a larger chainlike molecules (polymers).

Popper, Karl (1902-1994)
One of the greatest philosophers of science of the 20th century. Credited as establishing the 'falsifiable' element of science that can be used as a criterion under Daubert to establish whether something is scientific knowledge.

Pores
Small openings on friction ridges through which body fluids are released.
SWGFAST, Glossary - Consolidated 09-09-03 ver. 1.0
A minute opening in tissue, as in the skin of an animal, serving as an outlet for perspiration, or in a plant leaf or stem, serving as a means of absorption and transpiration.

The American Heritage® Dictionary of the English Language, Fourth Edition http://dictionary.reference.com/search?q=pore 06-11-2003

Poroscopy
A study of the size, shape, and arrangement of pores.
SWGFAST, Glossary 07-28-2009 ver. 2.0

Poroscopy was established by Dr. Edmond Locard of Lyon, France in 1912.

Porous
Absorbent.
SWGFAST, Glossary - Consolidated 09-09-03 ver. 1.0

Positive Print
A positive print is when the ridges of an image are a different color from the background and the furrows of an image are the same color as the background, as opposed to a negative image.

Potassium Thiocyanate
A chemical processing technique used to visualize friction ridge impressions. Potassium Thiocyanate works particularly well with impressions that are left in iron-rich dust or soil.

Prehensile
The ability to hold or grasp.

Pressure Distortion
Lateral pressure during deposition of a fingerprint.
Quantitative-Qualitative Friction Ridge Analysis, David R. Ashbaugh 1999 CRC Press

Prickle-cell Layer of Epidermis
See Stratum Spinosum.

Primary
A numerical formula derived from the presence of any whorl pattern as they appear on the fingers.
SWGFAST, Glossary - Consolidated 09-09-03 ver. 1.0

Primary Image
The first recording of an image onto media.
SWGFAST, Glossary 07-28-2009 ver. 2.0

See Original Image.

Primary Ridges
Ridges on the bottom of the epidermis under the surface friction ridges; the root system of the surface ridges.
Quantitative-Qualitative Friction Ridge Analysis, David R. Ashbaugh 1999 CRC Press

The term 'primary ridge' can be used to describe many different areas in the skin. It is not important to discern whether one is right or wrong, just to understand the area that is being referred to. How this term is used will also effect how the terms 'papillary ridges' and 'secondary ridges' are used.

1) Hale: The ridges at the bottom of the epidermis that correspond to the surface ridges.

2) All ridges at the dermal-epidermal junction, in the respect that they appear first. The surface ridges would be considered to be secondary ridges, appearing later. It seems to be interpreted this way in the U.S. vs. Carlos Ivan Llera Plaza opinion dated 1/7/2002.

3) In "Bloom and Fawcett's Concise Histology" primary ridges and secondary ridges refer to the ridges of the dermis.

Principle

A rule or law concerning the functioning of natural phenomena or mechanical processes: the principle of jet propulsion.

The American Heritage® Dictionary of the English Language, Fourth Edition
http://dictionary.reference.com/search?q=principle 03-08-2003

See Theory. See Laws.

Principle of Exchange

See Locard's Principle of Exchange.

Probability Based Fingerprint Evidence (PBFE)

The reporting of a fingerprint comparison using a mathematical model to assess the likelihood that the corresponding features have the same donor. Tools currently under development use minutia (ridge endings and bifurcations) and generate Likelihood Ratios.

Probative Value

A legal term indication something is offered as evidence of proof of a supposition.

Proficiency

The ongoing demonstration of competency.

SWGFAST, Glossary 07-28-2009 ver. 2.0

Proliferate

To grow or multiply by rapidly producing new tissue, parts, cells, or offspring.

The American Heritage® Dictionary of the English Language, Fourth Edition
http://dictionary.reference.com/search?q=proliferation 03-10-2003

2-Propanol
Solvent used in preparation of reagents.
SWGFAST, Glossary - Consolidated 09-09-03 ver. 1.0

Prosecutor's Fallacy
The subtle flip in logic results in a misinterpretation of the data.

See Transposing the Conditional.

Proximal
Situated at the closest point of attachment; direction toward the body.
SWGFAST, Glossary - Consolidated 09-09-03 ver. 1.0

Proximal Inter-Phalangeal Flexion Crease
The crease which separates the fingers from the palm.

Proximal Transverse Crease
The crease that separates the distal transverse crease and the radial longitudinal crease.

Nearest the central portion of the body or point of origin.
Quantitative-Qualitative Friction Ridge Analysis, David R. Ashbaugh 1999 CRC Press

Pure Science
Uses the experimental method in order to formulate theoretical constructs, explicate natural laws, and expand knowledge.
Feibleman, J.K. 1972 Pure science, applied science and technology: An attempt at definitions. In C. Mitcham and R. Mackey (eds.). Philosophy and technology. New York: Free Press.

Purkinje, Jan (1787-1869) (AKA Purkinje, Johannes Evangelist or Purkyne)
A Bohemian (Czech Republic) Physiologist who made numerous contributions to the field of histology. He devised new methods for preparing microscope samples, discovered sweat pores, introduced the term plasma and is most known for his discoveries about vision. He was the first person to name the patterns on the fingers, but never mentioned using them for personal identification. In 1823, Purkinje named 9 different patterns.

Quality/Quantity
The two factors that combine in an inverse relationship to form the basis for determinations of suitability or sufficiency of a friction ridge impression. The more quality that is present, the less quantity is necessary, and vice versa.

Qualitative
The clarity of information contained within a friction ridge impression.
SWGFAST, Glossary 07-28-2009 ver. 2.0

Concerned with quality or fundamental form and construction.
Quantitative-Qualitative Friction Ridge Analysis, David R. Ashbaugh 1999 CRC Press

Quality Assurance Measures for the Comparison Process
General procedures to ensure a quality product. Procedures may include documentation of the method used (look for predictive qualities, look for other possible conclusions), the data used (specific justification behind the conclusion), the principles used (don't ignore what doesn't fit, try to falsify your conclusion) and the tests used (verification for reproducibility, blind verification for reproducibility, consultation, independent examinations, and/or peer review for checking reproducibility along with validity).
Quality assurance measures may also include tests and audits that should be done. These can include having competency tests, proficiency tests, case audits, testimony audits, cv audits; having equipment maintenance logs.

Quality Control Measures
A Quality Control Measures is a test that checks a specific incidence (verification, peer review, or an audit).

Quantitative
The amount of information contained within a friction ridge impression.
SWGFAST, Glossary 07-28-2009 ver. 2.0

Concerned with quantity or quantities.
Quantitative-Qualitative Friction Ridge Analysis, David R. Ashbaugh 1999 CRC Press

R

R. v. Mohan (1994)
On appeal to the Supreme Court of Canada from the Ontario Court of Appeal, a decision on the admissibility of expert evidence and the nature of expert evidence and how it pertains to disposition. A Canadian decision similar to the American Daubert Hearings, the Mohan decision has set the parameters and application for the admission of expert in Canada.

Admission of expert evidence depends on the application of the following criteria:
a) Relevance
b) Necessity in assisting the trier of fact (judge or jury)
c) The absence of exclusionary rule
d) Must be by a properly qualified expert

In R. v. Mohan, four counts of sexual assault on female patients ages 13-16 were laid against a practicing paediatrician. His counsel indicated that he intended to call a psychiatrist who would testify that the perpetrator of the alleged offences would be part of a limited and unusual group of individuals and that the accused did not fall within that narrow class because he did not possess the characteristics of the group (profile) however the evidence was ruled inadmissible.

The original conviction was stayed by the Court of Appeals and opened a new hearing. At issue was the determination of the circumstances in which expert evidence is admissible to show that the character traits of an accused person do not fit the psychological profile of the putative perpetrator of the offences charged. The resolution of the issue involved the examination of the rules relating to (i) expert evidence, and (ii) character evidence.

In summary, expert evidence which advances a novel scientific theory or technique is subjected to special scrutiny to determine whether it meets a basic threshold of reliability and whether it is essential in the sense that the trier of fact will be unable to come to a satisfactory conclusion without the assistance of the expert.

The Supreme Court allowed the appeal but decided that the evidence should be excluded as nothing in the court record supported a finding that the profile of a paedophile or psychopath (as alleged by the psychologist) has been standardized to the extent that it could be said that it matched the supposed profile of the offender depicted in the charges. The expert's group profiles were not

seen as sufficiently reliable to be considered helpful.
http://www.canlii.org/en/ca/scc/doc/1994/1994canlii80/1994canlii80.pdf
08-01-2009
Courtesy of Cst. Jonathan BALTZER and Sgt. Tim Walker, RCMP

RAM
Combination of Rhodamine 6G, Ardrox and MBD dyes, which fluoresce when exposed to selected wavelengths of light; used to visualize cyanoacrylate fumed friction ridge detail.
SWGFAST, Glossary - Consolidated 09-09-03 ver. 1.0

Developed in 1990 by four FBI Latent Print Examiners: Harless Cummins, Felix Peigare, Mitchell Hollars and Tim Trozzi.

RAY
A fluorescent dye stain (a combination of Rhodamine 6G, Ardrox, and Basic Yellow 40) used to visualize cyanoacrylate ester fumed friction ridge detail. Optimum viewing is done with an alternate light source (450-550nm) and orange or red goggles.

R6G
See Rhodamine 6G.

RTX
See Ruthenium Tetroxide.

RUVIS
Reflective Ultra-Violet imaging system that allows visualization of friction ridge detail in the ultraviolet spectrum.
SWGFAST, Glossary - Consolidated 09-09-03 ver. 1.0

Radial
The smaller of the two bones of the forearm, on the same side as the thumb.
SWGFAST, Glossary - Consolidated 09-09-03 ver. 1.0

Radial Longitudinal Crease
The crease that encloses the thenar area and interdigital pad 1. Below the proximal transverse crease. Known as the 'line of life'.

Rarity
Fewness or scarcity of an item, thing, or shape.
Quantitative-Qualitative Friction Ridge Analysis, David R. Ashbaugh 1999 CRC Press

Reagent
Substance used in a chemical reaction to detect, examine, measure, or produce other substances.
SWGFAST, Glossary - Consolidated 09-09-03 ver. 1.0

Red Flags
Danger signs, common in latent fingerprints that may indicate a distortion in the ridge path.

Quantitative-Qualitative Friction Ridge Analysis, David R. Ashbaugh 1999 CRC Press

Redox
Reduction-Oxidation. Chemical reaction in which one or more electrons are transferred from one atom or molecule to another. An important component of the Physical Developer and Multimetal Deposition processes.
SWGFAST, Glossary - Consolidated 09-09-03 ver. 1.0

Redwop ™
A fluorescent fingerprint powder developed by Ed German in 1986 and given to the Lightning Powder Company.

Re-examination
A re-examination is a reassessment of a conclusion(s) which can be done by the same individual or a different individual, and done with either the original evidence or reproductions of the evidence. The person doing the reassessment may or may not know of the original conclusion(s). A re-examination is different from normal verification (although it can verify the conclusion) because the intent of re-examination may be different. The intent of re-examination is to check if other conclusion can also be determined while the intent of verification is to check the reliability of the conclusion(s). Differing conclusions may arise due to the differing information.

Reh, Dr. Ludwig (1894)
Dr. L. Reh was an early researcher on the hands and feet of mammals. Reh classified many of the various epidermic formations as scales but separated the fine lines that covered the pads. He wrote "Die Schuppen der Saugetiere" ("The Scales of Mammals") in 1894 where he stated that ridges didn't evolve from scales, they are of secondary origin.

Reis, George
George Reis is one of the early users of digital imaging in forensics and is a knowledgeable and prominent forensic imaging expert in the United States.
Mr. Reis started his career as a photographer, photojournalist and photo lab technician. From 1989 to 2004 he worked for the Newport Beach Police Department in California as a forensic photographer. In 1991 he began experimenting with digital imaging technology and the following year NBPD started using this technology for fingerprint analysis. In 1995, George Reis founded Imaging Forensics, which provides training and consulting services in both digital imaging and photography. Through his company he has trained personnel from the Secret Service, FBI, US Army Crime Lab, state, county and municipal agencies.

In addition to training, Imaging Forensics provides consulting to police agencies in order to help them transition to digital imaging technology. They also provide litigation support on criminal and civil cases (for both plaintiff and defense).
Mr. Reis is certified by the IAI in Forensic Photography. He is a member of the Forensic Photography and Imaging Certification Board, and a member of the Journal of Forensic Identification editorial review board. Additionally, Mr. Reis is an alpha and beta tester for Adobe Photoshop.

Relative Position
Proximity of characteristics to each other.
SWGFAST, Glossary - Consolidated 09-09-03 ver. 1.0

Reliable
Yielding the same or compatible results in different clinical experiments or statistical trials.
The American Heritage® Dictionary of the English Language, Fourth Edition Copyright © 2000 by Houghton Mifflin Company. Published by Houghton Mifflin Company.
http://dictionary.reference.com/search?q=reliable 05-27-2006

Renoe, Alexander J. (A. J.) (1868-1939)
Renoe was a prominent United States identification expert in the early 1900's. He learned about personal identification from Capt. Michael P. Evans. In 1889, while working at the Illinois State Reformatory, Renoe was asked to organize a Bertillon identification unit for the reformatory. In 1904, he added a fingerprints system. In 1908, he was asked to implement a finger print system for the Minnesota State Penitentiary. Just a few months after this he was offered the position of records clerk for the US Penitentiary at Leavenworth, Kansas under the Warden, Major R. W. McClaughry. In 1914, he was appointed Chief of the Bureau of Identification for the US Department of Justice, which was located at Leavenworth. While working in this position, Renoe developed the extensions to the Henry System that were used by many police departments, including the FBI. He held this position until 1923 when this finger print section was combined with the National Police Bureau's records to form the Identification Section of the Federal Bureau of Identification in Washington D.C. Renoe was appointed technical expert in the reorganization. Among his other accomplishments, in 1921 Renoe was elected as the 2nd president of the IAI and served two terms in this position.

Reproducibility
Accuracy-extended to which a measurement agrees with the accepted or

correct value.
www.esb.utexas.edu/dbm/Teach/bot308/Unit1/02science.htm

Reticular Layer
One of the two layers of the dermis. The layer that is furthest from the epidermis.

Reversed Image
See Image Reversal.

Reversed Color or Tones of Print
See Tonal Reversal.

Reyes, Victor
See State of Florida vs. Victor Reyes.

Rhodamine(s)
Family of dyes that produce fluorescence when exposed to selected wavelengths of light; used to visualize cyanoacrylate fumed friction ridge detail.
SWGFAST, Glossary - Consolidated 09-09-03 ver. 1.0

Rhodamine 6G
A fluorescent dye stain used with an alternate light source to visualize cyanoacrylate ester fumed friction ridge detail. Optimum viewing is done with an alternate light source (495-540nm) and orange or red goggles.

Ridge (Friction)
See Friction Ridge.
SWGFAST, Glossary - Consolidated 09-09-03 ver. 1.0

Ridge Aplasia
Congenital absence of friction ridge skin.
SWGFAST, Glossary - Consolidated 09-09-03 ver. 1.0

Ridge Characteristics
See Characteristics
SWGFAST, Glossary - Consolidated 09-09-03 ver. 1.0

Ridge Count
The number of ridges between the core and the delta. Used in the Henry Classification System.

Ridge Detail in Nature
John Berry (Hertfordshire) commenced publication of this esoteric journal in 1979, dealing with his observations that the seven basic ridge detail characteristics appear throughout nature, obvious examples being zebra and wind-blown or tidal-formed ridges and furrows on sand surfaces. In the century prior to his research, a dozen or so discoveries had been noted in fingerprint publications. The first issue of RIDGE DETAIL IN NATURE was circulated with 'Fingerprint Whorld' in 1979, featuring over seventy discoveries, many being illustrated. Since then Berry has published twenty-five annual issues, many profusely illustrated, and with large page counts. The journal was

re-titled STRABISMUS in 1998. At the end of 2004, the total of ridge detail discoveries was 1,556. Alice Maceo, of the Las Vegas Metro Police Department, has lectured at I.A.I. conferences, citing many of Berry's reported discoveries, and proffering her theory for the phenomenon. Berry also lectured on the subject at fingerprint conferences in several countries before his retirement in 1991. John Berry expresses his appreciation for the reports of over thirty researchers in the last quarter century, especially his friends and ex-colleagues at Hertfordshire, Martin Leadbetter and Mike Walker.

Ridge Dissociation
See Dissociated Ridges
SWGFAST, Glossary - Consolidated 09-09-03 ver. 1.0

Ridge Dysplasia
See Dysplasia
SWGFAST, Glossary - Consolidated 09-09-03 ver. 1.0

Ridge Flow
1. The direction of one or more friction ridges.
2. See Level 1 Detail.
SWGFAST, Glossary 07-28-2009 ver. 2.0

Ridge Hypoplasia
Underdeveloped ridges associated with an excess of creases.
SWGFAST, Glossary - Consolidated 09-09-03 ver. 1.0

Ridge Path
1. The course of a single friction ridge.
2. See Level 2 Detail.
SWGFAST, Glossary 07-28-2009 ver. 2.0

Ridge Unit
Small section of a friction ridge containing one pore.
Quantitative-Qualitative Friction Ridge Analysis, David R. Ashbaugh 1999 CRC Press

A theoretical length to indicate a segment of a friction ridge. This length is approximately the same distance as the width of a friction ridge and signifies the area around one pore.

See Friction Ridge Unit.
SWGFAST, Glossary 07-28-2009 ver. 2.0

Ridgeology
The study of the uniqueness of friction ridge skin and its use for personal identification (individualization).
SWGFAST, Glossary - Consolidated 09-09-03 ver. 1.0

Ridgeology is a term developed in 1982 by Sgt. David Ashbaugh to describe the scientific evaluation process used for friction ridge identifications.

Roquerre, Donald Daring

In 1934, in an attempt to conceal his identity, Donald Daring Roquerre mutilated his fingerprints by conducting surgery on himself. He removed sections of skin and exchanged them with other areas. In some fingers he merely changed the direction of the skin. In 1953 he was arrested, the alteration of his fingerprints was discovered and he was still easily identified.

Rosaniline Chloride
See Basic Fuschin.
SWGFAST, Glossary - Consolidated 09-09-03 ver. 1.0

Rose Bengal
A fluorescent dye stain used with an alternate light source to visualize cyanoacrylate ester fumed friction ridge detail. The results using this method were minimal and its use diminished in the 1980's.

Ross, Marion
Marion Ross was the murder victim in a 1997 SCRO murder case involving erroneous identifications.

See. McKie Case.

Rubber Lifter
A sheet of flexible rubber with a small amount of adhesive on one side used to lift latent prints for preservation. The advantage of using a rubber lifter is that because of it's flexibility, latents can be lifted off of textured and curved surfaces. Rubber lifters are also helpful in lifting latent prints off of paper items because they won't rip the paper. Latents lifted with rubber lifters will have reversed images.

Rubbing Technique
Powdering technique that can develop friction ridge detail when substrates are rubbed with gloves or cotton dipped in powder, usually after surfaces are cyanoacrylate fumed.
SWGFAST, Glossary - Consolidated 09-09-03 ver. 1.0

Rudimentary
1. Of or relating to basic facts or principles; elementary.
2. Being in the earliest stages of development; incipient.
3. Biology. Imperfectly or incompletely developed; embryonic: a rudimentary beak.
The American Heritage® Dictionary of the English Language, Fourth Edition Copyright © 2000 by Houghton Mifflin Company. Published by Houghton Mifflin Company.
http://dictionary.reference.com/search?q=rudimentary 05-13-03

Rudimentary Ridge
See Incipient Ridge.
SWGFAST, Glossary - Consolidated 09-09-03 ver. 1.0

Due to the definitions of Rudimentary, a rudimentary ridge could be referring to either the primary and secondary ridges or incipient ridges. It is more common to see them referred to as incipient ridges.

Ruga (plural: rugae)
A fold or wrinkle. In friction ridge identification the rugae refers to friction ridges.

Ruhemann's Purple
Colored compound that is the product of the reaction between amino acids and ninhydrin.
SWGFAST, Glossary - Consolidated 09-09-03 ver. 1.0

Rule 16
The United States Federal Rule of Criminal Procedures for Discovery and Inspection. In part, section (a)(1) (G), for expert witnesses, says, "At the defendant's request, the government must give to the defendant a written summary of any testimony that the government intends to use under Rules 702, 703, or 705 of the Federal Rules of Evidence during its case-in-chief at trial. If the government requests discovery under subdivision (b)(1)(C)(ii) and the defendant complies, the government must, at the defendant's request, give to the defendant a written summary of testimony that the government intends to use under Rules 702, 703, or 705 of the Federal Rules of Evidence as evidence at trial on the issue of the defendant's mental condition. The summary provided under this subparagraph must describe the witness's opinions, the bases and reasons for those opinions, and the witness's qualifications."

Rule 701. Testimony by Lay Witnesses
The United States Federal Rules of evidence state:
If the witness is not testifying as an expert, the witness' testimony in the form of opinions or inferences is limited to those opinions or inferences which are (a) rationally based on the perception of the witness, and (b) helpful to a clear understanding of the witness' testimony or the determination of a fact in issue, and (c) not based on scientific, technical, or other specialized knowledge within the scope of Rule 702 .

Rule 702. Testimony by Experts
The United States Federal Rule of evidence that state:
If scientific, technical, or other specialized knowledge will assist the tier of fact to understand the evidence or to determine a fact in issue, a witness qualified as an expert by knowledge, skill, experience, training, or education, may testify thereto in the form of an opinion or otherwise, if (1) the testimony is based upon sufficient facts or data, (2) the testimony is the product of reliable principles and methods, and (3) the witness has applied the principles and methods

reliably to the facts of the case. This rule went into effect in 1975 and supersedes Frye in Federal legal cases.

Rule 703. Bases of Opinion Testimony by Experts
The United States Federal Rule of evidence that states:
The facts or data in the particular case upon which an expert bases an opinion or inference may be those perceived by or made known to the expert at or before the hearing. If of a type reasonably relied upon by experts in the particular field in forming opinions or inferences upon the subject, the facts or data need not be admissible in evidence in order for the opinion or inference to be admitted. Facts or data that are otherwise inadmissible shall not be disclosed to the jury by the proponent of the opinion or inference unless the court determines that their probative value in assisting the jury to evaluate the expert's opinion substantially outweighs their prejudicial effect.

Rule 705. Disclosure of Facts or Data Underlying Expert Opinion
The United States Federal Rule of evidence that states:
The expert may testify in terms of opinion or inference and give reasons there for without first testifying to the underlying facts or data, unless the court requires otherwise. The expert may in any event be required to disclose the underlying facts or data on cross-examination.

Rule 1001. Definitions
The United States Federal Rule of evidence that states:
For purposes of this article the following definitions are applicable: (1) Writings and recordings. - "Writings" and "recordings" consist of letters, words, or numbers, or their equivalent, set down by handwriting, typewriting, printing, photostating, photographing, magnetic impulse, mechanical or electronic recording, or other form of data compilation. (2) Photographs. - "Photographs" include still photographs, X-ray films, video tapes, and motion pictures. (3) Original. - An "original" of a writing or recording is the writing or recording itself or any counterpart intended to have the same effect by a person executing or issuing it. An "original" of a photograph includes the negative or any print therefrom. If data are stored in a computer or similar device, any printout or other output readable by sight, shown to reflect the data accurately, is an "original." (4) Duplicate. - A "duplicate" is a counterpart produced by the same impression as the original, or from the same matrix, or by means of photography, including enlargements and miniatures, or by mechanical or electronic re-recording, or by chemical reproduction, or by other equivalent techniques which accu-

rately reproduces the original.

Rule 1002. Requirement of Originals
The United States Federal Rule of evidence that states:
To prove the content of a writing, recording, or photograph, the original writing, recording, or photograph is required, except as otherwise provided in these rules or by Act of Congress.

Rule 1003. Admissibility of Duplicates
The United States Federal Rule of evidence that states:
A duplicate is admissible to the same extent as an original unless (1) a genuine question is raised as to the authenticity of the original or (2) in the circumstances it would be unfair to admit the duplicate in lieu of the original.

Rule 1004. Admissibility of Other Evidence of Contents
The United States Federal Rule of evidence that states:
The original is not required, and other evidence of the contents of a writing, recording, or photograph is admissible if-- (1) Originals lost or destroyed. All originals are lost or have been destroyed, unless the proponent lost or destroyed them in bad faith; or (2) Original not obtainable. No original can be obtained by any available judicial process or procedure; or (3) Original in possession of opponent. At a time when an original was under the control of the party against whom offered, that party was put on notice, by the pleadings or otherwise, that the contents would be a subject of proof at the hearing, and that party does not produce the original at the hearing; or (4) Collateral matters. The writing, recording, or photograph is not closely related to a controlling issue.

Russell-Turner, William
Inventor of the Comparator.

Ruthenium Tetroxide (RTX)
Reagent used in the visualization of friction ridge detail, especially on fabrics.
SWGFAST, Glossary - Consolidated 09-09-03 ver. 1.0

A chemical used in a fuming method to develop friction ridge detail on porous items. RTX reacts with sebaceous material leaving dark gray images. This process can be used on thermal paper human skin, fabric, leather, glass, plastic, tape, wood, metal, stone, walls, and wet surfaces.

S

SAVED
Safe Approach Vapourized Evidence Device.

SCAFO
Southern California Association of Fingerprint Officers.

SCRO
Scottish Criminal Record Office. Founded in April 1960.

SKEET
An acronym for the requirement an expert must have; skills, knowledge, education, experience, and training.

SMANZL
Senior Managers Australian and New Zealand Forensic Laboratories.

SOCO
From the Greater Manchester Police, Scenes Of Crime Officer (now CSEO).

SPR
Small Particle Reagent. Suspension in which molybdenum disulphide adheres to fats and oils, allowing for visualization of friction ridge detail. SWGFAST, Glossary - Consolidated 09-09-03 ver. 1.0

SSO
An AFIS term meaning Sending Search to Other, referring to searching another AFIS system from your system.

SWGFAST
Scientific Working Group on Friction Ridge Analysis, Study and Technology. Established by the FBI in 1995 as TWGFAST. The name was changed to SWGFAST in 1999. This organization develops standards and guidelines in the area of friction skin identification. In 2007, it was officially recognized that SWGFAST represented both the tenprint profession as well as the latent print profession.

Safe Approach Vapourized Evidence Device (SAVED)
A robotic device developed by Sgt. Dave Wood from Calgary, Canada. This device is designed to find fingerprints on objects that are too dangerous for a person to handle. It fumes the object and photographs any latent prints found prior to the object being destroyed. To date, this device has never been used in actual casework but it is anticipated that it will be soon. In Nov. 2004 SAVED was shown on the television show CSI.

Safranin O
Red dye which produces fluorescence when exposed to selected wavelengths of light; used to visu-

alize cyanoacrylate fumed friction ridge detail.
SWGFAST, Glossary - Consolidated 09-09-03 ver. 1.0

Sampson, William C. and Karen L. William Sampson (1936-Nov. 28, 2007) is recognized as the most knowledgeable individual regarding the recovery of latent prints from human skin. He retired from the Miami-Dade Police Department after 38 years of service that included assignments to Radio Patrol, Foot Patrol, Traffic Homicide, Training Advisor, Training Bureau; Crime Scene Investigator; Interim Administrative Supervisor/Crime Scene Investigations Bureau, Liaison to Miami-Dade Police Department's Crime Laboratory and the Miami-Dade Medical Examiner Department. Bill Sampson's training and special projects include Coordinator for the Crime Scene Investigations Bureau; Certified Instructor by the Florida State General Police Standards Commission and has served as an adjunct professor at the Miami-Dade Community College. He has taught over 250 law enforcement entities, several universities, nine International Association for Identification International Conferences, numerous IAI Divisional Conferences, International Chiefs of Police Conference, and for the American Academy of Forensic Sciences. Several awards have recognized his contributions and accomplishments. He is the recipient of the Miami-Dade Police Department's Distinguished Service Award, recipient of 6 consecutive NACo (1990 thru 1995) Awards, the National Association of Counties for excellence in county government achievements in the field of Forensic Science, and the recipient of Ford Foundation Award. He's held an active role in the International Association for Identification; being a Certified Senior Crime Scene Analyst, Distinguished Member, recipient of the prestigious John Dondero Award, served on several committee positions and Past Chair Person of the Safety Committee, as well as a member of the Editorial Review Board. Mr. Sampson has also been involved in many other organizations. He is a retired Fellow of the British Fingerprint Society, Honorary Life Member of the Utah State Division of the IAI, member of the Florida Division of the IAI and has served on Board of Directors, Historian, District Director and served on various committees; recipient of Sustained Achievement Award and the Outstanding Science Award.
Karen Sampson is President of KLS Forensics Inc., which the Sampson's established in 1995. This company provides hands-on intensive training in various crime scene related subjects. KLS Forensics also assists law enforcement agencies when request-

ed. Her expertise includes the fields of textiles, Product Identification and it's origin and Photography. She is a past instructor and consultant for Miami-Dade Police department and the Miami-Dade Medial Examiner's Office. She has also taught at 4 International Annual Conferences of the IAI, numerous divisional conferences, American Academy of Forensic Sciences and numerous law enforcement entities and universities. Karen Sampson has attended and successfully completed specialized training in the fields of fingerprint comparison, Forensic Photography and Crime Scene Analysis. She is a member of the International Association for Identification, American Academy of Forensic Sciences, Florida Division of the IAI, Honorary Life member of Utah State Division of the IAI, and served on the IAI's 1995 committee on Management Issues.

Sandwich Method
The Sandwich Method is a dry process used to develop friction ridge detail on porous items. Transfer sheets are first prepared by soaking clean sheets of paper in the desired chemical and allowed to air dry (commonly ninhydrin or DMAC are used). Then the paper to be processed is placed between the transfer sheets and processed normally. The benefits to this method are that no bleeding of the ink or background discoloration occurs.

Santamaria Method
Florentino Santamaria Beltran, Chief of the Technical Police Laboratory in Madrid, Spain, was perhaps the first person to publish a quality and quantity approach to evaluating ridge characteristics. Santamaria did research in the 1940's and presented his findings in June of 1953 at the 22nd General Assembly of the International Criminal Police Commission in Oslo, Norway. Santamaria recognized that some characteristics were rarer than others and all characteristics shouldn't carry the same weight. Santamaria may have been the initial inspiration behind recognizing that a numerical standard was not the best approach in quantifying a fingerprint identification.

Scar
A mark remaining after the healing of a wound.
SWGFAST, Glossary - Consolidated 09-09-03 ver. 1.0

A mark left on the skin after an injury to the dermis or a mark left on the skin after an injury to the generating layer of the epidermis. If an injury to the generating layer of the epidermis removes sufficient regenerating cells, the cells cannot reproduce the original characteristics of the skin, leaving fibrous tissue or a scar.

Scarf skin
Dry or dead skin which has scaled and peeled away from the surface skin.
SWGFAST, Glossary - Consolidated 09-09-03 ver. 1.0

Science
The observation, identification, description, experimental investigation, and theoretical explanation of phenomena.
The American Heritage® Dictionary of the English Language, Fourth Edition Copyright © 2000 by Houghton Mifflin Company. Published by Houghton Mifflin Company. All rights reserved.
http://dictionary.reference.com/search?q=science 02-27-03

A way of gaining knowledge about a natural phenomenon and the body of knowledge derived from this approach. This systematic form of reasoning differs from other forms of reasoning, (like hearsay, intuition, a belief system or coincidence) by gaining knowledge through testable observations, peer review, and other scientific guidelines. These procedures insure objectivity resulting in a more reliable, credible and consistent type of knowledge.

Scientific Method
The principles and empirical processes of discovery and demonstration considered characteristic of or necessary for scientific investigation, generally involving the observation of phenomena, the formulation of a hypothesis concerning the phenomena, experimentation to demonstrate the truth or falseness of the hypothesis, and a conclusion that validates or modifies the hypothesis.
The American Heritage® Dictionary of the English Language, Fourth Edition Copyright © 2000 by Houghton Mifflin Company. Published by Houghton Mifflin Company. All rights reserved.
http://dictionary.reference.com/search?q=scientific%20method 02-27-03

The process by which we gain our knowledge (the most common form is hypothesis testing).
Based on evidence, not on belief. Make a distinction between other forms of explanation like emotions, chance, intuition, ignoring what does not fit, guessing. Used to support or disprove a hypothesis.
Not a set of rules, a way of gathering information impartially about natural phenomenon. Conclusions should be explainable, falsifiable and reproducible.

Scientific proof
It is a myth that scientific proof exists. The goal of science is not to provide proof but to find reasonable explanations of natural phenomenon.

Scientist
William Whewell first coined the word science in 1833. Before then, thinkers in science were known as 'natural philosophers'. The first of these natural philosophers that history records were Thales and his contemporaries, Anaximander and Anaximenes, who lived in Greece around 600BC, although there were also similar people to be found in China, India, Egypt and Mesopotamia. Whewell chose the terms 'science' and 'scientist' from the Latin scire 'to know'. So 'science' is the pursuit of knowledge.
http://www.sciencenet.org.uk/database/General/0104/x00046d.html
02-27-03

One who has a deep understanding of a certain body of knowledge and rigorously adheres to scientific principles, guidelines, and methodologies in order to formulate theoretical knowledge or conclusions.

Sebaceous Glands
Small subcutaneous glands, usually connected with hair follicles. They secrete an oily semi-fluid matter, composed in great part of fat, which softens and lubricates the hair and skin.
Webster's Revised Unabridged Dictionary, © 1996, 1998 MICRA, Inc

An oil-secreting gland generally associated with a hair follicle.
SWGFAST, Glossary - Consolidated 09-09-03 ver. 1.0

Sebaceous Sweat
See Sebum.

Sebum
A fatty secretion of the sebaceous glands.
Quantitative-Qualitative Friction Ridge Analysis, David R. Ashbaugh 1999 CRC Press

The secretion of the sebaceous gland. Composed of lipids, which are fats, oils and waxes.

Second Level Detail (also see Level 2 Detail)
Ridge path, major ridge path deviations, and paths caused by damage such as scars.
Quantitative-Qualitative Friction Ridge Analysis, David R. Ashbaugh 1999 CRC Press

Secondary
An alpha expression derived from the pattern type of the index fingers.
SWGFAST, Glossary - Consolidated 09-09-03 ver. 1.0

Secondary Ridges
Ridges on the bottom of the epidermis under the surface furrows.
Quantitative-Qualitative Friction Ridge Analysis, David R. Ashbaugh 1999 CRC Press

The term 'secondary ridge' can be used to describe many different areas of the skin. It is not important to discern whether one is right or wrong, just to understand the area that is being referred to. How this term is used will also effect how the terms 'primary ridges' and 'papillary ridges' are used.
1) Hale: Ridges at bottom of the epidermis that correspond to the surface furrows.
2) Surface ridges may be referred to as secondary ridges in the respect that the ridges at the dermal-epidermal junction grow first, considered as primary ridges, and the surface ridges appear later. It appears to be interpreted this way in the U.S. vs. Carlos Ivan Llera Plaza opinion dated 1/7/2002.
3) In "Bloom and Fawcett's Concise Histology" primary ridges and secondary ridges refer to the ridges of the dermis and the ridges in the epidermis that Hale refers to are considered epidermal grooves.

Secretor
The medical profession defines a secretor as someone who secretes their blood type antigens into their body fluids. When this happens the medical professionals can determine the blood type of a person just by analyzing a body fluid, like saliva or semen. A non-secretor is a person who doesn't secrete their blood type into their body fluids.
The fingerprint profession uses the term 'non-secretor' to describe a person who doesn't sweat. It's important to be aware of all the latent print recovery conditions in order to recognize that being a non-secretor doesn't imply a person is unable to leave a latent print. It also doesn't imply that just because latent prints weren't found doesn't mean a person is a non-secretor.

Sequential Processing
Use of a series of development techniques in a specific order to maximize development of friction ridge detail.
SWGFAST, Glossary - Consolidated 09-09-03 ver. 1.0

Set
See Perceptual set.

Shanndon-xylene
Technique used to separate adhesive surfaces.
SWGFAST, Glossary - Consolidated 09-09-03 ver. 1.0

Short Ridge
A single friction ridge beginning, traveling a short distance, and then ending.
SWGFAST, Glossary 07-28-2009 ver. 2.0

Shoulders
Where a recurving ridge tends to turn.

Side Cone
A term popularized by Ron Smith to describe the delta in the interdigital area that is below the little finger.

Silva, Dr. Rodolfo Xavier da
In November 1904, Dr. Xavier da Silva and a fingerprint expert of the Lisbon Anthropometric Office (Posto Antropométrico de Lisboa), Leonel Pereira, had identified the corpse of a stranger by his fingerprints. It seems to be the first corpse identification in Europe by this method. The first in the world belonged to the Juan Vucetich in 1895.
Dactiloscopia, 1938

Silver Nitrate
Chemical used in the Physical Developer, Multimetal Deposition and Silver Nitrate processes. Used alone, silver nitrate reacts with salt to develop friction ridge detail.
SWGFAST, Glossary - Consolidated 09-09-03 ver. 1.0

Early documentation reveals that the silver nitrate process was developed in the 1910's. In 1918, the IAI Conference gave a presentation on this process. Different people were experimenting with it but it's development is historically credited to Dr. Erastus Mead Hudson. The silver nitrate process became well known after Dr. Hudson recovered latent prints on a ladder used in the Lindbergh kidnapping case (1932). In later years, Dr. Hudson did additional research with the New York Police Department exploring other possible uses for the silver nitrate process, such as recovering latent prints from cloth and gloves.
Finger Print and Identification Magazine, Vol. 17, No. 3, September 1935.
The Federal Bureau of Investigation has also taken credit for the development of silver nitrate. They claim that it was first used in 1933 in the William Hamm kidnapping case (the president of the Hamm Brewing Company).

Silver Plate Transfer Method
See Iodine-Silver Transfer Method.

Simas, Alexandre Duarte de Cabedo (Dec. 20, 1945-present)
Mr. Simas is one of the most well known fingerprint experts in Portugal. He began his career in Criminalistics in 1981, specializing in fingerprints. During this time he took various courses such as "Teaching Techniques", "Crime Scene Photography", "AFIS", and "Biological Criminalistic".

After working for several years as Bureau's Chief in Sector de Identificação Judiciária, he became Professor of Criminalistics and Investigation for all courses at ISPJCC (Instituto Superior de Polícia Judiciária e Ciências Criminais), the equivalent to the FBI's Quantico.

Alexandre Simas has accumulated a long list of police agencies he has been responsible for training. He was the professor and training supervisor to the criminal police of São Tomé e Príncipe, Cape Verde Islands, and in charge of investigation courses for the rural and suburban police. Invited professor in after-graduation in "Criminal Sciences" in Universidade Internacional in Figueira da Foz, Professor in after-graduation in "Criminal Sciences" in "Universidade Moderna" and "Faculdade de Ciências do Sul", as well as supervisor of fingerprint courses in Polícia de Segurança Pública. Mr. Simas has also lectured in several attorney and judges courses.

Besides his teaching credentials, Mr. Simas is also an AFIS computer specialist. He was a technical assessor for installation and assembly of the Fingerprint Bureau of Cabo Verde and São Tomé e Príncipe criminal police.

He is recognized as being a mass disaster specialist and was instrumental in the identification of 144 corpses in an aerial disaster in the Santa Maria Island, Azores with an American Boeing 707, in 1989.

Alexandre Simas was a member of the Prevention Local Group in EXPO98 in Lisbon, participated in "100 years of fingerprints in Scotland Yard", in London, UK, participant in "Motorolla-Printrak Users Conference", in Los Angeles, USA, and was the representative of Polícia Judiciária in the "First International Conference and Exhibition on Forensic Human Identifications" in London.

Mr. Simas has authored the books "A identificação de A a Z" and "A Identificação em Grandes Catástrofes". He has also co-authored and collaborator on several others technical books.

Alexandre Simas has significantly contributed to the science of friction ridge identification and is recognized as one of the leading experts in his field.

Simian Crease
Single crease that crosses the palm in a place of the distal and proximal creases.
Quantitative-Qualitative Friction Ridge Analysis, David R. Ashbaugh 1999 CRC Press

Simultaneous Court Cases (not a complete list)
Commonwealth (of Massachusetts) v. Terry L. Patterson (1995)
Commonwealth (of Massachusetts) v. Terry L. Patterson (2005 - Massachusetts Supreme Judicial Court ruling)

Simultaneous Impression
Friction ridge impressions are simul-

taneous if they are deposited with one touch to the item. Individual segments of a simultaneous impression may not have sufficient value to arrive at a conclusion of identity on their own but may have sufficient value to arrive at a conclusion of identity in the aggregate (using all the information in the simultaneous impression). There is no scientific basis requiring that each segment of a simultaneous impression have sufficient value to arrive at a conclusion of identity individually.

Two or more friction ridge impressions from the same hand or foot deposited concurrently.
SWGFAST, Glossary 07-28-2009 ver. 2.0

Simultaneous Impression, factors of
Impressions are said to be simultaneous if sufficient factors are present. These factors can include: orientation (direction), spatial relationship (spacing and position), anatomical area, anatomical size, anatomical features (such as ridge width, flow, and creases), characteristics of the developmental medium, distortion (lateral and direct pressure, length of smearing, direction of smearing, curvature of smearing, and consistencies in ridge widths). Some impressions may easily be determined to have been left simultaneously because there is attachment of the ridges (a thenar and a hypothenar may have been left simultaneously and this is known because no space is present between the sections). Level 2 or Level 3 details are not factors in determining simultaneity.

Skin
The outer covering of the body consisting of the dermis and epidermis.
SWGFAST, Glossary - Consolidated 09-09-03 ver. 1.0

Skin Layers
The two main layers of the skin are the epidermis and dermis.

The epidermis consists of 5 layers (starting from the outer most layer):
Stratum Corneum (Horny Layer)
Stratum Lucidum (Clear Layer)
Stratum Granulosum (Granular Layer)
Stratum Spinosum (Prickly Layer)
Stratum Germinativum (Basal Layer or Malpighian Layer)

The dermis consists of 2 layers (starting closest to the epidermis):
Papillary Layer
Reticular Layer

Slaps
The images of the four fingers simultaneously usually taken on a fingerprint card. These images are taken to establish the correct order of the individual fingers.

Small Detail Axiom
"The smaller the detail found...progressively in agreement during comparison, the more individualizing power it has".
As stated by David R. Ashbaugh in United States of America vs. Byron C. Mitchell.

Small Particle Reagent
See SPR

Smith, David W. MD
Wrote "The Genesis of Dermatoglyphics" with Mulvihill, John J. MD for the Journal of Pediatrics, Oct. 1969 issue. It is said to be on of the most thorough discussions of fingerprint formation. Their findings were:
6-8 weeks after conception volar pads form
10-12 weeks volar pads begin to recede
13th week skin ridges begin to appear
21st week after conception fingerprint patters are complete
http://www.handanalysis.net/library/derm_history.htm 02-27-03

Smith, Ron
Ron Smith is a world-renowned authority on friction ridge identification. In 2001, he retired as the Associate Director of the Mississippi Crime Laboratory and established and directs "Ron Smith & Associates, Inc.". This company provides technical training to forensic specialists and criminal investigation. Mr. Smith is most well known for his educational seminars "Demystifying Palm Prints" and "Courtroom Testimony Techniques-Success instead of Survival". Through these seminars, his lectures and his international consulting he has established himself as an instrumental and essential part of the forensic science field. Ron Smith's research and contributions regarding palm print analysis have provided examiners worldwide with the fundamental tools needed for latent palm print recognition. In 2001, he received recognition for his numerous accomplishments when the IAI presented him with the John A. Dondero award, the IAI's highest honor. According to the IAI website, he is the 17th person to ever receive this award.

Snow Cones
A term popularized by Ron Smith to describe the middle deltas in the interdigital area.

Sodium Acetate
Chemical used in the preparation of reagents.
SWGFAST, Glossary - Consolidated 09-09-03 ver. 1.0

Sodium Bicarbonate
Chemical used in the preparation of reagents.
SWGFAST, Glossary - Consolidated 09-09-03 ver. 1.0

Sodium Chloride
One of the inorganic components of perspiration or eccrine sweat. Salt.

Sodium Hypochlorite (Household Bleach)
Solution used to clear ninhydrin stains and to darken the silver deposits of Physical Developer.
SWGFAST, Glossary - Consolidated 09-09-03 ver. 1.0

Source
Specific area of friction ridge skin.
SWGFAST, Glossary 07-28-2009 ver. 2.0

Source may also refer to the person a latent print impression is attributed to.

The Spa Murders © (State of Florida v. Stephen William Beattie (1978))
The spa murders occurred on July 23, 1978 in North Miami Beach, Florida. This case was the first case on record where a latent fingerprint developed from a homicide victim's skin was identified with an offender and introduced as evidence in court.
Three victims (1 male and 2 females) were found shot to death in the World of Health Spas. One of the victims, a young female, was found nude, posed and her clothing strewn about. It appeared as though she may have been sexually assaulted. She was processed for latent print evidence with black magnetic powder and three prints were developed on the left ankle area. One of the prints was determined to be identifiable and was identified to the subject. The other two victims were also processed for latent print evidence with KromeKote ® cards, yielding negative results.
There are many misconceptions connected with this case, which have perpetuated over the years, resulting in urban legend. One is that the print was deposited on the surface of the victim's skin with sun tan lotion or oil. This is unsubstantiated and unfounded but has contributed to over embellished statements that all prints recovered from human skin have been in the state of Florida and are due to sun tan oil.
The causative factor of the print is irrelevant and was definitely not sun tan oil. The fact was that a latent print was developed and recovered from the surface of the skin of a murder victim and was subsequently accepted in court as evidence.
On January 31, 1979, Stephen William Beattie was found guilty of three counts of 1st degree murder. On February 1, 1979 he was sentenced to three consecutive death sentences. Beattie committed suicide within three years of his sentence in prison while awaiting execution. He maintained his innocence even to the end.
By William C. Sampson and Karen L. Sampson

Sparks from the Anvil
Sparks from the Anvil was the second periodical of the IAI and was published from 1933-1937.

Specific Pattern
Pattern or path of the friction ridges used during identification; second level detail.
Quantitative-Qualitative Friction Ridge Analysis, David R. Ashbaugh 1999 CRC Press

Spinous Layer of Epidermis
See Stratum Spinosum.

Split Thumb
Thumb that has conjoined distal phalanges.
SWGFAST, Glossary - Consolidated 09-09-03 ver. 1.0

Sprue Marks
Marks that are made when casting metals or plastics. These marks can resemble friction ridge detail by replication ridges with bifurcations and ending ridges. These marks typically appear with a wavy motion and have no signs of pores or ridge edges. These marks have been called extrusion marks and/or false ridge detail.

Spur
A bifurcation with one short friction ridge branching off a longer friction ridge.
SWGFAST, Glossary 07-28-2009 ver. 2.0

Squamous
Resembling a scale or scales; thin and flat like a scale.
The American Heritage® Dictionary of the English Language, Fourth Edition Copyright © 2000 by Houghton Mifflin Company. Published by Houghton Mifflin Company. All rights reserved.
http://dictionary.reference.com/search?q=squamous

Stand-alone
A segment of a simultaneous impression that has sufficient value to arrive at a conclusion of identity directly from the information within this segment.

A segment of a simultaneous impression that has sufficient information to arrive at a conclusion of individualization independent of other impressions within the aggregate.
SWGFAST, Glossary 07-28-2009 ver. 2.0

Standard of Sufficiency for Conclusions
The general scientific standard is to have enough evidence and justification to eliminate doubt in others. Some people refer to this as general consensus conclusions or conclusions that will stand up to scrutiny or stand the test of time.

Starburst
A term popularized by Ron Smith to

describe the crease pattern in the top radial side of the thenar. These creases originate from the same area and then explode in different directions.

Starrs, Dr. James
A fingerprint critic. A professor of law and forensic science at George Washington University. Predicted the fall of fingerprints in 1996.

State of Florida v. Stephen William Beattie (1978)
The first case on record where a latent print was developed on a homicide victim's skin, identified to a suspect, and introduced as evidence in court. See The Spa Murders ©.

State of Florida v. Victor Reyes (2003)
This was the 4rd trial in the United States that considered the evidentiary value of computer enhancement with regard to latent evidence. In 1996, Victor Reyes was charged with a Broward County murder. Originally latent prints on some tape were analyzed as having no value, but in 1999 the latent images were reanalyzed by forensic analyst David Knoerlein using a computer enhancement technique known as 'dodge and burn', and identified as prints left by Victor Reyes. The State of Florida found that computer enhanced images did meet the Frye test and the latents were admitted as evidence in the trial. Reyes was acquitted at trial. The jury felt that the latent prints didn't prove that Reyes committed the murder. The significance of this case was that defense attorneys realized the importance of challenging digitally generated evidence.

State of Illinois v. Jennings (1910)
Aka People v. Jennings.
See Jennings. See Jennings, Thomas.

State of Maryland v. Bryan Rose (2007)
The second case to fail a fingerprint Challenge based on the reliability of the conclusion. Bryan (Brian) Rose was the suspect in a homicide case. Stephan Meagher testified for the prosecution and Ralph Haber testified for the defense. On Oct 19, 2007, Judge Souder published her decision, "...In conclusion, the proof presented by the State in this case regarding the ACE-V methodology of latent fingerprint identification showed that it was more likely so, than not so, that ACE-V was the type of procedure Frye was intended to banish, that is, a subjective, untested, unverifiable identification procedure that purports to be infallible. After impartial scientific testing, the establishment of an error rate and of objective criteria which when applied, are documented and can be verified, it may be that latent print identification opinion testimony as offered in this capital case will qualify for admission under Frye-Reed.

The State did not meet that burden in this case and, consequently, shall not offer testimony that any latent fingerprint in this case is that of the Defendant. In this case, the State did not show by a preponderance of evidence that a fingerprint examiner can reliably identify a fingerprint to an individual to the exclusion of all others using the ACE-V method."

In Oct. 2007, the prosecution filed a motion for reconsideration. It was denied on Feb. 21, 2008. On April 1, 2008, a federal grand jury indicted Rose on murder charges hoping that this would allow the fingerprint evidence into a trial. On Sept. 8, 2009, Judge Catherine Blake rendered her decision that the fingerprint evidence was admissible under the requirements set forth by the Supreme Court in Daubert v. Merrell Dow Pharmaceuticals and by Kumho Tire Co., Ltd. v. Carmichael. On Jan. 11, 2010, Bryan Rose accepted a plea deal.

State of Massachusetts v. Patterson (2005)
In 1995 Terry Patterson was found guilty of a 1993 armed robbery and the 1993 homicide of Det. John Milligan. In 2000, based on inefficient counsel, Patterson won an appeal to have new trail. Prior to the new trial, the defense asked for a Daubert Hearing regarding the use of simultaneous impression.
On Dec. 27, 2005, in Commonwealth (of Massachusetts) v. Terry L. Patterson, the Massachusetts Supreme Judicial Court determined "Consistent with the decisions of other courts that have considered the issue since Daubert, we conclude that the underlying theory and process of latent fingerprint identification, and the ACE-V method in particular, are sufficiently reliable to admit expert opinion testimony regarding the matching of a latent impression with a full fingerprint. In this case, however, the Commonwealth needed to establish more than the general reliability of latent fingerprint identification. It needed to establish that the theory, process, and method of latent fingerprint identification could be applied reliably to simultaneous impressions not capable of being individually matched to any of the fingers that supposedly made them. On the record before the judge below, the Commonwealth failed to meet its burden."
The prosecution offered Patterson a plea agreement of pleading guilty to a lesser charge with time served instead of risking a new trial and the potential longer sentence. Patterson took the plea agreement.

State of Michigan v. Les (1934)
In People v. Les, (255 NW 407) the defendant's palm print was recovered from the windowsill at the point of entry of a breaking and entering scene. Before trial, the defendant

contended that palm prints were not sufficient to sustain a conviction. The court ruled that the evidence was insufficient to hold the defendant for trial, quashed the information, and ordered the discharge of the defendant. The Government appealed that the trial court was in error in their ruling regarding the palm print evidence, and the Supreme Court of Michigan (1934) agreed that fingerprints and palm prints are both "considered physical characteristics" and therefore were "sufficient evidence to go to trial." The trial judge was directed to reinstate the information. http://www.clpex.com/Articles/TheDetail/TheDetail82.htm 10-20-2004

State of Nevada v. Kuhl (1918)
State vs. Kuhl was a significant court case regarding palm prints identifications. This case was an appeal for a conviction of a 1916 murder. It looked at 1) Was the court in error in allowing experts in fingerprint identification to testify as experts in palm print identification, 2) Was the court in error in admitting photographic enlargements of palm prints, 3) Was the court in error in allowing the use of a projectoscope, 4) Was the court in error in admitting photographs of palm prints where the experts drew lines upon them, and 5) Was the court in error in permitting the expert witness to make a positive statement as to the identity of the palm impressions. The Supreme Court of Nevada (1918) held "NO" on all counts.
http://www.clpex.com/Articles/TheDetail/1-99/TheDetail82.htm

State of New Hampshire v. Richard Langill (2007)
The first case to fail a Daubert Challenge based on the reliability of the conclusion. Richard Langill was suspected of burglary. Lisa Corson was the examiner in this case and Prof. James Starrs testified for the defense. The court determined, "Ms. Corson is qualified through training, experience, and proficiency testing to provide expert testimony at the defendant's trial. However, Ms. Corson's proffered testimony is inadmissible under Rule 702 because her application of the ACE-V (Analysis, Comparison, Evaluation, and Verification) methodology to the single latent print in this case was unreliable as a result of incomplete documentation and possibly biased verification." On Jan.19, 2007, Judge Coffey granted a motion to exclude the fingerprint evidence. Documentation was required in the NHDSFL Standard Operating Procedures but wasn't done in this case. The comment about 'possibly biased verification' was determined because blind verification wasn't done. Blind verification has become a policy of the FBI since the Mayfield mis-identification. Ms. Corson also testified in this case that Blind Verification was ideal but

not practical.

A motion to reconsider was entered and on April 11, 2007 Judge Coffey ruled that there was "insufficient information to support a finding that the application of the ACE-V methodology to the single latent print in this case was reliable." Judge Coffey affirmed her original decision.

On Feb 13, 2008, this was argued before the New Hampshire Supreme Court. On April 4, 2008, the court issued its opinion to reverse and remand.

State of New York v. Crispi (1911)
Aka People v. Crispi. Charles Crispi, aka Cesare J. Cella, was the defendant in this case, which is noted as being the first case that fingerprint evidence was the sole evidence. Fingerprint expert Joseph Faurot testified to the identification process. After hearing Faurot's testimony, Crispi pled guilty. The judge asked Crispi for a full confession, insuring him that no additional charges would be filed. The judge wanted to insure that the scientific evidence that was testified to was indeed correct.

State of New York v. Kent (1968)
Aka People v. Kent. Perhaps the first trial that a defense expert testified that although the identification had 12 (some articles say 14) points of similarity, the prints were not identical. Richard Stanley Kent was charged with murdering Joseph Murphy, a retired New York City Policeman. The key evidence against Kent, a latent print on a bed board, seemed to be irrefutable. William J. Ciolko, Dutchess County Public Defender, hired Dr. Vassilis C. Morfopoulos, director of the American Standards Testing Bureau, to look at the identification. Dr. Morfopoulos analyzed the identification using a 25x microscope. He testified that he found 3 differences, "One distinct and crucial difference destroys the validity of an identification", he said. Richard Kent was found not guilty of the murder. In 1970, the FBI and the IAI refuted Dr. Morfopoulos's analysis and sided with Wilfred Holick, the original examiner in this case. The defense attorney and the defense expert gave a presentation of this case at the 55th IAI Conference. There were two significant points to this case. This was the first time 'the prints are not identical' was used in court as a defense strategy, and the defense claimed that this case broke down the apparent ironclad status of fingerprints.

State of Ohio v. Betts (1917)
The Betts case may have been the first conviction based solely on palm print evidence. In 1917, Samual W. Betts was arrested and charged with burglary based on the fact that his palm print was found on a window-

pane. George Koestle (one of Ferrier's students) was the person who took and compared the palm prints. 'Fingerprint and Identification Magazine', Dec 1942.

Another palm print case that happened around the same time, and also said to be the first palm print case to have a conviction, was a murder trial in Nevada. The defendant was Ben Kuhl.

State of Ohio v. Hartman (1998)

The 3rd court case in the United States ruling on the computer enhancement of fingerprint images. In 1997, Brett X. Hartman was charged with murdering Winda Snipes by stabbing her 138 times, slitting her throat, and cutting off her hands. Due to numerous pieces of evidence, including latent print images on a chair and a bedspread, a jury found Hartman guilty of murder and kidnapping, sentenced him to death. In 2001, Hartman appealed his conviction stating 13 different challenges. The challenges dealing with the latent prints were 1) the admission of digitally enhanced fingerprint evidence, their reliability and the qualifications of the state's fingerprint expert, Patrick Warrick, to testify regarding such evidence and 2) the court failed to make a threshold determination concerning Patrick Warrick's qualifications stating that "It was error for the trial court to admit the opinion of witnesses who had not first been qualified as an expert". The court ruled that "the use of the computer in this instance is no different than ***would be the use of an overhead projector, microscope, a magnifying glass or anything else like that that would enhance an experts ability to make his determination...". It was ruled that since Warrick had used computer enhancement for approx. a year and a half this was not blazing new ground, Warrick's testimony was appropriate. The court also determined that although Warrick was not formally tendered as an expert witness, the defense did not challenge Warrick's qualifications and the court determined him to be qualified to identify defendants fingerprint on Snipes's bedspread. On Oct. 3, 2001, the appellate court affirmed Hartman's conviction. http://caselaw.lp.findlaw.com/scripts/getcase.pl?court=oh&vol=981475&invol=1 08-02-2004

State of Virginia v. Robert Douglas Knight (1991)

The first (case to establish a precedence for the acceptance of digitally enhanced evidence in American criminal proceedings) is Commonwealth of Virginia vs. Robert Douglas Knight. This 1991 murder case (murder was March of 1990, trial was in 1991) involved the enhancement of a bloody fingerprint found on a pillowcase at the crime scene. A company called Hunter Graphics (no longer in business) was contacted by the Henrico County Police Department to assist in the enhancement process. Experts from Hunter Graphics used a frequency filter known commonly as a Fast Fourier Transform (FFT) to subtract the fabric pattern that interfered with the identification of the fingerprint. The fingerprint was subsequently identified as belonging to Robert Knight. After being charged with the crime, Knight's attorney moved for a Kelly-Frye Hearing to determine the scientific validity and acceptance of the enhancement process. The determination of the court was that the techniques used were essentially photographic processes. Robert Knight plead guilty and was sentenced to four life terms. http://www.more-hits.com/forensics/dl/AboutForensicDigitalImaging.pdf 01-25-2005

State of Washington v. Eric Hayden (1998)
The 2nd court case in the United States ruling on the computer enhancement of fingerprint images. In 1995, Eric Hayden was charged with murdering a 27-year-old female. Her body was found with a bloody sheet wrapped around her head and neck. The examiner in this case, Dan Holshue, found latent prints on the sheet but they were too subtle to identify. Erik Berg, an expert in enhanced digital imaging, used enhancement techniques to filter out the background pattern and colors of the sheet. After enhancement, the latent prints were identified and Eric Hayden was found guilty of murder. His murder conviction was upheld on appeal and the court concluded that computer enhancement did meet the Frye test, setting new case law in this field.

Statistical Analysis of Error Rates
See Error Rate Studies.

Statistical Models on Fingerprint Individuality, etc.
Galton (1892)
Henry (1900)
Balthazard (1911)
Bose (1917)
Wentworth / Wilder (1918)
Pearson (1930)
Roxburgh (1933)
Cummins / Midlo (1943)
Amy (1946-48)
Trauring (1963)
Kingston / Kirk (1964)
Gupta (1968)
Osterburg (1977-80)
Stoney (1985)
Champod (1995-96)
FBI / Lockheed-Martin 50k x 50k study (1999)
Pankanti / Prabhakar / Jain (2001)
Neumann / Champod Liklihood Ratios (2007) (see PBFE)

Steegers, Juan (AKA Steegers y

Pereira or Steegers y Perera)(1856-1921)
Juan Steegers was a cuban civil servant honored by his government as a fingerprint pioneer.
"Fingerprint Techniques" Andre A. Moenssens, 1971 pg 26.

Sticky Side Powder ™
Product used to develop friction ridge detail on adhesive surfaces and/or tapes.
SWGFAST, Glossary - Consolidated 09-09-03 ver. 1.0

Stimac, Jon T. (1966-present)
Jon Stimac began his career in forensics after earning a Bachelor of Science Degree in Criminalistics/Criminal Justice from Weber State University in Ogden, Utah. Immediately after graduation, he began employment with Salt Lake City Police Department's Crime Laboratory.

In 1996, Jon left Salt Lake City to continue his career with the Oregon State Police Forensic Services Division. Since then, he has acted as a latent print examiner, temporary lab director, forensic scientist, and as the technical leader for the latent print discipline.

Jon supplemented early research on the 3M® solvent HFE-7100 and introduced to the forensic community the use of Un-du® as an alternative adhesive separator. For the development of latent print impressions on specialty papers (thermal and carbonless), he introduced a specialized ninhydrin formulation and the use of 1,2-Indanedione. Jon has published several technical articles covering these and other topics within international forensic identification journals, including the Journal of Forensic Identification. In addition, he has compiled and published a monthly newsletter on friction ridge individualization, FP Stuff, since 2001. In Feb. 2008, Jon Stimac became the editor of the IAI's Identification News.

In 2000, Jon became a member of the FBI sponsored Scientific Working Group on Friction Skin Analysis, Study and Technology (SWGFAST). He is also active within several regional and international forensic identification organizations.

Stock Solution
Concentrated solution diluted to prepare a working solution.
SWGFAST, Glossary - Consolidated 09-09-03 ver. 1.0

Stoney, Dr. David
A mild fingerprint critic. Directs the McCrone Research Institute in Chicago, PhD Forensic Science. Noted as being the person to state that conclusions of absolute certainty are based on a leap of faith.

Strabismus
A journal edited by John Berry (Hertfordshire) from 1979 dealing with the appearance of the basic seven ridge characteristics occurring throughout nature, the total at the end of 2004 being 1,556. Originally published under the title RIDGE DETAIL IN NATURE until 1998, this reference should be used for further information.

Stratify (Stratification)
Arranged in a sequence of grades or ranks.
WordNet ® 1.6, © 1997 Princeton University
http://dictionary.reference.com/search?q=stratified

Stratton Brothers (Alfred and Albert)
The Stratton brothers made legal history in May 1905 when fingerprint evidence was used against them in a British Court to convict them of murdering Thomas and Ann Furrow. Dr. Henry Faulds sided with the defense in this case due to a bitter controversy over Faulds contribution to the science of fingerprints.

Stratum Basale (Basal Layer)
The inner layer of epidermis that contains melanocyte cells, Merkel cells and keratinocyte cells. The layer of the epidermis where new keratinocytes are formed.
Known as the germinative or generating layer.

See Stratum Germinativum.

Stratum corneum epidermidis, horny layer of epidermis
The outermost layer of the epidermis, consisting of cells that are dead and desquamating.
Merck Source Health Library

Stratum germinativum, stratum germinativum epidermidis [Malpighii], germinative layer
The stratum basale epidermidis and the stratum spinosum epidermidis considered as a single layer. The term is also sometimes used to designate only the stratum basale epidermidis. Called also germinative layer of epidermis, malpighian layer or rete, mucous layer, and s. malpighii.
Merck Source Health Library

Stratum granulosum epidermidis, granular layer of epidermis
The layer of the epidermis between the stratum lucidum epidermidis and the stratum spinosum epidermidis.
Merck Source Health Library

Stratum lucidum epidermidis, clear layer of epidermis
The clear translucent layer of the epidermis, just beneath the stratum corneum epidermidis.
Merck Source Health Library

This layer of the epidermis is not always present. It is prominent in very thick skin. Also call the Hyalin layer of the epidermis.

This is an electronlucent skin layer between the stratum granulosum and stratum corneum in palmoplantar skin rather than what you have written.
Professor Julian Verbov 04-19-08

Stratum Malpighii
See Stratum Germinativum.

Stratum Mucosum
See Stratum Germinativum.

Stratum spinosum epidermidis, spinous layer of epidermis
The layer of the skin between the stratum granulosum epidermidis and the stratum basale epidermidis characterized by the presence of prickle cells. Called also prickle cell layer.
Merck Source Health Library

Protein synthesis happens in this layer of the epidermis, producing keratin.

Subcutaneous
Beneath or introduced beneath the skin.
Quantitative-Qualitative Friction Ridge Analysis, David R. Ashbaugh 1999 CRC Press

Subjective
Proceeding from or taking place in a person's mind rather than the external world: a subjective decision
The American Heritage® Dictionary of the English Language, Fourth Edition Copyright © 2000 by Houghton Mifflin Company. Published by Houghton Mifflin Company. All rights reserved
http://dictionary.reference.com/search?q=subjective 02-27-03

Influenced by a person's knowledge, state of mind, or ability.
Quantitative-Qualitative Friction Ridge Analysis, David R. Ashbaugh 1999 CRC Press

Subjective Probability
The user defines the probability (the probability of getting an A).

See Classical Probability and Empirical Probability.

Sub-Secondary
An alpha expression derived from the index, middle and ring fingers of both hands.
SWGFAST, Glossary - Consolidated 09-09-03 ver. 1.0

Substrate
Surface upon which a friction ridge impression is deposited.
SWGFAST, Glossary 07-28-2009 ver. 2.0

The surface upon which a latent fingerprint is deposited or placed.
Quantitative-Qualitative Friction Ridge Analysis, David R. Ashbaugh 1999 CRC Press

Sudan Black
Black dye that stains fats, oils, sebaceous components, and contaminants of friction ridge residue; can enhance cyanoacrylate fumed friction ridge detail.
SWGFAST, Glossary - Consolidated 09-09-03 ver. 1.0

A black dye used to visualize friction ridge detail. Can be alone or in conjunction with the cyanoacrylate process. Works best on waxy or greasy surfaces.

Sufficient
Enough or an adequate amount to justify a conclusion. test a conclusion, and/or eliminate doubt by others. This could be a conclusion of value or a conclusion of identity.

(SWGFAST uses sufficient and suitable interchangeably) The determination that there is adequate quality and quantity of detail in an impression for further analysis, comparison, or to reach a conclusion.
SWGFAST, Glossary 07-28-2009 ver. 2.0

Alternate definition: Used by friction ridge examiners to denote the quality and quantity of agreement or disagreement of friction ridge detail in an impression necessary to reach a conclusion of individualization or exclusion, respectively (e.g. "sufficient for identification" or "sufficient for exclusion").

Sufficient Recurve
The space between the shoulders of a loop, free of any appendages that abut upon the recurve at a right angle on the outside.
SWGFAST, Glossary - Consolidated 09-09-03 ver. 1.0

Suicide Ridges
A term popularized by Ron Smith to describe the ridge pattern on the underside of the distal transverse crease. Many times these ridges are found to be a series of vertically terminating ridges.

Suitable
(SWGFAST uses sufficient and suitable interchangeably) The determination that there is adequate quality and quantity of detail in an impression for further analysis, comparison, or to reach a conclusion.
SWGFAST, Glossary 07-28-2009 ver. 2.0

Alternate definition: The determination that there is adequate quality and quantity of friction ridge detail in an impression for some further process step such as retention in the case, further analysis by an examiner, comparison with inked impressions, or searching in AFIS.

Sulcus (plural: sulci)
A deep, narrow furrow or groove, as in an organ or tissue.
The American Heritage® Dictionary of the English Language, Fourth Edition Copyright © 2000 by Houghton Mifflin Company. Published by Houghton Mifflin Company. All rights reserved http://dictionary.reference.com/search?q=sulci

5-Sulfosalicylic Acid
Chemical used in fixative solutions for a variety of blood enhancement reagents.
SWGFAST, Glossary - Consolidated 09-09-03 ver. 1.0

Superglue
See Cyanoacrylate Ester.

SuperGlue Girl
For the 2006 California State Science Fair, 13 year old Avery L. Smith tried to add different coloring agents to superglue to enhance the visibility. She found that the ink from a pink highlighter produced the best results. Subsequent to the Science Fair, Miss Smith presented her conclusions at the 2007 IAI Conference in San Diego, California and became known as SuperGlue Girl. Her research was subsequently published in Forensic Magazine and Jan 2007 issue of The Print.
See Colored Superglue.

Superior Region
One of the 3 main areas of the palm. The area immediately below the fingers. In many countries this area is known as the interdigital area but in some countries, such as Portugal, this is called the superior region.

Supreme Court of Canada, Her Majesty The Queen v. Chikmaglur Mohan (1994)
(R. v. Mohan)
On appeal to the Supreme Court of Canada from the Ontario Court of Appeal, a decision on the admissibility of expert evidence and the nature of expert evidence and how it pertains to disposition. A Canadian decision similar to the American Daubert Hearings, the Mohan decision has set the parameters and application for the admission of expert in Canada.

Admission of expert evidence depends on the application of the following criteria:
a) Relevance
b) Necessity in assisting the trier of fact (judge or jury)
c) The absence of exclusionary rule
d) Must be by a properly qualified expert

In R. v. Mohan, four counts of sexual

assault on female patients ages 13-16 were laid against a practicing paediatrician. His counsel indicated that he intended to call a psychiatrist who would testify that the perpetrator of the alleged offences would be part of a limited and unusual group of individuals and that the accused did not fall within that narrow class because he did not possess the characteristics of the group (profile) however the evidence was ruled inadmissible.

The original conviction was stayed by the Court of Appeals and opened a new hearing. At issue was the determination of the circumstances in which expert evidence is admissible to show that the character traits of an accused person do not fit the psychological profile of the putative perpetrator of the offences charged. The resolution of the issue involved the examination of the rules relating to (i) expert evidence, and (ii) character evidence.

In summary, expert evidence which advances a novel scientific theory or technique is subjected to special scrutiny to determine whether it meets a basic threshold of reliability and whether it is essential in the sense that the trier of fact will be unable to come to a satisfactory conclusion without the assistance of the expert.

The Supreme Court allowed the appeal but decided that the evidence should be excluded as nothing in the court record supported a finding that the profile of a paedophile or psychopath (as alleged by the psychologist) has been standardized to the extent that it could be said that it matched the supposed profile of the offender depicted in the charges. The expert's group profiles were not seen as sufficiently reliable to be considered helpful.
http://www.canlii.org/en/ca/scc/doc/1994/1994canlii80/1994canlii80.pdf 8-1-2009
Courtesy of Cst. Jonathan BALTZER and Sgt. Tim Walker, RCMP

Supreme Court of The United States, Melendez-Diaz v. Massachusetts (2009)
The US Supreme Court decision that determined that forensic reports were not considered business records and therefore subject to confrontation (forensic practitioners must make themselves available to court testimony if asked).

Surfactant
Surface-active substance; detergent.
SWGFAST, Glossary - Consolidated 09-09-03 ver. 1.0

Sweat Glands
Both the eccrine and the apocrine glands are considered as sweat glands, as opposed to the sebaceous gland which is an oil gland.

Symphalangy
End to end fusion of the phalanges of the fingers or toes.
SWGFAST, Glossary - Consolidated 09-09-03 ver. 1.0

Another opinion: Synonymous with syndactyly and webbed fingers or toes.
The International Classification of Diseases, 9th edition, World Health Organization.
http://www.nber.org/mortality/1995/docs/ch14.txt 06-18-2003

Syndactyly
Refers to webbed fingers. Side-to-side fusion of digits.
SWGFAST, Glossary - Consolidated 09-09-03 ver. 1.0

Fusion of the fingers or toes. This may occur with or without fusion of the bone. Synonymous with symphalangy or webbed fingers or toes.
The International Classification of Diseases, 9th edition, World Health Organization.
http://www.nber.org/mortality/1995/docs/ch14.txt 06-18-2003

Synperonic-N
Chemical used in the preparation of the detergent solution in Physical Developer.
SWGFAST, Glossary - Consolidated 09-09-03 ver. 1.0

T

TEC
Thenoyl Europium Chelate. Treatment having fluorescent properties used with selected wavelengths of light to enhance cyanoacrylate fumed friction ridge detail.
SWGFAST, Glossary - Consolidated 09-09-03 ver. 1.0

TMB
Tetramethylbenzidene. Reagent used to detect / enhance bloody friction ridge detail.
SWGFAST, Glossary - Consolidated 09-09-03 ver. 1.0

TMB is a suspected carcinogen and has a very short shelf life (one day).

TWGFAST
Technical Working Group on Friction Ridge Analysis, Study and Technology. Established by the FBI in 1995. In 1999, the name was changed to better reflect the goals of this group. This organization develops standards and guidelines in the area of friction skin identification.

Taber, Isaiah West (Tabor) (1830-1912)
There are many books and articles that refer to a man named Tabor who was an eminent photographer of San Francisco who proposed using fingerprints to register the Chinese around 1880. One article was published by Jay Hambridge in October 1909 in Century Magazine titled "Fingerprints: Their Use by the Police". Hambridge states "Some 30 years ago….." but that is the only reference to a date. Tabors proposal wasn't accepted but it seems that this may have been the earliest trace of using fingerprints as a means of identification in the United States.

In 'Fingerprint Whorld', Volume 10 number 40, 1985, G.T. Lambourne wrote an article about Taber and included letters he received from the Smithsonian Institute. Due to Lambourne's research it appears that Taber's name had been misspelled throughout the years. Lambourne believes this misspelling originated from Galton's book 'Fingerprints' but it appears that his name was also misspelled in a letter from the House of Representatives, U.S. dated 1888. Lambourne also discovered the year that Taber suggested using fingerprints as a means of identification was the year 1886 and that his initials were I.W. Taber.

Due to the combination of reference material available the man referred to as Tabor seems to be the well-known San Francisco photographer Isaiah West Taber (1830-1912).

Tactile
Pertaining to the sense of touch.

Take Away Print
A 'take away' print, also referred to as a negative impression, is created when an object is touched and instead of the friction ridges leaving a matrix behind, the friction ridges take away a substance that is left on the substrate. This is common when the object being touched is covered with dust or another substance, such as blood. Frequently 'take away' prints are tonally reversed.

Target Group
A unique group of friction ridge details that stands out enough for an examiner to easily memorize. When the same group is location in an exemplar then recognition is triggered and a detailed comparison can begin.

See Focal Points.

Taylor, J.H. (James Herbert)
On May 1, 1910, Taylor was promoted to Chief of the Identification Section for the U.S. Navy. He wrote a book entitled "Finger Print Evidence" and in 1917 invented the metal identification tags for all the Navy men in WWI that had their fingerprints etched on them. In 1926, J.H. Taylor testified for the defense in the first known erroneous identification case, see Hall-Mills double murder case.

Taylor, Thomas (1877)
Microscopist at the U.S. Department of Agriculture, suggested that markings of the palms, the hands and the tips of the fingers could be used for identification in criminal cases. Although reported in the American Journal of Microscopy and Popular Science and Scientific American, the idea was apparently never pursued from this source.
Principle of Criminalistics: The Profession of Forensic Science, By Keith Inman and Norah Rudin, CRC Press, 2000.
http://www.courttv.com/onair/shows/forensicfiles/timeline1.html

Technical Review
A review to verify that conclusions are supported by suitable data, proper procedures, valid reasoning, and appropriate documentation.

Review of notes, documents, and other data that forms the basis for a scientific conclusion.
ASCLD/LAB 2008 Manual
SWGFAST, Glossary 07-28-2009 ver. 2.0

Technician
A person skilled in the details of a subject or task. especially a mechanical one.
Quantitative-Qualitative Friction Ridge Analysis, David R. Ashbaugh 1999 CRC Press

Technology
The science of the application of knowledge to practical purposes : applied science.
Merriam-Webster's Medical Dictionary, © 2002 Merriam-Webster, Inc. http://dictionary.reference.com/search?q=technology 10-14-2005

Tenprint
A recording of the friction ridge skin on the distal phalanges.

1. A generic reference to examinations performed on intentionally recorded friction ridge impressions, usually ten fingers.
2. A controlled recording of available fingers of an individual using black ink, electronic imaging, photography, or other medium on a contrasting background.
SWGFAST, Glossary 07-28-2009 ver. 2.0

Tension Crease
"Usually in crisscrossing patterns or at right angles to the ridges. These secondary creases are known as tension creases and are not normally found on the hands at birth. "
Scott's Fingerprint Mechanics. By Robert Olsen

See Creases, Flexion Creases and White Lines.

Tetramethylbenzidene
See TMB.

Thenar Area
The large cushion of the palm located at the base of the thumb.
SWGFAST, Glossary - Consolidated 09-09-03 ver. 1.0

Thenoyl Europium Chelate (TEC)
A fluorescent dye stain used with an ultraviolet light source to visualize cyanoacrylate ester fumed friction ridge detail.

Theory
A set of statements or principles devised to explain a group of facts or phenomena, especially one that has been repeatedly tested or is widely accepted and can be used to make predictions about natural phenomena
The American Heritage® Dictionary of the English Language, Fourth Edition Copyright © 2000 by Houghton Mifflin Company. Published by Houghton Mifflin Company. All rights reserved http://dictionary.reference.com/search?q=theory 02-27-03

An explanation of why a natural phenomenon occurs which has been tested and has gained general acceptance.

Explanations of observations (or of laws). The fact that we have a pretty good understanding of how stars explode doesn't necessarily mean we could predict the next supernova; we

have a theory but not a law.
http://www.madsci.org/posts/archives/oct99/940942724.Sh.r.html
02-27-03

(Authors note) This is a nonscientific definition, generally what people think of as a theory:
An assumption based on limited information or knowledge; a conjecture.
The American Heritage® Dictionary of the English Language, Fourth Edition Copyright © 2000 by Houghton Mifflin Company. Published by Houghton Mifflin Company. All rights reserved
http://dictionary.reference.com/search?q=theory 02-27-03

Theory of Differential Growth
The scientific theory that explains why fingerprints are unique. Internal and external pressures and stresses alter the volar pad development during the fetal stage. These pressures also effect how primary ridges grow. Since it is impossible to duplicate these pressures, no two fingerprints will ever be the same.

Besides the Theory of Differential Growth being based on embryonic biological formation, it is also supported by statistical probabilities (the probability of duplication is virtually zero) and empirical data (no two formations have been found to be the same in over 100 years).

Theory of Fingerprint Permanence (or Persistency)
The scientific theory that explains why fingerprints are permanent. Fingerprints develop on a fetus. Once the secondary ridges start growing, the primary ridges stop any further development and the blueprint for the friction ridge pattern is established. This pattern is permanent with the exception of scaring.

Thermal Paper
Thermal paper is paper that uses heat to produce its images. It has a chemical coating on one side that darkens when exposed to heat. The coated side of thermal paper is sensitive to the DFO and ninhydrin processes. DMAC, RTX, Hydrochloric Acid, Indanedione (HFE-7100 formulation) and physical developer are good alternatives to processing this kind of paper.

ThermaNin
A ninhydrin derivative, available from BVDA, used to recover latent prints on thermal paper. This chemical recovers latent prints without turning the thermal paper black.

Thermoplastic Powder
Toner powder used in copiers and printers.
SWGFAST, Glossary - Consolidated 09-09-03 ver. 1.0

Thick Skin
Thick skin refers to skin on the palms of the hands, fingertips or the soles of the feet. This skin lacks follicles, sebaceous glands and arrector pili muscles.
http://www.vcu.edu/anatomy/OB/Skin~1/tsld020.htm 08-07-2004

Thin Skin
Nonfriction ridge skin.

Thin skin is skin that covers most of the body. It contains hair follicles, sebaceous glands and arrector pili muscles. It also has thinner epidermis with less developed strata granulosa and lucida, and the stratum corneum may be quite thin.
http://www.vcu.edu/anatomy/OB/Skin~1/tsld020.htm 08-07-2004

Third Level Detail (also see Level 3 Detail)
Ridge shape, relative pore location, and some accidental details.
Quantitative-Qualitative Friction Ridge Analysis, David R. Ashbaugh 1999 CRC Press

Thompson, Gilbert (March 21, 1839-June 9, 1909)
A railroad builder with the U.S. Geological Survey in New Mexico, who in 1882 put his own thumbprint on wage chits to safeguard himself from forgeries.
http://www.forensicdna.com/Timeline020702.pdf 03-08-2003

Thompson was the first person to use fingerprints as a means of identification in the United States.

Tibia
A bone in the lower leg.
SWGFAST, Glossary - Consolidated 09-09-03 ver. 1.0

Tibial Area
The plantar area situated on the big toe side of the foot.
SWGFAST, Glossary - Consolidated 09-09-03 ver. 1.0

Titanium Dioxide
Titanium Dioxide is a white powder used as a coloring pigment. In 2003, Josh Bergeron published a paper in the Journal of Forensic Identification showing that when this powder is mixed with methanol it becomes a wonderful processing technique to develop friction ridge detail left in blood on dark surfaces.

Dave Wade also discovered that Titanium Dioxide can be mixed with water and photo-flo 200 to develop friction ridge detail on other items, including the adhesive side of tape. See WhitePrint© Titanium Dioxide.

Toeprint
Friction ridge impression left by a digit of the plantar surface.

Tolerance
The acceptance of dissimilarity

caused by distortion, usually involving an individualization; the opposite of the un-acceptance of differences caused by different friction ridge sources involving an exclusion. Generally expressed as "within tolerance" or "out of tolerance" for the level of clarity that is present in both impressions.

Within an acceptable range.

Tonal Reversal
Tonal Reversal is when the color of the ridges is reversed from the standard of dark ridges on a light background, also referred to as inverted ridges. Some reasons tonal reversal may occur are a) because of the developmental medium (such as CA'd or ardroxed latents)
b) excess moisture is present in the furrows
c) excess moisture is present on the substrate
d) pressure
e) take away prints are usually tonally reversed

Top-Down Influences
One of the two cognitive influences with respect to observational knowledge. Top-down influences are subjective in nature, guided by prior knowledge, expectations, or emotions.

See Bottom-Up.

Transferred Print
A transferred print is a true friction ridge impression that has been transferred to another surface. This may happen intentionally (as with fabricated or forged prints) or unintentionally (by the original substrate coming in contact with another surface). If a transfer occurs unintentionally, the transferred print will be a reversed image.

Transient Crease
Creases which are not permanent.

Transitive Property of Equality
The mathematical principle: If a = b and b = c, then a = c. This relates to friction skin identifications in establishing that if a print (a) was identified to print (b) and print (b) was identified to print (c) then it is known that print (a) was left by the same person as print (c) without the need of doing an additional comparison.

Transitory Print
A latent print seen by breathing on it.

Transposing the Conditional
The statistical equivalent of the Prosecutors Fallacy. In Bayes Theorum, the conditional probability of an event happening, given that another event has happened is expressed as P(a/b). Transposing the conditional is when someone misinterprets this to be the same as P(b/a), whether intentional or unintentional. Example:

While looking at the probability of someone speaking Spanish, given that they are from Spain it may be misrepresented as the probability of someone being from Spain, given that they speak Spanish.
Transposing the conditional can be related to fingerprints identifications in many different ways. One example is that Examiners may be reluctant to testify to any minimum point standard. This is often because people misinterpret the minimum number of points you may have used to make an identification with the minimum number of points that you would use to make an identification. Of course, this is not correct because there are other conditions that an identification is based on.

See Prosecutors Fallacy.

Trauma
Injury or damage.
SWGFAST, Glossary - Consolidated 09-09-03 ver. 1.0

Trifurcation
The point at which one friction ridge divides into three friction ridges.
SWGFAST, Glossary 07-28-2009 ver. 2.0

Triketohydrindine Hydrate
See Ninhydrin.

Tripartite Rule
Published in the 1910's, by Edmund Locard, The Tripartite Rule gives 3 different conclusions to a fingerprint identification.
If more than 12 Galton points exist, then the certainty of a positive identification is beyond debate.
If 8-12 Galton points exist, an identification will then be dependent on other items, such as rarity.
If less than 8 Galton points exist, then the print cannot provide a certain identification.

Triradius
Area on the friction ridges where three ridge systems meet.
Quantitative-Qualitative Friction Ridge Analysis, David R. Ashbaugh 1999 CRC Press

This term was introduced by one of the authors of the book "Personal Identification". It suggests a 3 point star and includes both the delta and the 3 radiating lines where ridges deviate in different directions.
Personal Identification, Wentworth and Wilder 1918 pg. 117.

Troup Committee
In 1894, Britain's Troup Committee established adding fingerprints to Bertillon Identification Cards. At this time, the fingerprints weren't used for identification purposes but their value was recognized.

See Bepler Committee.

True Skin
Another term for the dermis.

Turner, William Russell
See Russell-Turner, William.

Type 1 Error
The error in a system to overreact, a false positive result. An erroneous individualization.

Type 2 Error
The error in a system to underreact. Some view this type of error as either "false negative results" or "inconclusive results when a definitive result could have been found". Others view a type 2 error only a "false negative results" stating that inconclusive results cannot be an erroneous conclusion because inconclusive results are not conclusions, but the absence of a conclusion.

Type Lines
The two innermost friction ridges associated with a delta that parallel, diverge, and surround or tend to surround the pattern area.
SWGFAST, Glossary 07-28-2009 ver. 2.0

Typica
A Greek word which is synonymous with characteristic.

U

Ulna
The larger of the two bones of the forearm, on the palmar side of the little finger.
SWGFAST, Glossary - Consolidated 09-09-03 ver. 1.0

The inner and longer of the two bones of the human forearm on the same side as the little finger.

Ultraviolet
Wavelengths of light shorter than that of the visible spectrum, between 10 and 400 nm.
SWGFAST, Glossary - Consolidated 09-09-03 ver. 1.0

Un-Du®
Product used to separate adhesive tapes.
SWGFAST, Glossary - Consolidated 09-09-03 ver. 1.0

Unique
Being the only one of its kind.
The American Heritage® Dictionary of the English Language, Fourth Edition Copyright © 2000 by Houghton Mifflin Company. Published by Houghton Mifflin Company. All rights reserved
http://dictionary.reference.com/search?q=unique 02-27-03

Having no equal; one.
Quantitative-Qualitative Friction Ridge Analysis, David R. Ashbaugh 1999 CRC Press

Unique Characteristics
Characteristics used to individualize; specific details.
Quantitative-Qualitative Friction Ridge Analysis, David R. Ashbaugh 1999 CRC Press

Uniqueness
Very uncommon, unusual, atypical, or remarkable; a degree of distinguishing distinctiveness.
Quantitative-Qualitative Friction Ridge Analysis, David R. Ashbaugh 1999 CRC Press

United States v. Byron Mitchell (1999)
This was the first legal case where fingerprints evidence was challenged at a Daubert hearing. The defense claimed that the state had failed to establish the scientific validity of latent prints stating, "Is there a scientific basis for a fingerprint examiner to make an identification, of absolute certainty, from a small distorted latent fingerprint fragment". The US District Court for the Eastern District of Pennsylvania's decision was that the defense's motion to exclude fingerprint evidence was denied.

United States v. Henthorn (1991)
An extension of the Giglio decision

which applies to requests for the personnel records of government witnesses.

See Brady and Gilgio v United States.

United States v. Parks (1991)
"The only known fingerprint case in which a federal trial court has performed the type of analysis that is now mandated by Daubert, the district court excluded the government's fingerprint identification evidence. United States v. Parks (C.D. Cal. 1991) (No. CR-91-358-JSL) (Ex. 48). The district court in Parks reached its determination after hearing from three different fingerprint experts produced by the government in an effort to have the evidence admitted. In excluding the evidence, the district court recognized, among other things, the lack of testing that has been done in the field, the failure of latent fingerprint examiners to employ uniform objective standards, and the minimal training that latent fingerprint examiners typically receive."
http://www.goextranet.com/Seminars/Federal/FingerprintReply.htm
08-12-2004

The judge decided not to admit the evidence in this case because he had several concerns. The initial examiner, Diana Castro, testified to a point standard (8 points) but couldn't state why that standard was used. The judge concluded there were no written documents or studies to support this standard and therefore the conclusion wasn't scientific. The supervisor, Darnell Carter, testified that the office standard was 10 points but could be reduced with a supervisor's approval. The supervisor could offer no literature to support this policy. The 3rd expert was an IAI Certified Examiner that worked for the United States Postal Inspection Service, Steven Kasarsky. He testified that no studies on errors had been done but he knew of cases where 10 points of agree were found in different prints. He stated that practitioners all have independent standards and that practitioners don't know if a dissimilarity exists in an area that wasn't left, they must guess.

United States v. Plaza (2002)
Plaza was one of four people being charged as being a hit man. There were latent prints in the case and the defense decided to challenge the fingerprint evidence. A Daubert hearing was held. Federal Judge Louis Pollak ruled that fingerprint experts could not tell juries that two fingerprints matched. It was noted that fingerprints were unique and permanent but the science didn't meet the Daubert test. Judge Pollak reversed his decision two months later.

University of Applied Science
See Institute of Applied Science.

Urea
One of the organic elements in eccrine sweat.

V

VMD
Vacuum Metal Deposition. Process of selective condensation of metals under vacuum conditions; used to visualize friction ridge detail.
SWGFAST, Glossary - Consolidated 09-09-03 ver. 1.0

A number of metals when deposited by VACUUM METAL DEPOSITION will delineate fingerprints on some surfaces. Some of these work as single metal treatment while others must be used in combination. The currently recommended combination is GOLD followed by ZINC. Lead, zinc, silver, gold, magnesium and a few other metals develop fingerprints when deposited as single metals. Some of the known metal combinations are gold, silver or copper followed by cadmium or zinc.
http://www.crimetechlabs.com/vacuummetal.asp 07-17-2005

Vacuum Cyanoacrylate Ester
Fuming method, conducted under vacuum conditions, in which cyanoacrylate polymerizes on friction ridge residue; used to visualize friction ridge detail.
SWGFAST, Glossary - Consolidated 09-09-03 ver. 1.0

Vacuum Metal Deposition
See VMD.

Vaidya M.C.
Wrote "The Dermal Papillae and Ridge Patterns in Human Volar Skin" in 1968 with L.W. Chacko.

Valid
Well grounded, produced the desired results.
The American Heritage® Dictionary of the English Language, Fourth Edition Copyright © 2000 by Houghton Mifflin Company. Published by Houghton Mifflin Company. All rights reserved
http://dictionary.reference.com/search?q=valid

Validate
To make valid by checking the accuracy of a system.

Validation Study
An experiment to assess the usefulness of a technique (capabilities, benefits, limitations, and optimal conditions) compared to currently used methods.

An adequate validation study should include testing the reliability of the technique on realistic, ideal, and aged samples. Realistic samples are those that apply to real situations. Testing should be repeated multiple times. A validation study should include comparing the technique to current processes used, stating the limitations and values of the technique, and reviewing available literature. Factors to assess include: abilities compared to other methods, ease of use, expense, and safety concerns.

See Performance Check.

Value
The value of a friction ridge impression is determined by the context in which the term is used. An impression can have identification value, exclusionary value, value for determining how an object was touch, value in determining whether or not impressions were left simultaneously, investigation value, analytical value, or probative value. An impression can be of value in one area but not another, for instance an impression may have value in determining how an object was held but not have sufficient value to determine the identity of the source. Additionally, an impression can have identification value but not have probative value.

Vanderkolk, John
John Vanderkolk received a Bachelor of Arts degree in Forensic Studies and Psychology from Indiana University in 1979. He worked as an Indiana State Police Trooper from 1979-1983, became a Crime Scene Technician in 1983, and then a Criminalist (latent prints, footwear/tire-track, physical comparisons) from 1984-1996. He has been a Laboratory Manager/Criminalist since 1996.

John is a distinguished member (2005) of the International Association for Identification (IAI), and currently serves on the Editorial Review Board for the Journal of Forensic Identification since 1991 and the Forensic Identification Standards Committee. He is also a member of the Scientific Working Group for Friction Ridge Analysis, Study and Technology (SWGFAST) since 1996. John is also a member of the Canadian Identification Society, the Indiana Division IAI, and the Illinois Division IAI.

He has presented at a variety of international, national and regional seminars and has been published in The Journal of Forensic Identification and the Cognitive Psychology Journal Vision Research. The topics include: "Ridgeology, Animal Muzzleprints and Human Fingerprints", "Class Characteristics and 'Could Be' Results", "Identifying Consecutively Made Garbage Bags Through Manufactured Characteristics", "Forensic Individualization of Images Using Quality and Quantity of Information", "Levels of Quality and Quantity in Detail", "ACE+V: A Model" and "Behavioral and Electrophysiological Evidence for Configural Processing in Fingerprint Experts" by Dr. Tom Busey, Indiana University Department of Psychology with John Vanderkolk, Vision Research, 45 (February, 2005) 431-448.

Verbov, Professor Julian MD FRCP FRCPCH CBiol FSB FLS
Professor Julian Verbov is Professor of Dermatology at the University of Liverpool UK and has been a Consultant to The Fingerprint Society since 1991. His MD Thesis in 1971 was on "Dermatoglyphics and Other Findings in Health and Disease". He is author or contributor to more than 300 publications including 29 books and his particular specialty is Pediatric Dermatology. He founded the journal, Pediatric Dermatology, is a founding father of British Pediatric Dermatology, is a past Editor-in- Chief of the British Journal of Dermatology. He was awarded the Sir Archibald Gray Medal in 2006 by the British Association of Dermatologists, their highest accolade, for outstanding services to Dermatology. His invited lectures include visits to USA, Canada, Norway, Greece, France, Germany, Israel and the UK. He was keynote lecturer at the inaugural meeting of the Israel Society for Pediatric Dermatology in 2004. He is an Honorary Member of the British Association of Dermatologists, the British Society for Paediatric Dermatology, the North of England Dermatological Society, and the Dr Henry Faulds- Beith Commemorative Society, Scotland. He has been a Magistrate for the City of Liverpool since 1983.

Apart from his dedication to Dermatology, he has also been a teacher in Old Testament Studies at the University of Liverpool Dept of Philosophy. A polymath, some of his other many interests include his family, classical and brass band music, editing, teaching all age groups, writing poetry, etymology, clichés, humour, ties and tie design, apes and lay preaching.

His publications include:

* Hypohidrotic (or Anhidrotic) Ectodermal Dysplasia – an appraisal of diagnostic methods. Br J Dermatol 1970;83:341-348
* Editorial: Dermatoglyphics in Medicine Lancet 1972:1:417
* Anonychia with Bizarre Flexural Pigmentation – an autosomal dominant dermatosis Br J Dermatol 1975;92:469-474 (now sometimes referred to as Verbov Syndrome)
* Palmar Ridge Appearances in Normal Newborn Infants, and Ridge Appearances in Relation to Eccrine Sweating. Br J Dermatol 1975;93:645- 648
* Mummified Skin – An Exercise in Preservation Int J Dermatol 1983;22:46- 60
* Many contributions to Fingerprint Whorld and Educational Lectures

and advice to The Fingerprint Society.

Verification
"Verification is a form of peer review and is part of most sciences. Many organizations erroneously use verification as a method of protecting against errors in place of adequate training. While verification may prevent the occasional error, its purpose is to verify process and objectivity as opposed to only check results. It is also an excellent vehicle for training." David Ashbaugh Detail 28 http://www.clpex.com

Verification insures objectivity and unbiased results, it does not insure accurate results or conclusions.

Proof; confirmation of a process.
Quantitative-Qualitative Friction Ridge Analysis, David R. Ashbaugh 1999 CRC Press

The final step of the ACE-V method. A review and independent analysis of the conclusion of another examiner.
SWGFAST, Glossary 07-28-2009 ver. 2.0

See Blind Verification and Double Blind Verification.

More definitions listed under ACE-V.

Verification Shopping
Seeking verification that is in agreement with the desired outcome.

Vestiges
Erratic local disarrangements of ridges not conforming to surrounding ridge formations.
Quantitative-Qualitative Friction Ridge Analysis, David R. Ashbaugh 1999 CRC Press

Virgin Islands v. Austin Jacobs (2001)
A burglary case that failed a Daubert challenge. The judge decided to exclude the fingerprint testimony because the prosecutor hadn't provided information to the defense to determine if the fingerprint evidence was scientifically reliable. The defense asked for the CV of the examiner (Maureen Richardson) and for an explanation of the methodology to determine if a basis and reason existed for the findings. The prosecutor failed to provide these items.

Visible Light
Visible light is a series of electromagnetic wavelengths that we can see. These wavelengths range in frequency from 400-700nm and are seen as different colors. The combination of all the colors in the visible light spectrum is referred to as white light.

Volar
Related to the palmar and plantar surfaces.
SWGFAST, Glossary - Consolidated

09-09-03 ver. 1.0

To do with the palms of the hands or the soles of the feet.
Quantitative-Qualitative Friction Ridge Analysis, David R. Ashbaugh 1999 CRC Press

Volar Pads
Palmar and plantar fetal tissue growth that affects friction ridge skin development and patterns.
SWGFAST, Glossary - Consolidated 09-09-03 ver. 1.0

Swelling of the mesenchyme cells during fetal growth. There are 11 volar pads are on each hand of a fetus.

Vollmer, August (1876-Nov. 4, 1955)
A Chief of Police in Los Angeles, California who started the first crime laboratory in the United States. Vollmer, along with Paul Kirk, also established criminology and criminalistics as an academic discipline. In 1950 the University of California Berkeley began offering criminal justice degrees.
Vollmer's obituary appears in the January 1956 issue of Fingerprint and Identification Magazine.

Vucetich, Juan (AKA Vucetic, Ivan and Vucetic, Josip and Vucetic, Ivo) (1858-1925)
Working in Argentina, Vucetich is credited with deriving the classification system used in South America. His classification system was originally called 'The Icnofalangometric(ia) system' but after some modifications the name was changed to 'Dactiloscopy' or 'Dactiloscopia', at the suggestion of another fingerprint pioneer- Dr. Francisco Latzina,. Vucetich is also credited as being the first person to use a latent fingerprint to solve a crime. The real person who collected the evidence and made the identification was Inspector Eduardo Alvarez, in 1892, but historically Vucetich is given the credit because it is felt that Alvarez would have never done this without the influence of Vucetich. Confronted with the fingerprint evidence, Francesca Rojas confessed to murdering her two sons.

Walker, Michael David (1937-present)

Written by John Berry.

Michael David Walker was born in 1937 at Stroud, Gloucestershire, England and joined the New Scotland Yard Fingerprint Bureau in 1960, duly obtaining his expert status. Later he transferred to the Hertfordshire Constabulary Fingerprint Bureau, thence to the Cambridgeshire Bureau, where he is presently employed. I was an amazed witness to an absolutely outstanding memory identification in the eighties. In Hertfordshire, fingerprints of persons likely to commit crimes were filed in separate bundles, right hand, left hand, and plain impressions held together with elastic bands. One day I concluded a search and was about to put the fingerprint bundle in a drawer and I stopped to talk to Mike. My elastic band snapped and fingerprint forms cascaded to the floor. Mike instinctively grabbed one, looked at it and did a double take. He rushed to the Scenes of Crime Collection, flipped through the cards and with a wide smile handed me the crime scene imprint and the fingerprint slip. It was an identification in the brief flash of time as the form fell to the ground and he grabbed it, his mind, computer-like, recognized the crime scene imprint. Mike Walker has also made many Ridge Detail in Nature discoveries, via photograph or report, duly published in STRABISMUS. – John Berry, Jan. 2005

Watling, William

William Watling of the Internal Revenue Service was one of the first people to use imaging technology in forensics. Bill Watling was involved in the first Kelly-Frye hearing on this kind of technology, VA vs. Robert Douglas Knight 1991.

Personal Correspondence with George Reis 05-2005

Mr. Watling began his career in law enforcement with the Arizona Highway Patrol in 1969. He was assigned to the newly formed Latent Print Section of the newly created Department of Public Safety in 1970. Much of his fingerprint training was from various classes and workshops at the FBI Academy in Quantico, VA. In 1976 he was promoted to head the section. He expanded the Latent Print Section and oversaw the design and construction of three latent print laboratories for the State of Arizona. He went to work for the IRS Criminal Investigation Division, National Forensic Laboratory in 1987 as a Forensic Investigator, where he headed up their Latent Print Section. He went into private practice in late 1996. Coming out of private practice he went to work at the US Department of Homeland Security Fingerprint Identification Center in San Diego, California in 2003 as a latent print examiner supervisor. He has received many commendations and accolades from various organizations, prosecutors and others including a special commendation from the Governor of The State of Arizona.

He has authored and had published in various scientific journals many papers related to latent print development, identification and forensic image enhancement. He has given presentations related to fingerprints, forensic handwriting and forensic image enhancement to conferences/meetings and workshops of the IAI, various divisions of the IAI, the American Academy of Forensic Science and other symposiums throughout the US, Canada and Great Britain. He has also instructed workshops related to latent print development, evidence/crime scene photography and digital image enhancement for a number of law enforcement agencies though out North America. He was an instructor at Glendale Community College in Glendale, Arizona for both day and evening classes related to evidence technology for several years. He also served on the Curriculum Advisory Board for Community Colleges in Arizona. He was one of the pioneers in using computerized image enhancement on both fingerprint and document evidence. He is one of the three cofounders of the Arizona Identification Council, which is a division of the IAI. He is a life member of the AIC and the IAI and has served in various positions for both organizations. He served several terms on the AIC Latent Finger Print Certification Committee in addition to being President and on the Board of Directors several times. He is a distinguished member of the IAI and has served several terms on the Board of Directors as well as various committees. He has also been a member of several other divisions of the IAI and several other forensic related organizations.

While at the Arizona DPS, Mr. Watling along with Kenneth O. Smith, Jr. (now in charge of the USPIS Latent Print Section, Dulles, VA.) experimented with and developed several different formulas for developing latent fingerprints on various surfaces. They were the first to publish a paper on a HEPTANE based carrier for developing latent fingerprints on porous surfaces to keep inks from bleeding or running. Mr. Watling has also specialized in detecting fabricated latent fingerprint evidence and/or fabricated enhancement of such evidence. He has been successful in discovering a number of fabrications as well as erroneous fingerprint identifications - some by renowned fingerprint experts.

Mr. Watling testified to the validity of digital image enhancement used to enhance fingerprints in the first Kelly-Frye Hearing in the United States (VA vs. Robert Douglas Knight 1991.) He also provided testimony in the first similar type hearing in Canada also in 1991 and in San Diego, California (People vs. Jackson 1991). He has consulted with many latent print examiners and prosecutors when they prepare(d) cases involving digital image enhancement for trial. He also consults with defense attorneys in cases where it is believed image enhancement has been mis-used or to validate the identification.

Weaver, David
In 1990 David Weaver invented the CA fuming wand. 3M patented this as the Cyanowand™ and in 1993 they launched the new product. In 2005, David patented the Fuma-Dome™ and the Press & Fume™. In 2006, Mountain State University received an NIJ grant that, under the guidance of David Weaver, will research dyed superglue for better visualization.

Webbed Fingers
Two or more fingers connected along the sides by skin.
SWGFAST, Glossary - Consolidated 09-09-03 ver. 1.0

See Syndactyly.

Wentworth, Bert (1857-1938)
Born George Herbert (or Hebert) Wentworth. An early researcher in the field of friction skin identification. Wentworth was a police commissioner for Dover, New Hampshire in the early 1900's. In 1918 he co-authored the book "Personal Identification" with Dr. Harris Hawthorne Wilder. Wentworth went on to become a board member of the Institute of Applied Science in the 1930's.

Wertheim, Kasey (June 11, 1973-present)
Kasey Wertheim began looking at fingerprints with his father, Pat, while in grade school. During his undergraduate studies in chemistry and criminal justice at Northern Arizona University, he volunteered in the fingerprint section of the Arizona DPS Crime Laboratory, and successfully completed two summer internships with the Forensic Services Unit of the United States Secret Service in Washington DC. From 1997 to 2003, he worked as Forensic Scientist for the Mississippi Crime Laboratory, followed by a one-yea r effort with a small forensic technology company, LumenIQ, as their Director of Forensic Services. In 2004, Kasey was hired by Lockheed Martin to develop

an examination services team for the federal government. 2 years and 11 new employees later, Kasey had established the DoD Biometric Examination Services Team and earned his Masters in Business Administration, Technology Management. In 2007, he accepted a broader scale position with Harding Security Associates as a Senior Principal Analyst to continue DoD work on multiple forensic projects in different parts of the world. Concurrently, in 2004, Kasey Wertheim formed Complete Consultants Worldwide with a vision to bring examination services from non-centralized but incorporated experts in their home-offices to government clients who need superior skills to accurately and efficiently contribute to national security. By 2008, CCW provided the services of qualified, educated, and experienced scientific research and Subject Matter Expertise to the Department of Defense (DoD) biometric centers of excellence. It was in 2008 that Kasey Wertheim resigned his position with Harding Security Associates and exclusively worked as the President and Chief Executive Officer of Complete Consultants Worldwide.

Kasey has lectured, conducted workshops, published papers, and enhanced government and coalition forensic operations internationally. He has earned "Distinguished Member" status with the International Association for Identification (IAI), served as the Chair of the Latent Print Subcommittee of the IAI for 2 years, was an IAI Certified Crime Scene Analyst for 5 years, currently serves on the Editorial Board for the Journal of Forensic Identification (JFI), and is currently a "re-tested" IAI Certified Latent Print Examiner (CLPE).

Kasey Wertheim is also known for co-writing "Friction Ridge & Pattern Formation During the Critical Stage" with Alice Maceo, JFI, Jan/Feb 2002, Vol 52, No. 1. This article is one of the most comprehensive papers on this subject available to friction ridge practitioners.

Wertheim, Pat A. (March 23, 1948-present)
is one of the most prominent and influential latent print examiners in the latent print community. He began his career as a patrol officer in 1973 and has since been involved in every aspect of latent print work. He's been a distinguished representative of the IAI holding various positions such as Librarian, a member of the editorial review board, a board member for several years, and he's served in different Vice President positions. He worked for Lightning Powder as an instructor of identification and crime scene courses, as well as being their Vice President. In 1999, Mr. Wertheim founded "Forensic Iden-

tification Training Seminars" and has taught over 100 forensic courses. He has also written and presented over 40 educational papers and articles. He has been active in setting industry standards and has been a member of SWGFAST since 1996. Among his long list of noteworthy cases, he worked in Scotland with David Grieve in exposing the erroneous identification in the Shirley McKie case, he worked with Allan Bayle in England exposing mistakes made in the Alan McNamara case and he was a key witness for the United States Daubert hearings. In 2007 he testified to fabricated fingerprint evidence in the murder of Inge Lotz in South Africa. This is just a brief summary of the contributions and accomplishments Pat Wertheim has brought to the latent print community

West, Will and William
To some, the Will West / William West case in 1903 is noted as the demise of the Bertillon Method of Identification. Two men had the exact same measurements but different fingerprints. This incident happened at Leavenworth Penitentiary in Kansas.
Others claim that this case was not the demise of the Bertillon System. Fingerprints replaced the Bertillon System following the fingerprint exhibit at the 1904 Worlds Fair. Fingerprints were found to be more convenient to use and could be used to identify latent prints found at crime scenes. The West case did establish that fingerprints were more reliable than anthropometry or photographs.

Wet Print™
A premade solution of small particle reagent that can be purchased through the Lynn Peavey Company. This solution can be sprayed on wet items to develop latent fingerprints.

Wetwop ™
Kjell Carlsson of Sweden developed this product to develop friction ridge detail on adhesive surfaces and/or tapes. It is a power suspension mixture that has been found to work better than other staining methods and better than sticky side powder.

Whipple, Inez L. (1871-1929) (AKA Whipple-Wilder)
Inez Whipple-Wilder is noted for her research with the evolutionary development of volar pads in mammals, the evolutionary development of friction ridges, and ridge patterns. She found that these patterns are affected by internal and external forces on a fetus during development. She wrote, "The Ventral Surface of the Mammalian Chiridium, with special reference to the conditions found in man" in 1904. She is also noted as being an assistant to Harold Wilder and later becoming his wife.

White Light
White light is a combination of all the colors in the visible light spectrum. Visible light is sometimes referred to as white light.

White Lines
Creases which are not formed with other friction ridge detail. Usually associated with age. According to David Ashbaugh's book "Quantitative-Qualitative Friction Ridge Analysis, "white lines disrupts the stratum corneum (horny layer) of the epidermis. These creases do have ridge detail with-in the crease. They are usually permanent but do have the ability to shrink and grow. Also known as tension creases.

See Creases, Tension Creases and Flexion Creases.

WhitePrint© Titanium Dioxide
A processing technique used to develop friction ridge detail on both sides of electrical tape, the non-adhesive side of duct tape, plastic bags, cellophane, and other non-porous surfaces. Developed by Dave Wade in 2001-2002.
http://www.whiteprint.com/TiO2.htm

Whorl - Accidental
1. With the exception of the plain arch, a fingerprint pattern consisting of two different types of patterns with two or more deltas.
2. A pattern that possesses some of the requirements for two or more different types.
3. A pattern that conforms to none of the definitions.
SWGFAST, Glossary 07-28-2009 ver. 2.0

Whorl - Central Pocket Loop
A type of fingerprint pattern that has two deltas and at least one friction ridge which makes, or tends to make, one complete circuit, which may be spiral, oval, circular, or any variant of a circle. An imaginary line drawn between the two deltas must not touch or cross any recurving friction ridges within the inner pattern area.
SWGFAST, Glossary 07-28-2009 ver. 2.0

Whorl - Double Loop
A type of fingerprint pattern that consists of two separate loop formations with two separate and distinct sets of shoulders and two deltas.
SWGFAST, Glossary 07-28-2009 ver. 2.0

Whorl – Plain
A type of fingerprint pattern that consists of one or more friction ridges which make, or tends to make, a complete circuit, with two deltas, between which, when an imaginary line is drawn, at least one recurving friction ridge within the inner pattern area is cut or touched.
SWGFAST, Glossary 07-28-2009

ver. 2.0

Wilder, Dr. Harris Hawthorne (April 7, 1864-Feb. 27, 1928)
A fingerprint pioneer associated with his research into what is now known as differential growth. Dr. Wilder claims to be the first person to recognize that the 'center of disturbance', center of a ridge pattern, is always where a volar pad exists. He also claims to have proved that the large cats volar pad is really three pads fused together. This point was stated by Klaatsch earlier but Wilder claims that Klaatsch offered no proof. Wilder is also noted for the idea that ridges are ridge units fused together, a hypothesis which still remains unproven. He wrote numerous articles and published the book "Personal Identification" with Bert Wentworth in 1918.

First American to study dermatoglyphics. Named the A, B, C, D triradii points, invented the Main Line Index, studied thenar hypothenar eminencies, zones II, III, IV.
http://www.handanalysis.net/library/derm_history.htm 03-08-2003

Writer's Palm
The outer edge of a palm print typically left on a document when people write. This includes the outer portion of the hypothenar and may include the outer edge of interdigital section and the outer edge of the little finger.

Working Solution
Solution at the proper dilution for processing.
SWGFAST, Glossary - Consolidated 09-09-03 ver. 1.0

X

Xanthull v. State

In Xanthull v. State (403 SW.2d 807) the defendant was convicted of the burglary of a lumber company. A hammer on the floor behind the counter at the crime scene had been used to pry open the cash box and the defendant's palm print was found on the hammer. As in Kuhl, the deputy (who qualified as an expert in fingerprints based on his education, training, and experience) testified that palm prints were "biologically the same as the bulbar ridges on the end of the finger". The issue on appeal involved the question "was the court in error in allowing a fingerprint expert to testify on palm prints". The court (Court of Criminal Appeals of Texas, 1966) held that because he was qualified as a fingerprint expert and fully explained the fundamental similarity between fingerprints and palm prints, the court did not err in permitting him to testify as an expert on palm prints. http://www.clpex.com/Articles/TheDetail/TheDetail82.htm 10-20-2004

Xylene and Xylene Substitutes

A laboratory solvent used as a carrier in reagents, also used as a clearing agent. Xylene is considered a hazardous chemical. Over exposure can produce headaches, nausea or dizziness. Xylene substitutes are available under different names that are less hazardous to the user.

Xylene is also known as xylol, dimethylbenzene, or mixed xylenes.

Z

Zinc Chloride

A fluorescent technique used to develop friction ridge detail on porous surfaces. Also used to enhance latent prints that were developed with other methods.

A metal salt used to treat ninhydrin developed latent prints.
SWGFAST, Glossary - Consolidated 09-09-03 ver. 1.0

Zinc Nitrate

A metal salt used to treat ninhydrin developed latent prints.
SWGFAST, Glossary - Consolidated 09-09-03 ver. 1.0

Made in the USA
Charleston, SC
12 March 2011